DICTIONARY

OF

COMPUTER WORDS

DICTIONARY
OF
COMPUTER
WORDS

Houghton Mifflin Company

Boston · New York

Library of Congress Cataloging-in-Publication Data

Dictionary of computer words.

p. cm.
Includes bibliographical references and index.
ISBN 0-395-67426-3
1. Computers — Dictionaries.
QA76.15.D5259   1993
004.16'03 — dc20   93-4646
CIP

Manufactured in the United States of America

BP 10 9 8 7 6 5 4 3 2 1

Book design by Anne Chalmers

Picture credits: Library of Congress/Pre-Press Company: halftone
Library of Congress/Tech-Graphics: pixel
Lotus Development Corporation: spreadsheet
Maureen Kieffer/Cheryl Snyder: range
Microsoft Corporation: character-based, graphical user interface, and range reprinted with permission from Microsoft Corporation
Tech-Graphics: antialiasing, Bézier curve, chip, computer, connector, DIP switch, Dvorak keyboard, floppy disk, hard disk, hierarchical, landscape, letter-quality, mouse, network, outline font, overlaid windows, printed circuit board, programming language, QWERTY keyboard, resolution, sector, software, text wrap, trackball, write-protect

CONTENTS

EDITORIAL STAFF

Editors

Donna Cremans, Project Editor
Martha F. Phelps, Editorial Coordinator
Paul G. Evenson

Associate Editors

Ann-Marie Imbornoni
Nina Judith Katz

Assistant Editor

Michael H. Choi

Editorial Assistants

Rachel King
Beth G. Rowen

Administrative Assistant

Alisa Stepanian

In Memory of
Donna Cremans
1952–1993
Good Friend, Fine Editor

ACKNOWLEDGMENTS

Adobe, Adobe Illustrator, Adobe Type Manager, and Post-Script are registered trademarks of Adobe Systems, Inc. Aldus Freehand and PageMaker are registered trademarks of Aldus Corp. Apple, AppleTalk, FDHD, ImageWriter, LaserWriter, Mac, Macintosh, and MultiFinder are registered trademarks of Apple Computer, Inc. Apple Desktop Bus, Finder, Geneva, Macintosh II, Newton, PowerBook, QuickDraw, QuickTime, SuperDrive, System 7, and TrueType are trademarks of Apple Computer, Inc. Ashton-Tate is a registered trademark of Ashton-Tate Corp. AST is a registered trademark of AST Research. Hobbit is a registered trademark of AT&T. AutoCad is a registered trademark of AutoCad Development System. BIT-NET is a registered trademark of BITNET, Inc.

Centronics is a registered trademark of Centronics Data Computer Corp. FileMaker, HyperCard, and HyperTalk are registered trademarks of Claris Corp. CMOS is a trademark of CMOS Corp. Amiga is a registered trademark of Commodore-Amiga Inc. Intellifont is a registered trademark of Compugraphic Corp. CompuServe is a registered trademark of CompuServe, Inc. GIF is a service mark of CompuServe, Inc. DEC, DEC vt-52, DEC vt-100, and DEC vt-200 are trademarks of Digital Equipment Corp. Dow Jones News/Retrieval Service is a registered trademark of Dow Jones & Company, Inc. Mylar is a trademark of E. I. du Pont de Nemours & Co., Inc.

Epson is a registered trademark of Epson America, Inc. XTree is a registered trademark of Executive Systems, Inc. Hayes is a registered trademark of Hayes Microcomputer Products, Inc. Hercules is a registered trademark of Hercules Computer Technology. DeskJet, Hewlett-Packard, LaserJet, PCL, and Vectra are registered trademarks of Hewlett-Packard Co.

DVI is a registered trademark of Intel Corp. 386, i386, i860, i960, Intel287, Intel386, Intel486, and Pentium are trademarks of Intel Corp. AT, IBM, Micro Channel, OS/2, Personal Computer AT, Personal System/2, Presentation Manager, PS/1, PS/2, ThinkPad, and XGA are registered trademarks of International Business Machines, Inc. IBMPC, PC-DOS, PCjr, PC/XT, and PowerPC are trademarks of International Business Machines, Inc. ITC Zapf Dingbats is a registered trademark of International Typeface Corp. InterNet is a registered trademark of InterNet Corp. Bernoulli Box is a trademark of Iomega Corp. Helvetica, Times, and Times Roman are registered trademarks of Linotype Co. Lotus and 1-2-3 are registered trademarks of Lotus Development Corp.

MCI and MCI Mail are service marks of MCI Communications Corp. LEXIS and NEXIS are registered trademarks of Mead Data Central, Inc. GW-BASIC, Microsoft, MS, MS-DOS, and XENIX are registered trademarks of Microsoft Corp. Microsoft Windows, QBasic, Visual Basic, Windows, Windows NT, and Windows/386 are trademarks of Microsoft Corp. Times New Roman is a registered trademark of The Monotype Corp. PLC. Motorola is a registered trademark of Motorola Corp. NeXTStep is a registered trademark of NeXT Computer, Inc. NetWare and Novell are registered trademarks of Novell, Inc.

Pantone Matching System is a registered trademark of Pantone, Inc. Philips is a registered trademark of Philips International, B.V. PIC is a registered trademark of PIC Business Systems, Inc. QuarkXPress is a registered trademark of Quark, Inc. DESQview and QEMM386 are registered trademarks of Quarterdeck Office Systems.

Norton Utilities is a registered trademark of Symantec Corp. NuBus is a trademark of Texas Instruments. EEMS is a registered trademark of United Technologies Corp. UNIX is a registered trademark of UNIX System Laboratories. DrawPerfect and WordPerfect are registered trademarks of WordPerfect Corp. Ethernet and Xerox are registered trademarks of Xerox Corp. Paintbrush is a trademark of ZSoft Corp.

PREFACE

With the growing popularity of personal computing in the 1980s and 1990s, computers have become commonplace in offices, schools, and homes. Advances in technology have allowed the computer to become gradually lighter, smaller, and thus more portable so that laptop, notebook, and palmtop models are seen in use almost everywhere, from the passenger doing a business report on a transcontinental flight to the student sitting under a tree on campus finishing a term paper. As more people come into contact with personal computers, the need for for every user to understand the special language surrounding computers becomes more compelling. The *Dictionary of Computer Words* makes this language accessible to those who may have previously been put off by its apparent technical complexity.

The science of creating and operating these wondrous electronic devices has produced a special and in many ways mysterious vocabulary — a vocabulary that even the novice user must become familiar with. Indeed, the proliferation of computer-related terms has been one of the most notable developments in American English over the past ten years. Many terms, such as *byte* and *software*, are entirely new. Others, such as *menu*, *mouse*, and *window*, are familiar English words that have taken on new, specialized meanings. To the novice, the language surrounding computers can be intimidatingly complex, and that is where the *Dictionary of Computer Words* is a lifesaver, demystifying these special terms with clear, exact, and plain-spoken definitions.

For both the newcomer to computers and the user who simply needs more information, the *Dictionary of Computer Words* is a convenient and accessible way to become familiar with the terrain. It has been designed both to answer specific questions and to encourage browsing. The areas it covers are many: software, such as word processing and desktop publishing, operating systems, and viruses; hardware, such as printed circuit boards, CPUs, and architecture; artificial intelligence; networks; multimedia; and much more.

The vocabulary defined in this dictionary was chosen for its high utility: this is the language that is bound to be encountered most often by the average computer user and is most in need of elucidation. It is also up-to-the-minute: the reader will find full definitions of such terms as *virtual reality*; Apple's new laptop computer, *PowerBook*; and the *Pentium* microprocessor, released by Intel in March 1993. Sources for the Dictionary include the database of *The American Heritage Dictionary of the English Language, Third Edition* (1992), as well as computer journals and magazines and newspaper articles and columns on computers and computer applications. Advertisements for hardware and software have also been used as sources, since the abbreviations and technical specifications in such advertisements can be a significant cause of mystification to the newcomer.

The entries in the *Dictionary of Computer Words* are allowed as much space as is necessary for complete coverage, instead of being restricted to brief definitions. The defining language is clear and precise, free of unnecessary technical jargon. Examples of usage enhance the reader's understanding by putting a word in a context in which it is commonly heard or read. For example, at the entry for the verb *import*, the definition is augmented with an example of the word used in context: a graphics file can be *imported* into a desktop publishing program.

Cross-references are used extensively throughout the *Dictionary of Computer Words* in order to deepen the user's access to the broad range of information in its pages. Important words in the Dictionary are italicized when they occur in other entries, as a form of internal cross-reference. A term that is closely related to another important word or words is given a "see also" cross-reference at the end of its entry. Thus, at *increment*, the reader will find a cross-reference to a related term: "See also *decrement.*" When appropriate, cross-references are also provided to tables and illustrations. For example, at the words *head* and *platter*, cross-references will lead the reader to the illustration at *hard disk*. In addition to these cross-references, an entry for a term that often goes by another name or names will include these names listed at the end of the entry — for example, at *absolute address*, the last line of the entry reads, "Also called *real address.*"

An especially useful feature of the *Dictionary of Computer Words* is the **Subject Index** at the back of the book. In this Index related entry words have been gathered together and listed at a common topic or category. For example, the category hardware has listed under it *architecture, brownout, motherboard, port,* and *soundboard.* By reading the entry for each of those words and following the cross-references at the entry, the user can gain a useful overview of the category and begin to see interconnections in the language of computer technology.

As computers and computer technology continue to evolve, computer language — "computerese" — will continue expanding. *The Dictionary of Computer Words* covers the essential language. It will give the new and not-so-new computer user a solid grounding in a way that will be interesting, informative, and even, we hope, fun.

DICTIONARY

OF

COMPUTER WORDS

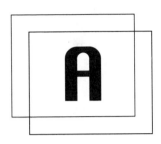

abort To cancel a procedure or program while it is in progress. A procedure or program can be aborted on request or unexpectedly because of a *bug*, an error, or a hardware malfunction. When this happens, you are usually returned to the *operating system shell*. See also *crash*.

absolute address An *address* expressed as a specific location in memory, as opposed to a *relative address*. Also called *machine address, real address*.

accelerator board A *printed circuit board* that can be added to a computer to enhance its performance by substituting a faster *microprocessor* without replacing the entire *motherboard* and associated components. For example, a 286 accelerator board containing an *Intel* 80286 *microprocessor* could be added to an old IBM PC-compatible that used the slower Intel 8088. Also called *accelerator card*. See also *expansion board, graphics accelerator*.

access *n.* The ability to locate, gain entry to, and use a directory, file, or device on a computer system or over a network. —*v.* To locate and be able to use a directory, file, or device on a computer system or over a network.

access code   An *alphanumeric* sequence that permits *access* to a computer system, a *network*, or an *on-line service.*

access time   In general, the time required for a program or device to locate and retrieve a piece of data, as from a computer's *memory* or from a *storage device.* Often, it specifically refers to *disk drives* and is the amount of time needed for a disk drive to respond to a request to read or write data. When such a request is made by the operating system, the disk drive must move the read / write heads over the proper location on the disk, settle the heads into position, and wait for the desired location on the disk to rotate under them. The fastest current hard drives for personal computers have average access times under 10 milliseconds; average values for older, slower models range from 30 to 100 milliseconds. Table 1 lists typical access times for various devices.

Table 1. Typical Access Times for Various Devices

Device	Typical Access Times
Static RAM	15–50 nanoseconds
Dynamic RAM	50–120 nanoseconds
EPROM	55–250 nanoseconds
ROM	55–250 nanoseconds
Hard disk drive	9–100 milliseconds
Erasable optical disk drive	20–200 milliseconds
CD-ROM	300–800 milliseconds
DAT drive	About 20 seconds
QIC drive	About 40 seconds

active   Of or relating to a file, device, or portion of the screen that is currently operational and ready to receive input. An active *window* is the window that is receiving *mouse* and *keyboard* input and in which the *cursor* is currently located; an active program is the program currently running.

active cell   In a *spreadsheet*, the *cell* that is currently highlighted or selected and ready to be acted upon, as by entering or editing data. Also called *current cell.*

active-matrix   Designating a type of *LCD* (liquid-crystal display) that uses individual transistors to control the charges on each cell in the liquid-crystal layer, as opposed to *passive-matrix* LCDs that use electrodes that extend the full length of the layer. Active-matrix LCDs produce a brighter display and better color, but they are currently difficult to produce and hence more expensive.

Ada   [AY-duh]   A high-level *programming language*, based on *Pascal* and developed for the U.S. Department of Defense in the late 1970s. Ada was designed to be a standard, general-purpose language that would save the military the expense and trouble of maintaining many incompatible computer systems. It utilizes program *modules* that aid in the writing of large, complex programs. It also supports *real-time* applications necessary for control processes, such as launching a guided missile. Several versions of Ada are available for personal computers.

   Ada is named after Augusta *Ada* Byron (1815–1852), Countess of Lovelace and daughter of Lord Byron. She worked with Charles Babbage in developing programs for the Analytical Engine, the first mechanical computer. She is often called the world's first computer programmer.

adapter   A *printed circuit board* or *interface card* that can be installed in a personal computer to allow it to use additional *peripheral* devices or hardware. A network adapter, for example, allows a computer to be connected to a *network*. See also *expansion board, video adapter.*

ADB   Abbreviation of **Apple Desktop Bus.**

add-in   An accessory program designed to be used in conjunction with an existing *application* program to extend its capabilities or provide additional functions. For example, the *spreadsheet* application Lotus 1-2-3 can be supplemented with add-ins to analyze the logical structure of a spreadsheet, view spreadsheet files before actually retrieving them, or change the values in a spreadsheet formula to produce a desired outcome.

add-on A hardware device that is added to a computer to increase its capabilities. Common add-ons include additional hard drives, tape backup and *CD-ROM* drives, *graphics accelerators, sound boards,* and *modems.* See also *expansion board.*

address *n.* The name assigned to a location in memory where a specific *byte* of data is stored.
—*v.* To locate data in *memory* or to find places in memory where data can be written.

One source of failures in personal computer systems is address conflicts, which can occur when a program attempts to address a memory location that is unavailable or is being used by another program. Input/output ports such as serial ports are also assigned specific addresses so that they can be located and identified by the *operating system* and *BIOS* (basic input/output system). Addresses are usually expressed in *hexadecimal* notation. An absolute address is a fixed location in memory. A relative address is a memory location at a specified distance from some other location, called the base address. See also *base address, physical address, relative address, virtual address.*

address bus A *bus* that carries the addresses of data storage locations back and forth between the *CPU* (central processing unit) and *RAM* (random-access memory). The address bus enables the CPU to select a specific location in memory for the transfer of data (via the *data bus*) that the CPU needs in order to execute a specific instruction.

address space The set of all memory *addresses* that are available for a *microprocessor* or an *application* program to store and retrieve data. In early microprocessors, the available address space was limited to the system's actual, physical memory. More recent microprocessors can make use of *virtual memory* to create address spaces much larger than the available physical memory.

AI Abbreviation of **artificial intelligence.**

alert box In a *graphical user interface*, a *window* or box that appears on the screen to alert the user to an event requiring attention. For example, an alert box might display a message stating that the program cannot locate a needed file. An alert box does not request user input, unlike a *dialog box*, although you may need to *click* on it or press the *Enter key* to close it. Also called *message box*.

algorithm A procedure for solving a given problem using an established, finite sequence of unambiguously defined steps. People use algorithms constantly to perform everyday tasks and determine when they are finished. Good examples of everyday algorithms are recipes for cooking and the procedure for placing a telephone call. One advantage to this method of problem solving is that it is not necessary to understand each step in the procedure in order to arrive at the correct result; if the steps are followed in the right order and valid data are provided, the answer will be correct. Algorithms are the basis for most computer programming.

aliasing [AY-lee-uh-sing] In computer graphics, the appearance of jagged distortions called *jaggies* in curves and diagonal lines. Aliasing occurs because of limited display screen *resolution*. *Pixels* (dots on a screen) are arranged in rows and columns. If the pixel grid is too coarse, the pixels cannot be turned on in a pattern that will be perceived as a smooth curve or diagonal. See also *antialiasing*.

alphanumeric Consisting of any combination of alphabetic characters and the decimal numerals 0 through 9. In some contexts certain punctuation characters and other symbols are also included.

Alt key On keyboards for IBM PC and compatible computers, a key that is pressed in combination with another key to execute an alternate *function*. In Microsoft Windows applications, for example, Alt-F4 exits and closes a running program. See also *Control key, Shift key*.

analog **1.** Measuring or representing data by means of one or more physical properties that can express any value along a continuous scale. Analog modes are contrasted with *digital* modes, in which a variable must assume one of a number of discrete values and can only approximate values that lie between these points. A mercury thermometer and a clock with hands, for example, are analog devices. Most computers are strictly digital devices; they can accept input and produce output in analog form, but only with the help of digital-to-analog and analog-to-digital converters. Analog computers, which operate on continuously varying input data, are primarily used in specialized industrial and scientific contexts. **2.** Designating a type of display, as on a watch or radio, that makes use of a pointer or other indicator moving against a fixed scale rather than a series of changing numerical digits.

analog monitor A monitor that can accept continuously varying or *analog* signals from the computer's video adapter. This allows the monitor to display a continuous range of colors rather than a limited number of color values. *CGA* and *EGA* monitors are digital; *VGA* and *Super VGA* monitors are analog. VGA monitors combined with advanced graphics *adapters* can now display as many colors on screen as the human eye can distinguish. See also *digital monitor, fixed-frequency monitor, multifrequency monitor, multiscanning monitor.*

AND A *Boolean operator* that returns the value TRUE if both of its *operands* are TRUE. If either operand is false, AND returns the value FALSE. Table 2 shows the results of the AND operator.

Table 2. **Results of AND Operator**

a	b	a AND b
FALSE	FALSE	FALSE
FALSE	TRUE	FALSE
TRUE	FALSE	FALSE
TRUE	TRUE	TRUE

answer mode   An operating condition in which a modem is ready to answer an incoming call and establish a connection with the calling modem.

antialiasing   [an-tee-AY-lee-uh-sing]   In computer graphics, a software process for removing or reducing *jaggies*, the jagged distortions of characters in a *bit-mapped font* created by a graphic display with limited *resolution*. Antialiasing diminishes the conspicuousness of jaggies by surrounding them with shades of gray (for *gray scale* images) or color (for color images). This makes the jaggies less prominent but makes the character's edges fuzzier. Another method for reducing jaggies is called *smoothing*. See illustration. See also *aliasing*.

BIT MAP   ANTIALIASING   SMOOTHING
(with jaggies)

antialiasing

append   *v.* To add data or another file to the end of a file or string.
—*n.* A *DOS* command that instructs the operating system where to search for *data files*, analogous to the PATH command for *executable files*. See also *path*.

Apple Desktop Bus   Abbreviated **ADB**   A trademark for an *interface* built into Macintosh computers. The Apple Desktop Bus allows up to sixteen *serial* input devices (mouse, keyboard, trackball, etc.) to be connected to the computer through two 4-pin *ports* on the back. When more than two devices are to be connected, they are linked together in a configuration called a daisy chain. To avoid conflicts, each device on the bus listens to be sure the line is clear before attempting to access the computer.

AppleTalk   A trademark of Apple Computer Inc. for a *local area network* (LAN) standard that is built into *Macintosh* computers. AppleTalk uses a *bus topology* to link other Macintosh computers and *LaserWriter* printers. Although considerably slower than other LAN systems, it has the advantage of being easy to set up and connect with standard telephone cable. It is also possible to connect IBM PC and compatible computers to AppleTalk if they are provided with suitable hardware; also, AppleTalk can be linked to other networks through *gateways*.

application   A program or set of programs that enables people to use the computer as a tool to accomplish some task. A huge variety of applications software has been developed, including *word processors* and *text editors, spreadsheet* and accounting packages, *database* management programs, *communications software*, and programs for entertainment and education. In addition to specialized applications written for specific jobs, there are also *integrated* applications packages that provide relatively less comprehensive tools for a wider variety of tasks. Many programs fall between these extremes; for example, WordPerfect includes some *graphics* and *desktop publishing* capabilities, and some database programs include basic word processing facilities. See also *systems software, utility.* See illustrations at *programming language, software.*

architecture   The overall design or structure of a computer system. In general, it is applied to the entire system including all the *hardware* components and *systems software* needed to make it run. More specifically, it refers to the internal structure of a *microprocessor*, either in terms of its data-handling capacity (8 bits, 16 bits, or 32 bits) or the type of *instruction* set it uses. The instruction set consists of all instructions or commands in the computer's *machine language* that the microprocessor can recognize and execute. See also *CISC, closed architecture, open architecture, RISC.*

archival backup   1. See **full backup**.   2. See **incremental backup**.

archive   1. A long-term storage area, often on magnetic tape, for *backup* copies of files or files that are no longer in active use.   2. A file containing one or more files in compressed format for more efficient storage and transfer, which must be decompressed by a *file compression program* in order to be used. See also *data compression, packed file*.   3. An *attribute* in *DOS* that indicates files that have been changed since the last backup.

arg   Abbreviation of **argument**.

argument   Abbreviated **arg**   In *spreadsheet* programs and in programming languages, a value that is passed to a *function* so it can be operated on to produce a result. For example, if a function called LOG computes the common logarithm of a number, then the statement LOG(100), where the argument is 100, would return the value 2. The term is often used as a synonym for both *option* and *parameter*, as in the phrase "command line argument," which refers to an option to a *command*.

arithmetic expression   An *expression* that can be calculated to yield a numerical value. Arithmetic expressions can contain *constants* and *variables*. Examples are 6 * (5 + 4) and PRICE * QUANTITY * 0.05.

arithmetic operator   A symbol that stands for a numerical operation, such as addition or multiplication. Table 3 lists arithmetic operators and their results. See also *Boolean operator, relational operator*.

array   1. A group of many single elements, all of the same kind, arranged in a regular pattern and connected together to perform a single task.   2. In mathematics and computer programming, a structure consisting of a collection of single elements or pieces of data, all having the same *data type*, any of which can be located and retrieved by specifying the name of

Table 3. Arithmetic Operators and Their Results

Operator	Operation	Example	Result
^	Exponentiation	+D2^3	Raises the value in cell D2 to the third power.
*	Multiplication	+D2*D3	Multiplies the value in cell D2 by the value in cell D3.
/	Division	+D2/100	Divides the value in cell D2 by 100.
+	Addition	+D2+D3	Finds the sum of the values in cells D2 and D3.
−	Subtraction	+D2−10	Subtracts 10 from the value in cell D2.

the array and the element's location within the array. A one-dimensional data structure, with values arranged in a single row or column, is known as a *vector*. A two-dimensional array, with values in both rows and columns, is a *matrix*.

arrow keys   A set of four or more keys labeled with arrows pointing left, right, up, and down, that control the movement of the *cursor* or *insertion point* on the display screen. Depending on which program is running, the arrow keys may have additional functions when combined with the *Shift*, *Control*, or *Alt keys* (on IBM PC computers) or the Shift, *Option*, or *Command keys* (on Macintosh computers). For example, Shift-Up arrow may send the cursor to the beginning of a *document*. Also called *cursor control keys*.

artificial intelligence   Abbreviated **AI**   A branch of computer science that attempts to develop electronic devices that can operate with some of the characteristics of human intelligence. Among these properties are logical deduction and inference, creativity, the ability to make decisions based on past experience or insufficient or conflicting information, and the ability to understand *natural language*.

One of the earliest goals of AI research was to create rapid, accurate machine translation of natural languages. Although this effort attracted a great deal of attention, it has never progressed beyond a rudimentary and mostly unreliable stage, because few researchers were prepared to recognize the enormous complexity and subtlety of human language. More recent work in the modeling and emulation of *neural networks* and in *speech recognition* has shown some promise, however.

Although many of the early hopes of AI have yet to be fulfilled, this fact in itself has helped to reveal how much still remains to be understood about the processes of human thought and intelligence. See also *expert system, LISP, PROLOG, translation software.*

ascender The part of a lowercase letter that rises above the main body of the letter, as in a *b*, a *d*, or an *h*. See also *descender, x-height.*

ascending sort A *sort* in which the items are listed from first to last or smallest to largest, as from A to Z or from 0 to 9. See also *descending sort.*

ASCII [AS-kee] Acronym for **American Standard Code for Information Interchange.** A code that assigns the numbers 0

Table 4a. Standard ASCII Character Set—Control Codes and Space Characters

Decimal Value	Hexadecimal Value	Character & Meaning	Decimal Value	Hexadecimal Value	Character & Meaning
0	00	NUL Null	18	12	DC2 Device control 2
1	01	SOH Start of heading	19	13	DC3 Device control 3
2	02	STX Start of text	20	14	DC4 Device control 4
3	03	ETX End of text	21	15	NAK Negative
4	04	EOT End of transmis-			acknowledge
		sion	22	16	SYN Synchronous
5	05	ENQ Enquiry			idle
6	06	ACK Acknowledge	23	17	ETB End transmission
7	07	BEL Audible bell			block
8	08	BS Backspace	24	18	CAN Cancel
9	09	HT Horizontal tab	25	19	EM End of medium
10	0A	LF Line feed	26	1A	SUB Substitute
11	0B	VT Vertical tab	27	1B	ESC Escape
12	0C	FF Form feed	28	1C	FS File separator
13	0D	CR Carriage return	29	1D	GS Group separator
14	0E	SO Shift out	30	1E	RS Record separator
15	0F	SI Shift in	31	1F	US Unit separator
16	10	DLE Data link escape	32	20	SP Blank space character
17	11	DC1 Device control 1			

Table 4b. Standard ASCII Character Set—Alphanumeric Characters

Decimal Value	Hexadecimal Value	Character	Decimal Value	Hexadecimal Value	Character
33	21	!	81	51	Q
34	22	"	82	52	R
35	23	#	83	53	S
36	24	$	84	54	T
37	25	%	85	55	U
38	26	&	86	56	V
39	27	'	87	57	W
40	28	(	88	58	X
41	29	)	89	59	Y
42	2A	*	90	5A	Z
43	2B	+	91	5B	[
44	2C	,	92	5C	\
45	2D	-	93	5D	]
46	2E	.	94	5E	^
47	2F	/	95	5F	_
48	30	0	96	60	`
49	31	1	97	61	a
50	32	2	98	62	b
51	33	3	99	63	c
52	34	4	100	64	d
53	35	5	101	65	e
54	36	6	102	66	f
55	37	7	103	67	g
56	38	8	104	68	h
57	39	9	105	69	i
58	3A	:	106	6A	j
59	3B	;	107	6B	k
60	3C	<	108	6C	l
61	3D	=	109	6D	m
62	3E	>	110	6E	n
63	3F	?	111	6F	o
64	40	@	112	70	p
65	41	A	113	71	q
66	42	B	114	72	r
67	43	C	115	73	s
68	44	D	116	74	t
69	45	E	117	75	u
70	46	F	118	76	v
71	47	G	119	77	w
72	48	H	120	78	x
73	49	I	121	79	y
74	4A	J	122	7A	z
75	4B	K	123	7B	{
76	4C	L	124	7C		
77	4D	M	125	7D	}
78	4E	N	126	7E	~
79	4F	O	127	7F	△
80	50	P			

Table 4c. IBM Extended ASCII Character Set

Decimal Value	Hexadecimal Value	Character	Decimal Value	Hexadecimal Value	Character
128	80	Ç	177	B1	▒
129	81	ü	178	B2	▓
130	82	é	179	B3	│
131	83	â	180	B4	┤
132	84	ä	181	B5	╡
133	85	à	182	B6	╢
134	86	å	183	B7	╖
135	87	ç	184	B8	╕
136	88	ê	185	B9	╣
137	89	ë	186	BA	║
138	8A	è	187	BB	╗
139	8B	ï	188	BC	╝
140	8C	î	189	BD	╜
141	8D	ì	190	BE	╛
142	8E	Ä	191	BF	┐
143	8F	Å	192	C0	└
144	90	É	193	C1	┴
145	91	æ	194	C2	┬
146	92	Æ	195	C3	├
147	93	ô	196	C4	─
148	94	ö	197	C5	┼
149	95	ò	198	C6	╞
150	96	û	199	C7	╟
151	97	ù	200	C8	╚
152	98	ÿ	201	C9	╔
153	99	Ö	202	CA	╩
154	9A	Ü	203	CB	╦
155	9B	¢	204	CC	╠
156	9C	£	205	CD	═
157	9D	¥	206	CE	╬
158	9E	P_t	207	CF	╧
159	9F	f	208	D0	╨
160	A0	á	209	D1	╤
161	A1	í	210	D2	╥
162	A2	ó	211	D3	╙
163	A3	ú	212	D4	╘
164	A4	ñ	213	D5	╒
165	A5	Ñ	214	D6	╓
166	A6	ª	215	D7	╫
167	A7	º	216	D8	╪
168	A8	¿	217	D9	┘
169	A9	¬	218	DA	┌
170	AA	⌐	219	DB	█
171	AB	½	220	DC	▄
172	AC	¼	221	DD	▌
173	AD	¡	222	DE	▐
174	AE	«	223	DF	▀
175	AF	»	224	E0	α
176	B0	░	225	E1	β

Table 4c. IBM Extended ASCII Character Set (continued)

Decimal Value	Hexadecimal Value	Character	Decimal Value	Hexadecimal Value	Character
226	E2	Γ	241	F1	±
227	E3	π	242	F2	≥
228	E4	Σ	243	F3	≤
229	E5	σ	244	F4	⌠
230	E6	μ	245	F5	⌡
231	E7	τ	246	F6	÷
232	E8	Φ	247	F7	≈
233	E9	θ	248	F8	°
234	EA	Ω	249	F9	•
235	EB	δ	250	FA	·
236	EC	∞	251	FB	√
237	ED	φ	252	FC	η
238	EE	ε	253	FD	²
239	EF	∩	254	FE	■
240	F0	≡	255	FF	

through 127 to letters, the digits 0 to 9, punctuation marks, and certain other characters. For example, uppercase D is coded as decimal 68 (*binary* 1000100); an exclamation point is coded as decimal 33 (binary 0100001). By standardizing the values used to represent text, ASCII enables computers to exchange information.

Basic, or standard ASCII uses 7 *bits* for each character code, giving it 2^7, or 128, unique symbols. Various larger character sets, called *extended ASCII*, use 8 bits for each character, yielding 128 additional codes numbered 128 through 255. *EBCDIC* is another set of codes that is used on IBM *mainframes* and *minicomputers*. Table 4 lists the standard ASCII and IBM extended ASCII character sets.

ASCII file   A text file that contains only characters in the standard *ASCII* character set, without extended characters or formatting codes.

ASCII sort   A sort in which items are listed in order according to their numerical position in the *ASCII* character set. Numbers precede uppercase letters, which precede lowercase letters. See also *dictionary sort*.

aspect ratio   The ratio of width to height of a display screen or an image. Images will become distorted if forced into a different aspect ratio during enlargement, reduction, or transfer.

assembler   A program that converts a set of *instructions* written in *assembly language* into *machine language*.

assembly language   A programming language that is only one step removed from *machine language*. Assembly languages have the same structure as machine language, the major difference being that commands and functions are expressed in words rather than in numbers. Programs are converted into machine language by an *assembler*. Assembly language has certain advantages over *high-level languages*, including high speed, relatively low memory demands, and the ability to act directly on the system's hardware. For this reason many *operating systems* and *utility* programs are written in it. For everyday programming, however, assembly language code is difficult and tedious to write. All procedures must be spelled out in minute detail, and repeating an operation requires writing its entire block of *code* again. Assembly programs also must be rewritten if they are transferred from one type of microprocessor to another. See illustration at *programming language*.

asterisk   **1.** A character (*) used to indicate multiplication, as in 4 * 2 = 8.   **2.** In file names, a character (*) used as a *wild card* that can stand for any number of unspecified characters. For example, *.EXE specifies all files with the *extension* .EXE.

asynchronous   Of, related to, or being a telecommunications mode that does not rely on an independent timing signal to identify the beginning and end of each *byte* of data that is transmitted. In asynchronous mode, the communicating devices are free to send data in a continuous stream whenever both devices are ready. The beginning of each byte is identified by a *start bit*, and the end by a *stop bit*. Most communications between personal computers is asynchronous, because the relatively lower transmission speeds permit the use of standard telephone lines. See also *modem, parity, synchronous*.

attribute **1.** In *applications*, a characteristic of a block of text or of a database *field*. Style and size are text attributes; a database field's attribute might specify that the field contains only numerical data in the form of percentages. **2.** In *DOS* file management, a property that can be assigned to a *file* to indicate whether it is a read-only file, a *system* file, or a *hidden file* or whether it has been changed since the last *backup*.

audit trail **1.** In accounting and database management software, a complete record of all transactions and changes made to a document. This allows the document's history to be reconstructed in case of data loss or error. **2.** In systems management, a record of all activity on a network, used primarily for security purposes.

authoring language A computer language or application designed to help create *graphics* and *multimedia* presentations, *hypertext* documents, and *CAI* (computer-aided instruction) programs. Authoring languages provide tools for linking together text, graphic, and sound objects to create new application programs. A well-known authoring language for writing instructional programs is PILOT. Macintosh computers include an authoring language called *HyperCard*. Also called *authoring tool*.

AUTOEXEC.BAT *Auto*matic *exec*ute *bat*ch file, a file that *DOS* automatically executes when you start or restart the computer. See also *batch file*.

auto-redial A feature that allows a *modem* to dial a number repeatedly when it receives a busy signal.

autorepeat A feature that allows a key on a *keyboard* to repeat its assigned keystroke continuously until the key is released.

autosave   A feature in *applications* that minimizes loss of data in the event of system failure by automatically saving an open file to disk at periodic intervals. Also called *timed backup*. See also *save*.

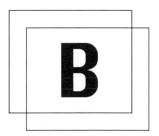

background   **1.** One or more operations that a computer is carrying out in addition to the one that is the main focus of the user's attention. Until recent years, the function that most commonly occurred as a background operation was printing, as most operating systems and word processors enabled the user to direct one document to a printer while returning to work on another document without having to wait for the printer to release control of the computer.

  With the more widespread use of *multitasking* operating systems, however, the concept of background processing has become more general. In a multitasking environment it is possible to have multiple programs running simultaneously and sharing *CPU* time. This allows a user to continue working while the CPU completes time-consuming operations such as large spreadsheet recalculations, file sorts, and modem-to-modem file transfers. It also makes it possible to leave facilities such as *electronic mail* and *fax modems* active and waiting to notify the user when a message is received. Background processes are often hidden from view and do not

allow the user to interact with them until they are switched
to the *foreground*. They typically receive a lower priority; that
is, a smaller amount of microprocessor time, so as not to slow
the operation of the current foreground process unduly. See
also *spooling*. **2.** The area of a *display screen* over which
characters and graphics appear. On many *monitors*, the user
can set the color, shading, or pattern of the background.

backlighting   A technique used in *laptop computers* and *notebook computers* to increase the legibility of an *LCD* display
screen by illuminating it from behind. This heightens the
contrast between the text and the *background*, but at the cost
of more quickly running down the computer's batteries.

back slash   A character (\\) used to indicate the *root directory*
and to separate *subdirectories* in *DOS* file names.

Backspace key   A key that moves the cursor one space to the left
and deletes whatever *character* is there. See also *Delete key*.

backup   **1.** The process or an instance of backing up.   **2.** A
disk or tape that contains files copied in a backup. See also
data compression, DMA.

back up   To copy files from one *storage* area, especially a *hard
disk*, to another to prevent their loss in case of disk failure.
For today's personal computers, where a typical hard disk can
easily contain 120–200 *megabytes* of data, regular *backups*
are crucial. Many professionals recommend that you make at
least two *backups* and keep the extra backup in another location in case of fire or theft. Files can be backed up by using
operating system commands or a backup *utility* program.
Backup utilities are faster and usually compress the data so
that fewer disks or tapes are required.

backward compatible   Of or relating to a computer system or
software program that does not make earlier versions obsolete. For example, IBM PC-compatibles based on the *Pentium
microprocessor* can run all software that will run on the ear-

lier 80486. Similarly, later versions of most *application* programs can read files generated with earlier versions.

Manufacturers strive to maintain backward compatibility
when they develop new hardware and software, because it
avoids the need for users to start from scratch every time they
upgrade to a new version. Occasionally, however, the capabilities of newer products become so far advanced that a certain
amount of compatibility has to be given up. Powerful new
operating systems and *graphical user interfaces* such as
Microsoft Windows and IBM's *OS/2*, for example, cannot be
run on many older machines because they take advantage of
operating modes available only in newer microprocessors.
Also called *downward compatible*. See also *compatible, forward compatible*.

bad break   In word processing and desktop publishing, a place
where a word, line, or page is improperly divided. Examples
include setting the second part of a hyphenated word at the
beginning of a left-hand page, hyphenating "minute" at the
end of a line as "min-ute" when the word in a document is
actually "mi-nute," and leaving a section title stranded at the
very bottom of a page.

bad sector   A *sector* of a hard disk or floppy disk that cannot be
used for reading and writing information because of a manufacturing defect or a flaw in the surface. It is normal for a new
hard disk to have a small number of bad sectors; the operating
system or a disk utility program can locate and mark these
areas so they will not be used. As a hard disk gets older, more
sectors may occasionally fail, but if this happens frequently it
is a sign of a malfunctioning disk drive or impending disk failure. If bad sectors appear on a floppy disk, some data will usually be lost and the entire disk may become unusable; the
safest policy generally is to copy the remaining files to a fresh
disk, if possible, and discard the one that has failed. See also
disk, format, head crash, sector.

bandwidth   A measure of the amount of data that can be
passed by a communications channel in a given amount of

time. For *analog* devices, bandwidth is the range of frequencies that can be transmitted and is expressed in *hertz* (cycles per second). A standard telephone line, for example, has a usable bandwidth of about 3,000 Hz. For *digital* devices, bandwidth is often measured in *bps* (bits per second). The bandwidth of a *data bus*, for example, is the number of *bits* of data the bus can transmit at one time. A 32-bit bus can transmit twice as much data as a 16-bit bus. In general, the bandwidth of a channel directly affects the speed of data transfer—the wider the bandwidth, the faster data can be sent.

base address　The beginning *address* for a sequence of *code* or data. The base address acts as a reference point. Another address in the sequence is specified by giving its distance, or *offset*, from the base address. An address in the form of a base address plus an offset is called a *relative address*.

base font　In word processing, the default *font* that is used in a document wherever a different font is not specifically selected.

BASIC　[BAY-sik]　Acronym for **Beginners' All-purpose Symbolic Instruction Code.** A simple, widely used high-level *programming language*. It was first developed in the mid-1960s by John Kemeny and Thomas Kurtz of Dartmouth College, and many other versions with *proprietary* extensions have also been developed over the years. Despite being criticized by professional programmers for its unwieldiness, BASIC is still widely taught to students as a first programming language. A recent version of BASIC, Microsoft's Visual Basic, eases the task of creating *applications* for *Microsoft Windows*. Programmers create on-screen objects using graphics tools and then write code in Visual Basic that specifies how the on-screen objects work and interact.

basic input/output system　See **BIOS.**

batch file　A *text file* that consists of a number of commands to be executed onc after the other. Batch files offer a convenient way to carry out a frequently executed sequence of commands by simply typing the name of the batch file. They are easy to create and can include a small number of programming functions, such as IF . . . THEN, GOTO, and FOR . . . IN . . . DO constructs, which make the command line interface much faster and more powerful. It is also possible to call one batch file from within another, executing the second file and then returning control to the first. All batch files in DOS have the extension .BAT; hence they are often called *BAT files.*

As the last step in the boot-up sequence, most DOS-based computers automatically run the file AUTOEXEC.BAT, which can be used to set a number of system parameters and install device *drivers* and *terminate and stay resident* (TSR) programs without the user's having to enter the commands one by one. See table at *file.*

batch processing   A mode of computer operation in which a complete program or set of instructions is carried out from start to finish without any intervention from a user. Batch processing is a highly efficient way of using computer resources, but it does not allow for any input while the batch is running, or any corrections in the event of a flaw in the program or a system failure. For these reasons it is primarily used for CPU-intensive tasks that are well established and can run reliably without supervision, often at night or on weekends when other demands on the system are low. See also *interactive, transaction processing.*

BAT file   [bat]   See **batch file.**

baud   A unit of speed in data transmission usually equal to one *bps* (bit per second). See also *baud rate.*

baud rate   In telecommunications, the number of switching events, or frequency changes in electrical state, that can occur in a given communications circuit in one second. At slower speeds, i.e. 300 to 1,200 baud, the data transmission rate is generally synonymous with the rate in *bps* (bits per second). In other words, at 300 baud, 300 bits per second are transmitted. At higher baud rates, however, it is possible to transmit more bits per second than the equivalent baud rate. For example, 9,600 bps can actually be transmitted at a baud rate of 4,800 by sending 2 bits of data with each frequency change. Note that, because the low-end modem speed is now closer to 9,600, the term "baud" is becoming outdated and bits per second, as a standard measure of transmission speed, is now more accurate.

bay   A space in the cabinet of a personal computer where a *storage device* such as a disk drive, tape drive, or CD-ROM drive can be installed. A bay is referred to as "internal" or "hidden" when it cannot be used for removable media, such as floppy disk drives; otherwise it is called "exposed" or "accessible." Also called *drive bay*. See also *disk drive*, *expansion board*, *slot*.

BBS   Abbreviation of **bulletin board system.**

benchmark   A standard by which the performance of hardware or software is measured. Benchmark tests typically measure efficiency and the speed at which a program or computer component performs a certain task, but these measurements are not reliable in gauging the actual performance of the whole computer system. For example, the output from a *microprocessor* that performs well in a benchmark test could be held up by slow disk drives. *Throughput*, a measurement of a computer's ability to send data through all of its components, is often a better overall indication of a computer's speed than individual benchmark measurements. See also *throughput*.

Bernoulli Box   [ber-NOO-lee]   A trademark of Iomega Corporation for a type of *mass storage* device that uses removable cartridges similar to floppy disks. The main feature of a Bernoulli Box is that the disk is flexible and spins at a high speed. As the disk begins to spin, the decreased air pressure along its surface causes it to be pulled nearly into contact with the read/write *head*, but a thin cushion of air remains to isolate the head from the disk's surface. This makes the drive unlikely to suffer a *head crash*, and the high rotation speed makes the Bernoulli Box significantly faster than traditional floppy drives. It also has a greater storage capacity of up to 44MB. Also called *Bernoulli disk drive*. See also *floppy disk, hard disk*.

beta test The final stage in the testing of new software, conducted by independent testers outside the company that developed it, before it is released commercially. The specific software product being tested is called a "beta version."

Bézier curve [BEZ-ee-ay] A smooth free-form curve used in nearly all *draw programs*. The shape of the curve is determined mathematically by the location of two midpoints called "control handles," or simply *handles*. Usually the handles appear on the screen as two small boxes. By clicking on the handles and dragging them with the mouse, you can change the shape of the curve. See illustration.

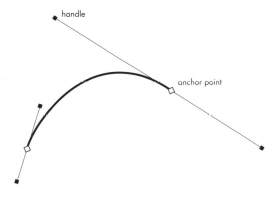

Bézier curve

binary Of or relating to a number system with a base of two. Each place in a binary number represents a power of two, in contrast with the *decimal* (base ten) system most of us use every day, in which each place in a number represents a successive power of ten. Thus the decimal number 165, which really stands for

$$(1 \times 10^2) + (6 \times 10^1) + (5 \times 10^0)$$

is written in binary notation as 10100101, which stands for

$$(1 \times 2^7) + (0 \times 2^6) + (1 \times 2^5) + (0 \times 2^4) +$$
$$(0 \times 2^3) + (1 \times 2^2) + (0 \times 2^1) + (1 \times 2^0).$$

This kind of notation is unnatural and difficult for humans to read, but it is ideal for computers, because an electronic circuit that only has to differentiate between two states—on or off, open or closed, 0 or 1—is easier to build and can operate faster than one that must detect and work with ten possible states. Table 5 lists decimal, binary, octal, and hexadecimal equivalents. See also *hexadecimal, octal*.

Table 5. Binary, Octal, and Hexadecimal Values

Decimal	Binary	Octal	Hexadecimal
0	000	0	0
1	001	1	1
2	010	2	2
3	011	3	3
4	100	4	4
5	101	5	5
6	110	6	6
7	111	7	7
8	1000	–	8
9	1001	–	9
10	1010	–	A
11	1011	–	B
12	1100	–	C
13	1101	–	D
14	1110	–	E
15	1111	–	F

binary file   A file containing numeric data or program instructions in a computer-readable form. See also *ASCII file, text file*. See table at *file*.

BIOS [BYE-ose]   Acronym for **basic input/output system.** A set of *instructions* and *routines* that enable the computer to communicate with the various devices in the system, such as memory, disk drives, keyboard, monitor, printer, and communications ports. Just as the *operating system* lets *applications* programs interact with the computer without having to tell it exactly how to carry out every operation, the BIOS mediates between the operating system and the *hardware*, taking care of the intricate details of getting the various devices to work smoothly together. The BIOS in IBM PC and compatible computers is contained in the system's *ROM* (read-only memory), making it available when the system boots up and keeping it safe in case of system failure. See also *I/O, shadowing.*

bit [bit]   Acronym for **binary digit.** The smallest unit of memory and therefore information within a computer. A bit can hold only one of two values, 0 or 1. In the *binary* number system, the digits 0 and 1 are also called bits. See also *ASCII, byte.*

bit map   A set of *bits* that represents a graphic image in *memory*. Each bit corresponds to a dot in a pattern. For a monochromatic image, the bit map consists of rows and columns of 0s and 1s. Each value determines whether its dot is to be filled in (1) or not (0). For a color image or one with shades of gray, each dot requires more than one bit of data. To print the image on a printer, the computer translates the bit map into ink dots. To display the image on a screen, the computer translates the bit map into *pixels* (dots of light). *Optical scanners* and *fax machines* convert text or pictures into bit maps. See also *dots per inch, resolution.*

bit-mapped font   A *font* in which each character is represented by a pattern of dots. To display or print a bit-mapped font, the computer or printer must have a *bit map* of each character in *memory*. This means bit-mapped fonts require huge amounts of memory and *disk* space. Furthermore, bit-mapped fonts cannot be scaled up or down, as from Times Roman 12 point to Times Roman 16 point, without developing *jaggies*. See also *antialiasing, scalable font.* See illustration at *outline font.*

bit-mapped graphics Graphic images that are stored in memory as *arrays* of bits that specify the appearance of each individual *pixel* on the screen. Bit-mapped graphics are commonly produced by *paint programs.* Because they are not mapped in memory as sets of objects but only as undifferentiated sequences of dots, it is difficult to pick out one element of a bit-mapped drawing for editing. The *resolution* of bit-mapped images is limited to that of the display screen, scaling them up or down to different sizes does not work very well, and they require large amounts of memory and storage space. See also *bit map, object-oriented graphics, raster graphics, vector graphics.* See illustration at *pixel.*

bits per second See **bps.**

blank character A character that produces no visible representation other than a space on the screen, usually generated by pressing the *space bar.*

block **1.** In word processing, a section of text that is marked so that some operation can be performed on it as a unit. The ability to manipulate marked blocks of text is perhaps the most important feature that distinguishes *word processing* from manuscript preparation with a typewriter. Marking is usually done by highlighting the desired text with the *arrow keys* or by using the mouse to *drag* the cursor over it. Once a block is marked, it can be *deleted, copied,* moved to another document or another location in the same document, *saved* as a named file, or *printed* with a few keystrokes or mouse clicks. Another powerful kind of operation that can be performed on a block of text is reformatting, in which the margins, spacing, and size and appearance of the type can be changed quickly for any portion of a document. See also *block protection, cut and paste.* **2.** In telecommunications, an amount of data transferred from one system to another as a unit. In general, the larger the block size, the faster the data transfer rate, but if noisy telephone lines or other disruptions cause errors that make it necessary to repeat blocks, smaller block sizes are more efficient. The most common transfer *protocols* use block sizes ranging from 128 bytes to 1,024 bytes.

block protection In word processing, a feature that allows a *block* of text to be kept together as a unit when moved to a location where it would otherwise be interrupted by page breaks.

board See **printed circuit board.**

boldface A typeface in which the letters are heavier and darker than normal. The entry words in this dictionary are printed in boldface. See illustration at *font family.*

bomb *n.* An abrupt and complete failure, especially of a running program.
—*v.* To fail suddenly and completely. See also *crash.*

Boolean expression [BOO-lee-en] An *expression* that yields a value of TRUE or FALSE. Boolean expressions can contain *relational operators* such as = for "is equal to"; < for "is less than"; and > for "is greater than." For example, the statement 26 > 30 returns the value FALSE. The other main type of operator in Boolean expressions is a *Boolean* (sometimes called logical) *operator,* such as *AND, OR, NOT, NOR,* or *XOR.* For example, if A is the statement "Ice is cold" (and we assume that the statement is true), the result of the expression NOT A is FALSE.

Boolean logic A form of algebra that employs only two values, TRUE and FALSE. Boolean logic, developed by the 19th-century English mathematician George Boole, is particularly well suited for use with computers because it works so well with the *binary* number system. A bit with value 1 corresponds to TRUE; a bit with value 0 corresponds to FALSE. See also *Boolean operator.*

Boolean operator   An operator whose result can only be one of two values, TRUE or FALSE. Boolean operators are widely used in programming, *spreadsheets*, and *databases*. Common Boolean operators are *AND*, *OR*, *XOR*, and *NOT*. For example, the database *query*

find all where last_name = "Jones" AND balance_owed > 100

would yield the records of everyone named Jones who owed more than $100. The query

find all where last_name = "Jones" OR balance_owed > 100

would yield the records of everyone named Jones regardless of the balance owed and the records of everyone who owed more than $100 regardless of last name. Also called *logical operator*.

boot   *v.* To load the *software*, usually the *operating system*, that starts the computer.
—*n.* The process of loading the software that starts the computer. See also *cold boot, warm boot*.

bps   Abbreviation of **bits per second.**   A measure of data transmission rate. For example, a common rate for a *modem* to transmit and receive data is 9,600 bps. See also *baud, baud rate*.

Break key   A key that causes a computer to pause in the middle of an operation, such as sorting a file, or to break a *modem* connection. Not all keyboards have a Break key, nor do all programs recognize it. In many cases a break is executed by pressing a combination of two keys. See also *Ctrl-Break*.

bridge   A device that connects two *local area networks* and makes it possible for them to exchange data, even though they may have different *topologies* or *communications protocols*.

broadcast   To simultaneously send one message to a number of receivers, as in an *electronic mail* system or over a *network*.

brownout   A reduction in electric power, usually as a result of a shortage, a mechanical failure, or overuse by consumers. A computer subject to these power interruptions can lose data or even *crash*. See also *surge protector, UPS.*

browse   To view information without manipulating it. Browsing enables the user to move through a large number of files or database *records* quickly, but usually does not allow the user to change data.

buffer   A temporary storage area for data, usually located in the computer's *RAM*, used to compensate for differences in rates of processing when data is being transmitted from one computer device to another. The *CPU* of a computer can process data much faster than a printer can, for example. When the user enters a print command, the *operating system* copies the data to a print buffer, from which the printer pulls characters at its own pace. A print buffer is often called a *spooler.*

Since writing to disk is another relatively slow task, many text *editors* and *word processors* save changes to text in a buffer. Then, at either set intervals or at the end of an editing session, they transfer the updated text from the buffer to the document's disk file. Saving the file during the editing session forces the editor or word processor to write the changes to disk.

Many operating systems, including *DOS,* employ a disk buffer to temporarily store data they have read from disk. DOS allows the user to specify the memory allocated to disk buffers by placing a BUFFER command in the *CONFIG.SYS* file. Each DOS buffer uses 528 *bytes,* so the command BUFFERS=10 reserves about 5 *kilobytes* of RAM for buffers. In Macintosh computers, the disk buffer is called a *cache,* and its memory allocation is set via the *Control Panel.*

bug   A defect in software or hardware that causes it to perform inconsistently, *crash,* or otherwise malfunction. The word was allegedly coined when a moth caused a short circuit in one of the earliest computers.

built-in font   See **resident font.**

bulletin board system Abbreviated **BBS** An electronic communication system that allows users to leave messages, review messages, play games, and upload and download software, especially *public domain software*. Computers are connected to a BBS by *modem*. Thousands of BBSs are active in the United States alone. BBSs are often good resources for tips and advice about various software products, but they can bring trouble to your system if you download software that has been contaminated with a *virus*. See also *SIG, SYSOP*.

bundled software 1. Programs that are included as part of the package when you buy a computer. 2. Several programs packaged and sold together.

burn-in *v.* To run a new computer continuously for an extended period, usually 24 to 48 hours, in order to test for defective memory chips, microprocessors, and other components.
—*n.* See **ghosting**.

bus 1. A circuit that connects the components of a computer, allowing the transfer of electric signals from one connected component to any other. The electric signals encode data, and the bus is the pathway on which data travels throughout the computer. Personal computers have three of these pathways— the *data bus*, the *address bus*, and the *expansion bus*. The data bus carries data back and forth between the computer's *RAM* (random-access memory) and its *CPU*. The address bus carries the *addresses* of data storage locations back and forth between RAM and the CPU. The expansion bus connects the CPU with the various computer components, including *expansion boards* and *peripherals* such as disk drives, keyboards, display screens, and printers. Each device connected to the expansion bus has its own *controller*. A controller regulates the transfer of data between the device and the bus.

The size of a bus, called its width, determines how much data it can carry at once. More technically, the width of the bus is the number of signal lines used to transmit data in parallel, each line carrying one data *bit*. A 16-bit bus transmits

16 bits of data at one time, just like 16 trucks traveling side by side on a 16-lane highway. Another characteristic of buses is that their *clock speed* is measured in *megahertz* (MHz). Table 6 shows a comparison of some popular buses. **2.** One of the three principal *topologies* for a local area network, in which all computers and devices, known as *nodes*, are connected to a central cable along which data is passed. See also *ring, star*. See illlustration at *network*. **3.** The central cable used in a bus topology.

Table 6. Types of Expansion Buses

Type	Computer(s) Designed for	Width (bits)	Backward Compatible?
ISA	IBM PC/XT	8	N/A
	IBM PC/AT	16	Yes
EISA	IBM PC-compatibles using Intel 80386 or 80486 microprocessors	32	Yes
Micro Channel Architecture	High-end versions of IBM PS/2	32	No
NuBus	Macintosh II and above	32	N/A

bus mouse A *mouse* connected to the computer through an *expansion board*, as opposed to a *serial mouse*, which is connected through a *serial port*. One advantage of using a bus mouse is that it does not tie up one of the computer's serial ports.

button **1.** In *graphical user interface* systems, a small outlined area within a *dialog box* that is clicked to select a command. **2.** In a *hypertext* database, an *icon* that when selected allows a user to view a particular associated object. Text, pictures, recorded music, and other forms of information are called objects; associated objects are linked together.

byte The amount of computer memory needed to store a single character. On most computers, a byte is made up of eight adjacent *bits*. Each bit has a value of either 0 or 1, and the various eight-bit combinations represent all of the data in a com-

puter. Amounts of computer memory are often expressed in
terms of *kilobytes* (1,024 bytes) and *megabytes* (1,048,576
bytes).

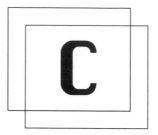

C A *high-level language* widely used in writing professional
software. Known as an efficient and flexible programming
language, C was developed by Dennis Ritchie and Brian
Kernighan of AT&T Bell Laboratories in the 1970s. C is closer
to *assembly language* than many other languages, making its
codes faster but also more difficult to learn than other high-
level languages. C is also known as a *portable* language, in
that C programs can be easily rewritten to run on computers
based on different *microprocessors*.

C++ A programming language originally based on C that uses
object-oriented programming. C++ was developed in the early
1980s by Bjarne Stroustrup at AT&T Bell Laboratories.

cache [kash] An area of *RAM* that stores frequently used data
or instructions for fast access. See also *disk cache, RAM
cache.*

CAD [kad] Acronym for **computer-aided design.** The use of
computer programs and systems to design detailed two- or
three-dimensional models of physical objects, such as me-

chanical parts, buildings, and molecules. Many CAD systems allow the user to view models from any angle, to move about inside of the model, and to change its scale. When the designer or engineer changes one part of a model, the CAD system is able to reconfigure the rest of the model around this new specification. CAD systems require fast microprocessors and high-resolution video displays. Until the last few years, all CAD systems were *dedicated*, or specially built, *minicomputers*. CAD software that runs on general-purpose *workstations* and powerful *personal computers* is now available.

CAD/CAM [KAD-kam] Acronym for **computer-aided design/ computer-aided manufacturing.** A computer system that designs and manufactures products. An object is designed with the CAD component of the system, and the design is then translated into manufacturing or assembly instructions for specialized machinery. See also *CAD, CAM.*

CAI Abbreviation of **computer-aided instruction.** The use of computer programs as teaching tools. CAI software usually offers tutorials, drills, and tests and allows the student to proceed at his or her own pace.

calculated field In a *database*, a *field* that contains results of calculations performed on other fields. In a database showing each country's area and population, for example, the calculated field could give population density figures.

calculator A program or a part of an *operating system* that enables the user to perform arithmetic calculations, usually on an on-screen representation of a hand-held calculator. The calculator is operated with the keyboard or with a mouse. See also *desk accessory.*

calendar An *application* that works as an electronic datebook. Besides allowing you to set appointments, many calendar programs can automatically set entries for weekly or monthly events. Some calendar programs can issue a signal to remind you of an important engagement or a significant day. See also *PIM.*

call *v.* In programming, to invoke and transfer control to a *routine, subroutine,* or *function.* When the called procedure is completed, program execution resumes at the next *instruction* after the calling point.
—*n.* An invocation of a routine, subroutine, or function.

CAM [kam] Acronym for **computer-aided manufacturing.** The process of using specialized computers to control, monitor, and adjust tools and machinery in manufacturing. See also *CAD/CAM, robotics.*

Caps Lock key A *toggle* key on a computer *keyboard* that when activated locks the keyboard so that you can enter *uppercase* letters without pressing the *Shift key.* The computer's Caps Lock key has no effect on number and punctuation keys, unlike a Caps Lock key on a typewriter. Most keyboards have a light that illuminates when the Caps Lock key is pressed.

card **1.** A *printed circuit board,* especially one designed to fit an *expansion slot* in a personal computer; an *adapter.* **2.** In *HyperCard* and similar programs, a card is an on-screen representation of an index card on which information can be written and "filed."

carriage The mechanism that feeds paper through a printer. On *dot-matrix* and *ink-jet printers,* the assembly that moves the print head across the page is called the print head carriage assembly.

carriage return Abbreviated **CR** On personal computers, a code that brings the *cursor* back to the beginning of the same line. (In the *ASCII* character set, a carriage return is coded as the *decimal* value 13.) To move the cursor to the beginning of a new line you press the *Enter key* or the *Return key.* Most word processing and desktop publishing programs feature *word wrap,* which automatically starts a new line once the current line is filled. See also *hard return, line feed.*

carrier   1. A telecommunications company.   **2.** A steady signal or tone of a specified frequency that is sent along a communications line. The carrier can be modulated, or changed,
as in frequency or amplitude, by a device such as a *modem* in
order to transmit information from one computer to another.

cartridge   1. A removable unit that contains a data storage
medium such as tape, disks, or memory *chips*. The term
removable cartridge generally refers to a type of portable hard
disk.   **2.** A removable unit used to load fonts into some
printers, giving you the option to print in other fonts besides
the *base font*. See also *font cartridge*.

cartridge font   See **font cartridge**.

cascading menu   A *submenu* that appears on the screen when
a choice from another menu is selected. See illustration at
menu.

cascading windows   See **overlaid windows**.

case-sensitive   Able to distinguish between *uppercase* (capital)
and *lowercase* (small) letters. Programs that are case-sensitive
and have a search feature will distinguish between "APPLE,"
"apple," and "Apple," for example. Case-sensitive programs
will respond differently to commands issued in uppercase versus lowercase letters. *DOS* is case-insensitive; its commands
can be typed in uppercase or lowercase.

cathode-ray tube   Abbreviated **CRT**   The basic element in
standard computer *monitors* and television sets. In a *monochrome* monitor, the *video adapter* sends signals to an electron gun at the back of the CRT. In response, the electron gun
shoots out a stream of electrons. Another mechanism, also
controlled by signals from the adapter, focuses and aims the
electron beams so that they strike the phosphors coating the
inside of the *display screen*. Phosphors are materials that
glow when struck by electrons. The electron beams sweep
across the screen about 60 times a second, continually re-illu-

minating, or *refreshing*, the appropriate phosphors. Color monitors work on the same principle, but use three electron guns (one each for red, blue, and green) and three different phosphor materials.

CD   Abbreviation of **compact disk.**

cdev   [SEE-dev]   Acronym for **control panel device.** Any of various *utility* programs for the Macintosh computer that appear as options in the *Control Panel* and work from the *system folder.*

CD-I   Abbreviation of **Compact Disk-Interactive.**   A standard format for combining and storing audio, video, and text on high-capacity *compact disks.* The technology is designed for *interactive* viewing of video images on a computer screen, using a CD-I drive. CD-I was developed by Philips International. *DVI* (Digital Video Interactive), owned by Intel, is a competing standard.

CD-ROM   [SEE-dee-ROM]   Acronym for **compact disk–read-only memory.**   A *compact disk* that functions as *ROM* (read-only memory). CD-ROMs can store over 600 *megabytes* (MB) of data. The data must be input with special equipment, and it can be used only on a CD-ROM drive. Since they are read-only, CD-ROMs do not accept additional data or files and cannot be erased. At present, CD-ROMs are chiefly used to store large reference works, such as encyclopedias and dictionaries. See also *erasable optical disk, optical disk.* See table at *access time.*

cell   One box or unit for entering information within a *spreadsheet.* The information can be in the form of text, numbers, *formulas,* or *functions.* The spreadsheet is formed by intersecting rows and columns of cells. See illustration at *spreadsheet.*

cell block   See **range.**

central processing unit   See **CPU.**

Centronics interface   1. The *standard* for connecting the *parallel port* of an IBM PC or compatible computer with a *parallel* device, usually a printer. The standard provides for eight *bits* of data to be sent simultaneously over eight parallel lines. The cable connecting the computer's parallel port with the device uses a 25-pin *connector*. Eight of the pins are for the data lines; the rest are either lines for sending *control character* codes or simply ground lines.   **2.** The parallel port of an IBM PC or compatible computer. In this sense, also called *Centronics port*. See also *parallel interface*. See illustration at *connector*.

CGA   Abbreviation of **Color Graphics Adapter.**   The first color *video adapter* and *video standard* used with IBM PC and compatible computers, introduced in 1981. The CGA system has been superseded by the *EGA* (Enhanced Graphics Adapter) and *VGA* (Video Graphics Array) systems. See table at *video standard*.

character   A symbol, such as a letter, number, punctuation mark, or graphics symbol, that occupies one *byte* of memory. Each symbol represented by an *ASCII* or *extended ASCII* code is a character. See also *control character*.

character-based   Of or relating to programs that can display only *ASCII* and *extended ASCII* characters. Character-based programs for IBM PC and compatible computers treat display screens as an array of boxes, each of which can hold one character. Because the extended ASCII character set includes shapes for drawing pictures, character-based programs can simulate graphics objects that consist mostly of straight lines, such as *menus, windows,* and bar charts.

Many *DOS* applications, such as word processors and spreadsheets, are written as character-based programs so that they can be run on any IBM PC or compatible computer, even one with limited memory and graphics capabilities. Increasingly, software manufacturers are developing *graphics-based* applications that utilize *operating environments* such as *Microsoft Windows.* Graphics-based programs treat the display

```
 ┌─────────────────────────────────────────────────────────────────┐
 │ File  Edit  Search  Options                                Help   │
 │ ─────────────── HELP: Survival Guide ──────────────               │
 │ Using the MS-DOS Editor:                                          │
 │                                                                   │
 │   ■ To activate the MS-DOS Editor menu bar, press Alt.            │
 │   ■ To activate menus and commands, press the highlighted letter. │
 │   ■ To move between menus and commands, use the direction keys.   │
 │   ■ To get help on a selected menu, command, or dialog box, press F1. │
 │   ■ To exit Help, press Esc.                                      │
 │                                                                   │
 │ Browsing the MS-DOS Editor Help system:                           │
 │                                                                   │
 │   ■ To select one of the following topics, press the Tab key or the first │
 │     letter of the topic. Then press the Enter key to see information on: │
 │                                                                   │
 │   ◄Getting Started► Loading and using the MS-DOS Editor and the   │
 │                     MS-DOS Editor Help system                     │
 │     ◄Keyboard►      Editing and navigating text and MS-DOS Editor Help │
 │                                                                   │
 │ Tip: These topics are also available from the Help menu.          │
 │                                                                   │
 │ ───────────────────── Untitled ─────────────────────             │
 │ <F1=Help>  <F6=Window>  <Esc=Cancel>  <Ctrl+F1=Next>  <Alt+F1=Back> │
 └─────────────────────────────────────────────────────────────────┘
```

character-based program
The survival guide of the MS-DOS edit program

screen as a grid of millions of pixels. The Macintosh computer is graphics-based. See illustration. See also *graphical user interface.*

character mode A mode of *resolution* supported by a *video adapter* that allows the screen to display *characters* only, with no complex graphical images. In the character mode the screen is split into boxes. Each box can hold one *ASCII* character, and these characters do not necessarily look exactly as they will in print. The other display mode, *graphics mode*, splits the screen into millions of *pixels* rather than boxes, and is able to display text as it will appear in print, as well as complex graphics. See also *text mode.*

characters per inch Abbreviated **cpi** The number of characters that fit into a one-inch long line of type of a particular *font*. In *monospace fonts*, all characters have a constant width. But in *proportional fonts* characters have varying widths, so measurements of the number of characters must be averaged to compute characters per inch.

characters per second Abbreviated **cps** **1.** A measure of the speed of *dot-matrix* and *daisy wheel printers*. See also *pages per minute.* **2.** A measure of data transmission rate.

character string   See **string.**

checksum   A technique for detecting errors in the transmission of data. The computer transmitting information assigns a numerical value based on the number of bits in the data being sent and includes this in its transmission. The receiving computer does the same calculation. If the resulting numerical value is different, the receiving computer asks for the data to be resubmitted. Checksum is frequently used in modem transmissions. See also *communications protocol.*

chip   A minute slice of *semiconductor* material, usually silicon, arranged into positive and negative sections that form circuits when charged with electric current. These circuits are called *integrated circuits* because they are located on a single slice of a semiconductor. When electricity charges the semiconductor, it registers a binary 1. When no charge carries and the circuit is therefore not completed, this lack registers a binary 0. A chip smaller than a fingernail can hold millions of circuits. Computers consist of chips soldered onto *printed circuit boards* or inserted into appropriate sockets. Chips called *microprocessors* house an entire *CPU.* Memory chips contain blank *memory.*
  Chips are packaged in a variety of forms. A traditional package is the DIP (dual in-line package). DIPs have connecting pins protruding only from the sides. This design does not work well for modern chips that require very large numbers of connections. The PGA (pin-grid array) has pins that protrude from all along the bottom of the chip. PGA packages are preferred for chips needing many connecting pins. A SIP (single in-line package) has just one row of chips in a straight line. *SIMMs* (single in-line memory modules) contain up to nine chips packaged as a single unit. See illustration.

Chooser   A *desk accessory* for the Macintosh computer that enables the user to select a printer. The Chooser displays the *icons* of all *printer drivers* (programs that control a computer's communication with a printer) currently installed in the *operating system.* Since a Chooser printer driver is at the

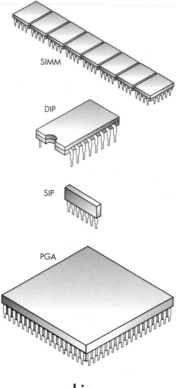

SIMM

DIP

SIP

PGA

chip
Four kinds of chip

operating system level, it works for any application on a Macintosh computer. With *DOS* computers, however, each application must supply its own printer driver.

circuit board   See **printed circuit board.**

CISC   [sisk]   Acronym for **complex instruction set computer.** A *CPU* (central processing unit) that recognizes and carries out a relatively large, complicated set of *instructions*. Most personal computers have CPUs with CISC *architecture*. *RISC* (reduced instruction set computer) architecture supports a smaller number of simpler instructions.

Class A   A standard, set by the FCC (*Federal Communications Commission*), for how much radiation a personal computer can emit. Computers with Class A certification are suitable for office and industrial use. See also *Class B*.

Class B   A standard, set by the FCC (*Federal Communications Commission*), for how much radiation a personal computer can emit. Class B is a tougher emissions standard than *Class A*. Computers with Class B certification are unlikely to interfere with radio and television reception in residential areas and are suitable for use in the home.

clear   To erase data from a display screen or document. The clear command in Windows and Macintosh *environments* deletes the selected data. The *cut* command copies the selected data to the *clipboard*. See also *undo*.

click   To press down and immediately release a button on a *mouse*. In *graphical user interfaces*, clicking the mouse when its *pointer* is touching an object on the screen will *select* that object. This operation is also called "clicking on." See also *double-click, drag, shift clicking*.

client/server network   The most common model for a *network* of personal computers. One centralized, high-powered computer, called the *server*, is the network's hub. It is connected to many less powerful *personal computers* or *workstations*, called clients, throughout an organization. The clients run programs that are stored on the server. They also access data stored there, such as a common schedule of meetings or a *database* of customers. The server typically acts as an *electronic mail* post office. See also *peer-to-peer network*.

clip art   In word processing and desktop publishing, illustrations that are stored on disk and can be inserted into a *document*. Many collections of professional-quality clip art are available.

clipboard   A file or an area in memory where *cut* or *copied* text and graphics can be temporarily stored before being moved to another location within the same document or into a new document. The information on the clipboard is lost if another unit of information is moved to the clipboard. See also *buffer, copy, cut, cut and paste, scrapbook.*

clock speed The speed of a computer's internal clock, which determines the shortest amount of time it takes the *CPU* to carry out each instruction. The clock in a computer is a circuit that generates a stream of evenly paced pulses. Clock speed is expressed in *megahertz* (MHz), and standard personal computer clock speeds range from about 4MHz to about 66MHz. Some computers have an adjustable clock speed, a useful feature if one is using software that runs poorly at a particular speed.

Clock speed alone does not determine the performance of a computer. An *expansion bus* has its own clock speed, which is often slower than the CPU clock speed. Also, the CPU must often wait for data it needs from slower memory chips or disk drives. These differences cause the faster components to lie idle while the slower components catch up. These idle periods are called *wait states*. See also *microprocessor.*

clone A computer, program, or component that resembles an original model in appearance and function. Personal computer clones often have the same components, run the same *software*, and use the same *peripherals* as the well-known (and more expensive) IBM PC computers that they imitate.

The *IBM PC* was cloned almost immediately after its development because both its operating system and many of its components came from outside companies. Cloners were able to purchase these components from the same places and build near-perfect replicas of the IBM PC. In some cases, cloners have improved upon the product that they are imitating. See also *compatible, EISA.*

close **1.** To exit a data file and save it. **2.** In *graphical user interfaces*, to exit a file and remove its *window* from the screen.

closed architecture   1. A computer system design whose specifications are *proprietary*; that is, not available to outside software developers and peripheral manufacturers. This prevents
outside companies from developing products for such a computer.   **2.** A computer design that does not include *expansion slots* to accommodate additional *printed circuit boards*.
See also *open architecture*.

cluster   A unit of storage on a disk. When a disk is *formatted*, it
is divided into *tracks*, concentric circles around the disk, and
sectors, sections of each concentric track. A cluster, typically
consisting of two to eight sectors in a single track, is the
smallest unit used by *DOS* to store data. Data from one file
may be fragmented and stored in many clusters throughout a
disk; the disk's file allocation table (FAT) keeps track of the
location of these clusters. See also *file, fragmentation, sector,
track*.

CMOS   [SEE-moss]   Acronym for **complementary metal oxide
semiconductor.**   A trademark for a memory chip that draws
very little power and is therefore used in battery-powered
devices, such as *laptop* computers. Most computers use a
CMOS to keep the time, date, and system setup data, since a
CMOS retains its data when the computer's power is turned
off, so long as it receives a trickle of energy from a battery.

COBOL   [KOH-bol]   Acronym for **common business-oriented
language.**   A *high-level language* developed in the late 1950s
and early 1960s. It is still widely used, especially in commercial data processing and business applications. COBOL is
closer to English than many other high-level languages, making it easier to learn.

code   *n.*   **1.** A set of symbols for representing characters in
binary form for storage in a computer. For example, most
computers recognize characters in *ASCII* code.   **2.** The instructions in a computer program. The instructions written
by a programmer in *programming language* are often called
source code. Instructions that have been converted into

machine language that the computer understands are called machine code or executable code.

—*v.* To write instructions in a programming language.

cold boot A computer start-up that begins when the power is turned on. The computer then automatically loads its operating system.

Color Graphics Adapter See **CGA.**

column A vertical arrangement of data. On a display screen in *character mode*, a column is a vertical line that is one character wide and extends from the top of the screen to the bottom. In a *spreadsheet*, a column is a set of vertically aligned *cells*. See illustration at *spreadsheet*.

COM file [kom] In *DOS*, a file with the *extension* .COM that indicates it is an executable command file. COM files are set up for programs and routines that are 64KB or smaller. To execute a COM file, you type the file name and press Enter. See also *executable file, EXE file*. See table at *extension*.

command A signal, given to a computer by a user, that tells the computer to do a specific task. In *command-driven* programs, commands are issued by typing a key or combination of keys. In *menu-driven* programs, commands are issued by selecting choices from an on-screen menu. See also *user interface*.

COMMAND.COM The *DOS* file that interprets and performs the commands keyed in by the user and displays prompts and messages. This file must be present on the hard disk or on a floppy disk to run DOS.

command-driven Of or relating to a program that recognizes and accepts keyed-in command statements. Command-driven software requires that you learn the commands and remember the correct syntax. See also *menu-driven*.

Command key   A key on *Macintosh* computer keyboards that is marked with a four-leaf clover and/or the Apple logo and functions in combination with other keys as a shortcut through *menu* choices. Table 7 lists some Command key combinations used as shortcuts on the Macintosh computer.

Table 7. Command Key Shortcuts for the Macintosh Computer

Key Combinations	Equivalent Menu Items
⌘-A	Select All
⌘-C	Copy
⌘-N	New
⌘-O	Open
⌘-P	Print
⌘-Q	Quit
⌘-S	Save
⌘-V	Paste
⌘-W	Close
⌘-X	Cut
⌘-Z	Undo

command line   1. The line on the screen that has the *prompt;* the line where the next command that is typed in will appear. 2. A *string* of *characters* comprising a command.

communications protocol   A set of rules that defines the way in which data is passed between two or more computers. The variables that have to be agreed upon for communication to take place include:

- baud rate (the speed at which modems transmit data)
- duplex mode (whether each computer will send and receive data simultaneously, or whether they will alternate between sending and receiving)
- number of *bits* per *byte*
- number of *stop bits* (bits inserted to signal the end of a byte of data.)

Table 8 lists widely used protocols for communication between modems. See also *handshaking, Kermit, on-line service, Xmodem, Ymodem, Zmodem.*

Table 8a. Common Communications Protocols

	Protocol	Maximum Transmission Rate (bps)	Duplex Mode
North American Standards	Bell 103	300 bps	Full
	Bell 212A	1,200 bps	Full
International Standards	CCITT V.21	300 bps	Full
	CCITT V.22	1,200 bps	Full
	CCITT V.22*bis*	2,400 bps	Full
	CCITT V.27*ter*	4,800 bps	Full
	CCITT V.29	9,600 bps	Half
	CCITT V.32	9,600 bps	Full
	CCITT V.32*bis*	14,400 bps	Full

Table 8b. Complementary Protocols

These protocols add additional functions, such as file transfer capability, error detection, and data compression, to the standard protocols.

Protocol	Features
Kermit	• Transfers information in blocks of 96 bytes • High transmission accuracy • Relatively slow
MNP (Microcom Networking Protocol)	• Very fast (can achieve throughputs of over 48,000 bps) • Class 4 automatically varies transmission speed according to the quality of the line • Class 5 provides data compression
Xmodem	• Transfers information in blocks of 128 bytes • Fairly high transmission accuracy • Relatively slow (can send only one file at a time)

Table 8b. Complementary Protocols

Protocol	Features
Ymodem	• Transfers information in blocks of 1,024 bytes (1 kilobyte) • High transmission accuracy • Supports batch file transfers
Zmodem	• High transmission accuracy • Includes "checkpoint restart" feature (resumes interrupted transmissions at point of interruption, not from the beginning)

communications software Software that enables a computer to communicate through a modem over telephone lines. Communications software can have a wide variety of features to speed the exchange of data, such as *auto-redial* and *macros* that automatically execute the *log on* sequence.

compact disk Abbreviated **CD** A small plastic disk on which data such as text or music is digitally encoded. CDs are read using laser optics, while conventional disks are read by magnetic means. Since CDs that have been encoded with information cannot be erased or changed, they are called *CD-ROMs* (compact disk–read-only memory) in computer applications. See also *disk, erasable optical disk, optical disk.*

Compact Disk-Interactive See **CD-I.**

compatibility The ability of one computer, *peripheral*, program, or file to work with the same commands and formats as another.

One must be careful to distinguish exactly what is meant by compatibility in a given case. Two printers may be compatible in that they can both be attached to the same computer, but that does not mean they will accept the same *font cartridges*. An *IBM PC-compatible* is a computer that can run the same software as an IBM PC; however, many manufacturers claim compatibility even though their machines cannot run 100% of this software. Programs are compatible if they can use files in the same data *formats*. This means files produced by one *application*, such as a *word processing* program, can easily be formatted so that they can be *imported* into another application, such as a *database* or *spreadsheet*. See also *compatible, emulate, plug-compatible*.

compatible *n.* A computer, *peripheral*, file, or program that can be used with or substituted for another. The term is especially used as shorthand for an *IBM PC-compatible*, a personal computer that is compatible with an *IBM PC*. See also *clone, compatibility, plug-compatible*.
—*adj.* Capable of being used with or substituted for another computer, peripheral, file, or program.

compile To translate a program written in a *high-level language* into *object code*. The object code may be *machine language* that can be directly executed by the computer, or it may be an intermediate *assembly language*. If the latter, the object code must then be transformed into machine language using *assemblers, linkers,* or *loaders*. See also *source code*.

compiler A program that translates another program written in a *high-level language* into *object code*. Compilers translate the entire program into executable code before it is run; *interpreters* translate and run a program line by line. Since object code is unique to each type of computer, there are many compilers available for each high-level language. See illustration at *programming language*.

complementary metal oxide semiconductor See **CMOS.**

complex instruction set computer See **CISC.**

COM port Acronym for **communications port.** A connection point on a computer for plugging in a *serial* device, such as a modem or a mouse. There can be up to four COM ports. The *DOS* operating system designates them COM1, COM2, COM3, and COM4.

compress To store data so as to minimize the space it requires. See also *data compression*.

compression See **data compression**.

computer A programmable machine that performs high-speed processing of numbers, as well as of text, graphics, symbols, and sound. Modern computers are *digital*. The computer's physical components are called *hardware*; its programs and data are called *software*. All computers include these components:

- a central processing unit, referred to as the CPU, that interprets and executes instructions
- input devices, usually a keyboard and/or a mouse, through which data and commands enter the computer
- memory that enables a computer to store programs and data
- mass storage devices, such as disk drives and tape drives, that store large amounts of data and
- output devices, such as printers and display screens, that show the results after data has been processed by the computer.

See illustration. See also *mainframe, minicomputer, personal computer, supercomputer, workstation*.

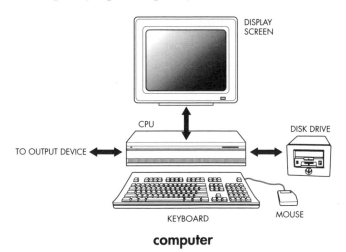

computer

computer-aided design   See **CAD.**

computer-aided instruction   See **CAI.**

computer-aided manufacturing   See **CAM.**

concatenate   To join together. For example, you can concatenate two *files* into a single file. You can also concatenate two or more database *fields* into one field. Or you can concatenate two or more character *strings*, such as "super" and "computer," into one string, "supercomputer," and then search for that concatenated string within your document or program.

condensed type   A *type* style that narrows characters and places them closer together than in ordinary type. Condensed type increases the number of characters that can fit into a single line.

CONFIG.SYS   A file that tells the *computer* what *configuration* to use for *DOS* or *OS/2* systems. For example, CONFIG.SYS may have a DEVICE statement to let the computer know that you're going to be using a *mouse* so that it can install the proper device *driver*. CONFIG.SYS tells the computer how many *files* can be open at the same time and how much *memory* to reserve for its *buffers*.

  CONFIG.SYS is one of the first files the computer checks when it *boots* up. If it finds this file, it immediately sets everything up according to the commands there. If there is no CONFIG.SYS file in the *root directory*, the computer follows the *default* configuration settings instead.

configuration   The way in which a *computer* is set up in terms of both *hardware* and *software*. For example, an IBM PC-compatible computer's configuration may consist of 4MB of *RAM*, a hard drive, a floppy drive, a *serial mouse*, a *VGA* monitor, and the *DOS* operating system with Microsoft Windows. When you configure your computer, you attach all the physical components with the necessary cables and *connectors*, set various switches and *jumpers*, and select the software *pa-*

rameters that tell the computer what the configuration looks like and how its various components should interact with each other. For example, the operating system needs to know whether you're going to be using a mouse and what type of *printer* the computer is hooked up to.

On DOS- and OS/2-based computers, the system is configured by placing commands in the file *CONFIG.SYS*. On Macintosh computers, the system's parameters are set with the *Control Panel*, a Macintosh *desk accessory*.

configuration file   A file that tells a computer what *configuration* to use for a specified *program*. The configuration file for *DOS* and *OS/2* is called *CONFIG.SYS*. Whenever you ask your computer to run a program, it checks the configuration file to find the current *parameters* for that program. In a word processing program, for example, the parameters would include the current settings for line spacing, margin width, and *font* specifications.

connector   A coupler used to join two cables or to plug a cable into a *port* or *interface*. There are several types of connectors. Three common ones are the *DIN connector*, the *DB connector*, and the *Centronics interface*. See illustration.

console   The portion of a computer that allows you to communicate with the *CPU* (central processing unit). In a personal computer, the console is made up of the *keyboard* and the *monitor*. In a network, the console is the *terminal* that controls the *mainframe* or *server*.

constant   A value, such as a number or a *string*, that does not change. *Programs* generally use both constants and *variables*.

context switching   See **task switching.**

continuous tone   A method of creating an image out of smoothly gradated colors or shades of gray, as in photography. Color *printers* and some color *graphics* programs use continuous tone, but some black-and-white printers and most black-

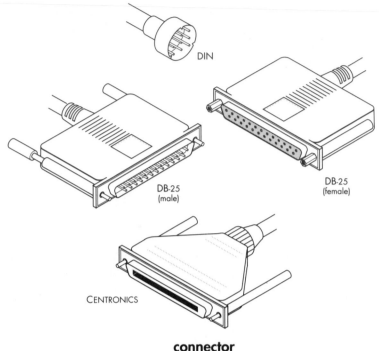

connector
Several kinds of connector

and-white graphics software use patterns of black dots of variable size and density to simulate continuous tone. See also *halftone*.

control character A *character* that can be pressed, usually in combination with the *Control key*, to give the computer a *command*. For example, in some *word processing* programs the control character *x* means "delete" and the control character *c* means "copy." The first 32 characters of the *ASCII* character set are defined as control characters, but a particular *application* may define its own control characters differently.

Control key Abbreviated **Ctrl** A key on IBM PC and compatible keyboards that is pressed in combination with another key to produce a *control character*. For example, when you type *x* in a word processing program the letter *x* appears as part of your text, but when you press the Control key while typing *x*, the computer will interpret *x* as a control character.

controller A unit that controls the flow of data along the *expansion bus* between a computer's *CPU* and devices such as a display screen, a disk drive, or a printer. Each component or device attached to the expansion bus has its own controller. Personal computers come equipped with controllers for standard components, but if additional devices are added, more controllers, which come installed on *expansion boards*, can be inserted. See also *bus, expansion bus.*

Control Panel In *Macintosh* computers and *Microsoft Windows*, a utility program used to set such system *parameters* as screen colors, speaker volume, the date and time in the computer's clock, the *double click* speed for a mouse, or the keyboard repeat rate.

control panel device See **cdev.**

control program 1. See **operating environment.** 2. See **operating system.**

conventional memory The amount of *RAM* available to *programs* running in *DOS* in *real mode.* Usually this amounts to 640KB *(kilobytes)* and is adequate if you want to run only one program at a time. If you want to run more than one program at a time, however, you will need more than conventional memory. See also *expanded memory, extended memory, protected mode, real mode.*

convergence The relative sharpness of each *pixel* on the *display screen* of a color monitor. On a color screen, each pixel is made up of red, blue, and green dots, and the sharpness of an individual pixel depends on how well these colored dots converge. See also *pixel.*

conversion A change, as from one format or program to another. For example, there are programs that let you change, or convert, a file from the format used by one word processing program to another.

coprocessor A *microprocessor* distinct from the *CPU*. A coprocessor will perform specified functions that the CPU either cannot perform or cannot perform as well and as quickly. For example, while CPUs can do mathematical calculations, certain *math coprocessors* have been designed to perform these calculations faster. Graphics coprocessors can speed the manipulation of graphics images.

copy To duplicate *data*. In word processing, for example, you can copy *text* from the document you're working on into a *buffer* (often known as the *clipboard*) in order to *paste* it into another document. You can also copy a *file* from one *directory* or *disk* to another.

copy protection Any of various methods of preventing *software* from being copied and given to unauthorized users. Copy protection usually prevents the user from making *backups* of software, so that if a copy-protected *program* becomes corrupted, the user has to contact the manufacturer to ask for a second copy. For this reason, most companies and software developers have stopped using copy protection. See also *piracy, shareware.*

corrupt To accidentally change or destroy the *data* in a *file*. This can happen because of a problem with the software, damage to the *disk* or *disk drive*, or because of a power fluctuation. Utility programs, such as PC Tools and Norton Utilities, can sometimes recover data from a corrupted file.

cpi Abbreviation of **characters per inch.**

cps Abbreviation of **characters per second.**

CPU Abbreviation of **central processing unit.** The part of a computer that interprets and executes instructions. A *mainframe* or a *minicomputer* has a CPU consisting of one or more *printed circuit boards*, but the CPU of a *personal computer* or small *workstation* consists of a single *chip* called a *microprocessor*.

The CPU fetches, decodes, and executes instructions, and transfers information to and from other components, such as *disk drives, expansion boards*, or the *keyboard*, over the computer's *bus*, its main data highway. The part of the CPU known as the Arithmetic Logic Unit (ALU) performs all arithmetic and logic operations on data. The CPU's Control Unit coordinates the steps necessary to execute each instruction. It tells the other parts of the CPU what to do and when. The data *registers* of the CPU function as a scratch pad for the ALU and as working memory for the CPU. In some instances, *CPU* is used more broadly to include *main memory*, or *RAM*. See illustration at *computer*.

CR   Abbreviation of **carriage return.**

crash   A failure of a *program* or a *disk drive*, usually causing the loss of *data*. A crash renders the entire system, including the *operating system*, unusable; the user generally has to *reboot* before he or she can continue working. See also *abort*.

crop   In a graphics or desktop publishing program, to cut away unwanted parts of an image. For example, you may want to crop a picture before inserting it into a *document* or *layout*.

cross-hatching   In a *graphics* program, a pattern created by intersecting lines and used to fill in an area. For example, you might select several different cross-hatching patterns to distinguish different parts of a pie graph.

CRT   Abbreviation of **cathode-ray tube.**

Ctrl Abbreviation of **Control key.**

Ctrl-Alt-Del   For IBM PC and compatible computers, a command that causes a *warm boot*, issued by pressing the *Delete key* while holding down the *Control* and *Alt keys*. If your program crashes, you can press Ctrl-Alt-Del instead of turning the computer off and doing a *cold boot*.

Ctrl-Break   A *DOS* command issued by pressing the *Break key* while holding down the *Control key*. Ctrl-Break cancels the previous command issued in DOS.

cursor   The bright, usually blinking indicator on a *display screen*, marking the position at which a *character* can be entered, changed, or deleted. A cursor may be a small rectangle, an underline, or a vertical bar. The cursor can be moved about the screen with the *mouse* or the *arrow keys*.

cursor control keys   See **arrow keys.**

cursor movement keys   See **arrow keys.**

cut   To remove part of a *document* or a *graphics* file and store it in a *buffer* (often called a *clipboard*). See also *cut and paste*.

cut and paste   To *cut* part of a *document* or a *graphics* file and then insert or *paste* it into another place in the document or into another document or file.

cut-sheet feeder   See **sheet feeder.**

cylinder   The set of all *tracks* (concentric circles) located in the same corresponding position on each recording surface of a disk or on each side of a *platter* in a hard disk drive. On a *double-sided disk*, a cylinder consists of 2 tracks, 1 from each side. On a *hard disk*, a cylinder consists of 2 tracks (1 from each side) from each platter. If a hard disk has 600 tracks on each of 4 platters, then it will have 600 cylinders, each consisting of a vertical set of 8 tracks.

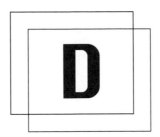

DA   Abbreviation of **desk accessory.**

daisy wheel printer   A *letter-quality* printer that consists of a hammer, a metal or plastic daisy wheel, and an inked ribbon similar to those in typewriters. The daisy wheel itself is a thin wheel with printing characters fixed at the end of its spokes. To print, the daisy wheel rotates until the right character is in between the hammer and the ribbon. Then the hammer strikes the character against the ribbon so that the ribbon prints the character on the page. The result looks typewritten. Daisy wheel printers are now sold only rarely. See table at *printer.*

DAT   [dat]   Acronym for **digital audio tape.**   A storage medium that uses *magnetic tape* to store *data* digitally. A DAT cartridge is smaller than a 3.5-inch *floppy disk* and can hold from 700MB (*megabytes*) to 2.3GB (*gigabytes*). Because DATs allow only *sequential access,* they are best used for *backups.* See table at *access time.*

data   Facts, as in the form of figures, characters, or words, especially when given to the computer as *input* to be stored in *machine-readable* form. When you type words or numbers into a *database,* for example, the computer stores this as data in *binary* form. The word "data" is actually the plural form of "datum," which means "a single fact," but "data" has taken on a life of its own. This means that you can treat it as a

database

plural out of respect to its origins or as a singular in deference to its independence. See also *information*.

database An organized collection of information that can be searched, retrieved, changed, and sorted using a collection of programs known as a *database management system*. Many databases are organized into *records* consisting of data that have been *input* into *fields*. For example, an address database may have one record for every person whose address is included. Each record might have one field for names, another field for street addresses, another for ZIP codes, and still another for phone numbers. See also *flat-file database, hypertext, relational database*.

database management system Abbreviated **DBMS** The program or programs that control a *database* so that the information it contains can be stored, retrieved, updated, and sorted. The scale and capabilities of DBMSs vary widely. There are database management systems that run on personal computers, such as FileMaker or dBASE. There are also huge, specialized applications that operate on *mainframes* and over large *networks* such as airline flight reservation systems.

Most database management systems let you request a *report* giving *information* from the database organized in a way that meets your specific needs. For example, to do a mailing to customers, you may need their names and addresses printed out on mailing labels and sorted by ZIP code. Often requests for information must be structured in the form of a *query* that specifies the criteria for the selection of information. Queries can be structured by simply choosing options from a menu or by *query by example*, in which the DBMS presents a blank record and the user specifies the fields and values he or she wants. More sophisticated DBMSs may require the user to use a special *query language*. Once the language is learned, the user has a great deal of power in structuring needed information. See also *report generator*.

database server A computer system on a *network* that stores a shared *database* and enables network users to retrieve the data they request. See also *server*.

data bus A *bus* that carries *data* back and forth between the *CPU* (central processing unit) and *RAM* (random-access memory). The width of the data bus is the number of signal lines used to carry data in parallel, each line carrying one *bit* of data. An eight-bit data bus transmits eight bits of data at once.

data compression The storing of *data* in a form that minimizes the space required. One system of data compression, for example, assigns special *binary* codes to frequently used words so that they take up fewer *bits* than they would if each letter were coded separately. Data compression can speed up transmission of data by *FAX machine* or *modem* because it enables these devices to transmit the same amount of data using fewer bits. Data compression is also used in *backup* utilities, in storing *bit-mapped graphics* files, and in storing video images. A type of *expansion board* called a compression board will automatically compress data as it is written to disk, then decompress it when it is read. The data compression is not noticeable to the user but can effectively double or triple the capacity of a disk drive. See also *CD-I, DVI, pack*.

data entry The process of putting *data* into a *computer*, especially the typing of text and figures into a *database* or *spreadsheet* from the *keyboard*.

data entry form In *database* applications, a single *record* appearing on-screen in a form that is easy for the user to fill in or update. Most database applications let the user create a custom data entry form, in addition to displaying a *default* form.

data file A *file* containing *data* created by an application, such as a *document*, a *graphics* design, or *database records*. See also *program file*. See table at *file*.

data processing Abbreviated **DP** The storing or processing of *data* by a computer, especially the storing or processing of numerical data by a *mainframe* or *minicomputer*.

data type   **1.** In programming, a declaration of the kind of data (floating-point or integer, for example) that is being used in a particular place within a program. The data type determines which operations can be performed on each data object. **2.** In *database management systems* and *spreadsheet* programs, a definition for the type of data (name, date, or dollar amount, for example) found in a specific data field.

daughter board   A *printed circuit board* that attaches either to a computer's main circuit board (the *motherboard)* or to an *expansion board.* Daughter boards are added to improve a computer's performance or enhance its capabilities. See also *expansion board, motherboard.*

DB connector   A *connector* used in *serial* or *parallel* transmission of *data,* as between a *computer* and a *printer.* See illustration at *connector.*

DBMS   Abbreviation of **database management system.**

DDE Abbreviation of **Dynamic Data Exchange.**

debug   **1.** To search for and eliminate errors in a *program.* **2.** To search for and correct malfunctions in *hardware.*

decimal   Of or relating to a number system with a base of ten. The number system we normally use is a decimal system, unlike the *binary* system that computers use. The decimal system uses the ten different symbols 0–9 for numbers. Each place in a decimal number represents a successive power of ten. Decimal numbers without decimal points are called *integers.* Decimal numbers with decimal points can be written in either *fixed-point* or *floating-point* notation. See also *hexadecimal, octal.* See table at *binary.*

decompress   See **unpack.**

decompression   The act or process of *unpacking.*

decrement *v.* To decrease a number by a given amount, usually repeatedly. For example, if you decrement 12 by 4 you get 8, then 4, then 0.
—*n.* The amount subtracted each time a number is decreased in this way. In the example above, 4 would be termed the decrement. See also *increment.*

decryption The process of unscrambling *data* so that the *information* you receive when you give the *password* or *key* is intelligible. Decryption, of course, is necessary only when a *file* has undergone *encryption.*

dedicated Designating a *computer, device,* or *program* reserved for one use. For example, a dedicated *server* may be a computer used only as a server for a particular *network.* If you have separate phone lines for your *modem* and your telephone, then your modem line is dedicated.

default A setting used by your *computer* unless and until you choose another one. For example, your *word processor* has a default *font* that it will opt for every time you begin a new *document* unless you choose a different one. It also has default margins. The *IBM PC* and its compatibles have default *directories* that they will call up unless you select a different directory. You can change the defaults on your computer if they don't suit your needs.

defragmentation The reorganization of a file to eliminate *fragmentation.* When a file becomes fragmented, the *read/write head* has to wander all over the disk in order to read that one file. This means that it takes longer to access the data than it would if the file were defragmented.
In *DOS,* defragmentation of a disk can be done by copying all the files to a new disk with the COPY or XCOPY command. *Utility* programs called disk optimizers will defragment files without copying files to a new disk. See also *fragmentation.*

Del Abbreviation of **Delete key.**

delete To erase. For example, you can delete a *character*, a *block*, or a *file*. You can delete using the *Delete key*, the *Backspace key*, or a *command*.

Delete key Abbreviated **Del** On IBM PC and compatible keyboards, a *key* that is pressed to erase the *character* indicated by the *cursor*. See also *Backspace key*.

delimiter A *character* marking the beginning or end of a unit of *data* or of one of a series of *commands*. For example, the backslash character (\) is used as a delimiter in *DOS pathnames*, such as C:\WP\MEMOS\CURPROJ.ABC.

demand paging In systems using *virtual memory*, a kind of swapping in which *pages* of *data* are not copied from your *disk* to *RAM* until they are needed. For example, if you're working on a 50-page *document*, not all of it will go into RAM when you first call it up. As you move from page to page in the document, RAM will swap data with your disk to make sure it has whatever page you need at the moment while leaving the rest of its *memory* free for use by other *applications*.

density A measure of how tightly *bits* of data can be packed together on a tape or disk. The bits are closer together on higher-density disks, making more *memory* available than in a low-density disk of the same size. The lowest-density *floppy disks* are single-density, then double-density, then high-den-

Table 9. **Floppy Disk Densities and Capacities**

		IBM	Macintosh
5.25-inch disk	Single-density	360K	N/A
	Double-density	720K	N/A
	High-density	1.2MB	N/A
3.5-inch disk	Single-density	N/A	400K
	Double-density	720K	800K
	High-density	1.44MB	1.2MB

sity, and then extra-high-density, but not every *disk drive* can support disks of every density. Table 9 shows the storage capacities of various kinds of floppy disks on the IBM PC and the Macintosh computers.

descender   The part of a lowercase letter that falls below the main body of the letter, as in a *j*, *g*, or *y*. See also *ascender, x-height.*

descending sort   A *sort* in which the items are listed from last to first or largest to smallest, as from Z to A or from 9 to 0. See also *ascending sort.*

desk accessory   Abbreviated **DA**   On *Macintosh* computers, a *program*, usually a *utility*, that can be accessed at any time from any *application*. For example, the *calculator*, clock, and *Control Panel* are desk accessories. On IBM PC and compatible computers desk accessories are called *memory resident* programs, *terminate and stay resident* programs (TSRs), or *pop-up utilities.*

desktop   **1.** In a *graphical user interface*, an on-screen *metaphor* of your work, just as if you were looking at a real desktop cluttered with folders full of work to do. The desktop consists of *icons* that show *files*, *folders*, and various *documents*. Common desktop programs come with a set of *desk accessories*, including such things as a *calendar*, *calculator*, and *notepad*. You can rearrange the icons on the desktop just as you can rearrange objects on a real desktop.   **2.** In *Microsoft Windows*, the background of the screen, on which *windows*, icons, and *dialog boxes* appear. See illustration.

desktop computer   See **personal computer.**

desktop configuration   A case for a personal computer system in which components such as the *CPU*, the *power supply*, the *motherboard*, and mass *storage devices* are housed in one compact box. See also *tower configuration.*

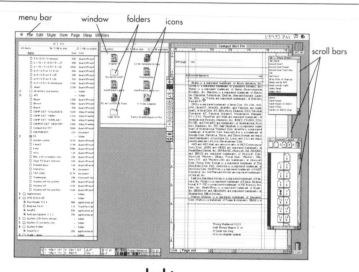

menu bar   window   folders   icons

scroll bars

desktop
On a Macintosh computer

desktop publishing   The design and production of publications, such as newsletters, trade journals, or brochures, using *personal computers* or *workstations* with *graphics* capability. Usually you work with three separate programs to do desktop publishing, namely the *word processing* program; the graphics program; and the *page layout program*, which lets you insert graphics into the text, organize the *layout*, make last-minute changes to the text or illustrations, and view the page as it will look when done. Some page layout programs let you create the text and graphics in the same program, which simplifies the procedure.

DESQview   [DESK-vyoo]   A trademark for a *character-based operating environment* for IBM PC and compatible computers using *DOS*. Developed by Quarterdeck Office Systems, DESQview features a windowing environment with *pull-down menus, icons*, and *pop-up utilities*. By taking advantage of *protected mode* and *extended memory*, DESQview supports *multitasking*, allowing the user to run more than one program at a time.

destination The location to which you *copy* a *file*. For example, in the *DOS command* "COPY C:\WP\MEMOS\ CURPROJ.ABC A:" A:, or the computer's floppy *disk drive*, is the destination to which the file "CURPROJ.ABC" will be copied.

device A *hardware* component or machine that attaches to your *computer*. *Printers, modems, disk drives, keyboards,* and *mice* are all devices. See also *peripheral*.

device driver See **driver**.

dialog box In a *graphical user interface*, an on-screen message box that presents information or requests input. A dialog box allows you to carry on a conversation with the program by selecting or deselecting option *buttons*, typing in text, or selecting from a list of files. Typically, dialog boxes disappear once you have entered the requested information.

In the Macintosh and Microsoft Windows interfaces, any menu option followed by an ellipsis (...) will bring up a dialog box if selected. See illustration. See also *alert box*.

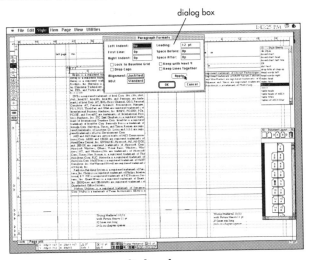

dialog box
On a Macintosh computer

dictionary sort A *sort* that disregards capitalization and places numbers where they would be if they were spelled out alphabetically. For instance, "80846" would be found in the Es. Also called *lexicographic sort*. See also *ASCII sort*.

digital Measuring or representing data by means of discrete digits. Digital modes are contrasted with *analog* modes, in which data is measured or represented by continuously varying physical quantities, such as voltage. A clock with hands is an analog device, because the hands moving continuously around the face can indicate every time of day. A digital clock uses a series of changing digits to represent time at discrete intervals, for example, every second. All modern computers are digital because they use the digits 0 and 1 to represent all data. Computers can accept input and produce output in analog form, but only by simulating analog events. See also *digitize, modem*.

digital audio tape See **DAT**.

digital monitor A *monitor* that takes *digital* signals from the *video adapter* and converts them to *analog* signals. The analog signals then control what is displayed on the screen. Unlike *analog monitors*, digital monitors display only a limited number of color values; they cannot display a continuous range of colors. *CGA* and *EGA* monitors are digital. *VGA* and *SVGA* monitors are analog.

Digital Video Interactive See **DVI**.

digitize To convert *analog* data or signals to *digital* form. For example, *optical scanners* digitize *continuous tone* images into *bit-mapped graphics*. Sound can also be digitized, as for storage on a *compact disk*, by sampling pitch and volume many times per second and then recording these measurements digitally.

digitizer **1.** A device that *digitizes* data. *Optical scanners* are digitizers. **2.** A input device consisting of an electronically sensitive tablet and a *light pen* or *puck* used to input drawings directly into the computer. A puck, also called a cursor, is a mouselike device with an attached plastic window with cross hairs to aid in precise placement and movement. The tablet records the movement of the puck or light pen and *digitizes* each point through which the puck or light pen passes. These points are then transferred to the display screen to be viewed or *stored* in a file on disk. In this sense, also called *graphics tablet*.

DIN connector   [din]   A *connector* that meets the standards of *Deutsche Industrienorm*, the organization that sets the standards for German *hardware*. DIN connectors are used to connect the *keyboard* to most IBM PC and compatible computers and as *serial port* connectors on many Macintosh computers. See illustration at *connector*.

dingbat   A typographical ornament or symbol, such as a bullet, check mark, or star, that can be inserted into a document. Many *clip art* packages contain dingbats. One of the most popular sets of dingbats is the Zapf dingbats, available as a PostScript font. See illustration.

dingbats

DIP switch   [dip]   A series of tiny rocker or slider switches contained in the housing of a DIP, or *dual in-line package*. The housing has downward-facing pins so that it can be inserted into a socket on a *printed circuit board* or soldered directly to the board.

DIP switches are *toggle switches;* that is, they have only two possible positions: on or off (sometimes labeled 1 and 0). They enable you to configure a circuit board for a particular type of computer, printer, or application. Installation instructions should tell you how to set the switches.

One of the advantages of *OS/2* over *DOS* is that OS/2 allows you to configure circuit boards by entering software commands instead of toggling DIP switches. See illustration.

ROCKER DIP SWITCH   SLIDE DIP SWITCH

DIP switch
Two types of DIP switch

direct access   See **random access.**

direct-access storage device   A *storage device,* such as a *disk,* that offers *random access* rather than *sequential access* to *data.* A disk is a direct-access storage device, but a *DAT* is not.

direct memory access   See **DMA.**

directory   A way to organize files into a *hierarchical* structure. IBM PC and compatible computers have a top directory called a *root directory* (or simply "root") that is usually labeled "C:\" on the hard disk. All directories below the root directory are its *subdirectories.* The last directory in a chain or *path* of directories leading from the root contains files. In the Macintosh computer world, directories are called *folders.* See illustration at *hierarchical.*

disk   The most common medium for permanent data storage. The two types of disks are *magnetic disks* and *optical disks.* A magnetic disk is a round plate, as of plastic or metal, covered with a magnetic coating. Data is encoded on the disk by magnetizing microscopically small iron particles that are scattered throughout the coating. Magnetic disks include *floppy disks, hard disks,* and *removable cartridges.*
    Optical disks are composed of a layer of reflective material encased in a protective plastic coating. Data is encoded by a

pattern of tiny pits or of aligned metal alloy crystals on the reflective layer. The data is read by means of a laser. The laser light is scattered by the pits or crystals, but when it strikes the flat reflective surfaces between them, it is reflected directly into a detector. The three kinds of optical disks are *CD-ROMs*, *WORMs* (write once read many), and *erasable optical disks*. See illustrations at *floppy disk, hard disk*.

disk cache A part of *dynamic RAM* set aside to facilitate access to the data most often read from a *disk*. Every time the *CPU* requests data from the disk, the disk cache intercepts the request. If the cache has the data on hand, it sends it on to the CPU. Otherwise, the cache takes the data from the disk and sends one copy to the CPU while storing another copy. A disk cache has a logic program built in that enables it to guess what data will be needed next, and when no data is being requested, the cache copies the data. If you want to *write* a file to disk and the file is in the cache, the cache compares the version on disk with its own updated version and writes only the data that has actually changed to disk. Some caches intercept all data to be written to disk and hold it until the CPU is free before actually saving it on disk. While this speeds up the computer's work, it also risks the loss of new or changed data in case of a *crash*, since the cache is *volatile memory*.

disk crash See **head crash**.

disk drive A device that reads *data* stored on a magnetic or optical *disk* and writes data to the disk for storage. A hard drive reads *hard disks*, a floppy drive reads *floppy disks*, and an optical drive reads *optical disks*.

Disk drives are distinguished by their data storage capacity and *access times*, or the amount of time it takes the drive to *access* a single piece of data. Optical drives can store much more data than floppy or hard drives, but are relatively slow. Hard drives are faster and have larger storage capacities than floppy drives. In practice, techniques such as disk caching and *interleaving* can significantly improve the performance of disk drives. See also *cache*. See illustration at *computer*.

diskette   See **floppy disk.**

diskless workstation   A *workstation* or *personal computer* on a *local area network* that has a *CPU* and *RAM*, but does not have its own *disk drive*. Its program and data files are stored on the network file *server*.

disk operating system   See **DOS.**

disk pack   A removable *storage device* consisting of a stack of several magnetic *disks* encased as a unit. Disk packs are used chiefly with *minicomputers* and *mainframes*.

display   *v.* To show *information* or *graphics* on a *monitor*. —*n.* A display screen.

display adapter   See **video adapter.**

display screen   The part of a *monitor* that gives *information* in visual form. Commonly, a computer's display screen uses a *cathode-ray tube* to show images, just as a television does. *Laptop* and *notebook* computers, however, use *flat-panel displays*, typically *LCDs* (liquid-crystal displays) or *gas plasma displays*. See illustration at *computer*.

dithering   In computer graphics, a technique for alternating the values of adjacent dots or *pixels* to create the illusion of intermediate values. In printing color or displaying color on a computer screen, making adjacent dots or pixels different colors gives the effect of a third color. For example, a printed field of alternating cyan blue and yellow dots appears to be green. On a *monochrome* display or printer, altering the ratio of black to white dots can create the illusion of a particular shade of gray. Thus dithering can give the effect of more colors on a color display or printer and of shades of gray on a black-and-white display or printer. See illustration at *halftone*.

DMA   Abbreviation of **direct memory access.**   A feature allowing the transfer of data between *memory* and a *peripheral* device, such as a *disk drive*, without involving the *CPU*.

Computers with DMA can transfer data to and from peripheral devices faster than computers without DMA. DMA is
handy for *real-time* applications and making *backups* in less
time.

document A piece of work created with an *application*, especially a *word processor*, and, if saved on disk, given its own
file name.

documentation The instructions, *tutorials*, and reference materials that come with a program or a piece of hardware.
Documentation is usually in the form of printed manuals, but
most software includes *on-line* documentation that can be
displayed on a screen or printed out with a printer. Often software also has an on-line help system that can be summoned
from the application with a *Help* command or by pressing a
designated *Help key*.

DOS [doss] Acronym for **disk operating system**. The widely
used term for *MS-DOS* and *PC-DOS*, the standard *operating
systems* for IBM PC and compatible computers. MS-DOS
(Microsoft disk operating system) was developed by Microsoft
for IBM. PC-DOS is virtually the same operating system, but
marketed by IBM.
  Like all operating systems, DOS oversees and coordinates
such operations as reading from and writing to disk, interpreting input from the keyboard and mouse, and executing commands from *application* programs. DOS is a *command-driven*
operating system that requires the user to type commands at
the keyboard.
  There have been a dozen or so versions of MS-DOS and PC-
DOS, each increasingly sophisticated because of the additions
of features from *minicomputer* operating systems. DOS, however, still does not support *multitasking* or multiple users. It
is also limited to using 1MB (*megabyte*) of memory—an
amount that seemed prodigious when the system was first
designed, but, with the advent of memory-hungry *applications* and *terminate and stay resident* (TSR) programs, is now
barely adequate. Special memory systems, known as *ex-*

dot-matrix printer

panded or *extended memory,* can surmount this limitation. See also *DESQview, Microsoft Windows, OS/2.* See table at *operating system.*

dot-matrix printer An *impact printer* that prints text and graphic images by hammering the ends of pins against an ink ribbon. This produces characters made up of a *matrix,* or pattern, of dots. Dot-matrix printers are relatively cheap, relatively fast, and able to print graphics. They are also a necessity for printing on multi-layer forms, which a nonimpact *laser printer* can't do.

On the other hand, dot-matrix printers can be noisy and their print quality is generally poor compared with the typeset look produced by laser printers. Most dot-matrix printers can print at different speeds, depending on desired print quality. The fastest speed produces *draft-quality* text. *Near-letter quality* is a tradeoff between reduced speed and improved text quality. In near-letter quality mode, the printer passes over a line several times, offsetting the dots slightly to form more solid characters. Print quality is also determined by the number of pins used to print the dots—the more pins, the better the quality. Print heads in dot-matrix printers typically have 9, 18, or 24 pins.

Some dot-matrix printers can interpret commands from *PostScript* or some other *page description language,* but most are designed to work with *bit-mapped fonts* controlled by *ASCII* codes sent to the printer from a personal computer. See table at *printer.*

dot pitch A measure of the distance between each *pixel* on a *display screen,* given in millimeters—the lower the dot pitch, the higher the *resolution* of the display screen. The best high-resolution color monitors have dot pitches of 0.28 mm or less.

dots per inch Abbreviated **dpi** A measure of the *resolution* of a *printer;* the more dots per inch, the higher the resolution. A *laser printer* with a resolution of 300 dpi can print 300 dots per linear inch, or 90,000 (300 × 300) per square inch. See illustration at *resolution.*

double-click To click a *mouse* button twice in quick succession without moving the mouse. Double-clicking is a way of rapidly selecting an item and initiating an action, such as selecting and opening a *file*. Both *Microsoft Windows* and the Macintosh computer *interface* let you set the double-click speed, which indicates the longest interval between clicks that the computer will interpret as double-clicking rather than as two separate clicks.

double-density disk A *floppy disk* that can hold twice the data of the now obsolete *single-density disk*. Double-density 3.5-inch disks hold 720KB (*kilobytes*) of data; double-density 5.25-inch disks hold 360KB of data. Double-density disks have less data storage capacity than *high-density disks*. See table at *density*.

double-sided disk A *floppy disk* that can hold data on both its top and bottom surfaces. You need to use a double-sided *disk drive* to read from or write onto a double-sided disk. See table at *density*.

down Malfunctioning or not operating, especially temporarily.

download To transfer a copy of a *file* from a central source to a *peripheral* device or computer. You can download a file from a *network* file *server* to another computer on the network, or from a *bulletin board system* to a personal computer. You can also download a font from disk to a laser printer. Such a font is called a *soft font*, as opposed to a *hard* font that is built into the printer by the manufacturer.

downloadable font See **soft font**.

downward compatible See **backward compatible**.

DP Abbreviation of **data processing.**

dpi Abbreviation of **dots per inch.**

draft-quality   Of or producing a low-quality printed output suitable for drafts of documents. *Dot-matrix printers* generally support both a draft-quality mode that sacrifices print quality for speed of output and a relatively slow *near-letter quality* mode. On some printers, draft quality is good enough for most print jobs, excluding business correspondence. See illustration at *letter-quality*.

drag   To hold down the *mouse* button while moving the mouse. In many word processing programs, for instance, dragging the mouse selects a block of text. In a *graphical user interface*, an *icon* or graphics object can be moved by dragging it across the screen.

DRAM   [DEE-ram]   See **dynamic RAM.**

draw program   A graphics program that allows the user to create line art using objects such as lines, circles, squares, and *Bézier curves*. Draw programs employ *object-oriented graphics*; that is, they represent each graphic object with a mathematical formula. Objects created in draw programs can be sized and scaled without introducing distortions and moved without affecting surrounding objects. This is in contrast to images created with *paint programs*, which treat images as *bit maps*.

drive   See **disk drive.**

drive bay   See **bay.**

driver   A program that enables the computer to communicate with a *device* such as a printer, mouse, CD-ROM drive, or *RAM disk*. Every device needs a driver to tell the computer how to send commands to it. Some drivers are built into the *operating environment*; *Microsoft Windows*, for example, provides *printer drivers* for all Windows applications. But most drivers must be installed for the device to work. In DOS, this can be done by loading the driver in the *CONFIG.SYS* file with the DEVICE or DEVICEHIGH command, so that it is loaded automatically on startup. For example, if you wish to use a mouse with DOS, a statement such as DEVICE = MOUSE.SYS (it varies depending on the type of mouse you have) must be included as a line in CONFIG.SYS. On the other hand, this line is not needed if you use Microsoft Windows and desire mouse support only when Windows is running, because Windows contains its own mouse driver.

When installing many applications programs, it is possible to choose from a list of drivers, especially printer drivers, to match the equipment on your system. When a system does not print or another device does not work, it is often because the wrong driver was installed during the setup procedure. Also called *device driver.*

drop-down menu   See **pull-down menu.**

DTP   Abbreviation of **desktop publishing.**

dumb terminal   A *terminal* that contains no internal micro-processor or local data storage facilities. It is simply an output device that accepts data from the *mainframe* or *minicomputer* that it is connected to. See also *smart terminal.*

dump   To send a copy of the data in a portion of the computer's *RAM,* its *main memory,* to the screen or to a printer. Memory contents are often dumped to the screen while *debugging* a program to enable the programmer to examine exactly what is happening in memory at a particular stage in the program's execution. See also *screen dump.*

duplex   See **full duplex.**

DVI   Abbreviation of **Digital Video Interactive.**   A trademark for a system developed by RCA, General Electric, and Intel that makes use of *data compression* to enable computers to store and display moving video. Because of the size of video images, which can easily take up more than 1MB per frame, storing enough of them to make a reasonably long motion video on the hard disk of a typical personal computer would be impractical without some kind of data compression. See also *CD-I*.

Dvorak keyboard   An alternative keyboard designed for faster typing. Unlike the *QWERTY keyboard*, the Dvorak keyboard is designed so that most English words fall in the middle row of keys. Common letter positions are placed together for quicker typing.

Some computers let you choose between QWERTY and Dvorak keyboards. You can redefine QWERTY keys with *macros* to turn them into Dvorak keys.

The Dvorak keyboard was designed in the 1930s by August Dvorak and his brother-in-law William Dealy. See illustration.

Dvorak keyboard

dynamic   Occurring immediately as needed, as opposed to fixed and provided for in advance. For example, in dynamic *memory* allocation, a program is allowed to call for memory space on demand, rather than being assigned a fixed block of memory when it starts. The program can then yield the memory space if it is later needed by another program. Although this process is somewhat slower than an arrangement using fixed blocks of memory, it provides more flexibility when running multiple programs. See also *static*.

Dynamic Data Exchange   Abbreviated **DDE**   A system that allows two applications programs to be linked together so that a change made in one application, which is called the "server," is immediately reflected in the other, which is called the "client." A common example of this process is the use of a communications program to monitor an *on-line* service for stock prices and trading information, while a *spreadsheet* program receives the new data as it comes in, makes changes in its tables, and recalculates its formulas automatically. Applications must be specifically designed as DDE servers or clients for this technique to work. DDE was developed by Microsoft and IBM for the *Windows* and *OS/2* systems and is also used by the Macintosh computer *System 7*.

dynamic RAM Abbreviated **DRAM** [DEE-ram] A type of memory chip that stores information as electrical charges in capacitors. Because a capacitor can hold a charge for only a limited time, the RAM chips must be periodically *refreshed*. If the *CPU* tries to access the memory during this process, one or more *wait states* may have to be introduced until the memory can catch up, causing the system to slow down. The fastest current personal computers use DRAM *access times* on the order of 70 or 80 *nanoseconds* to avoid excessive wait states. Although it is slower than *static RAM*, dynamic RAM is generally used in personal computers because it is simpler and less expensive. See table at *access time*.

dynamic random-access memory Abbreviated **DRAM** See **dynamic RAM.**

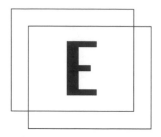

EBCDIC [EBB-see-dik] Acronym for **Extended Binary-Coded Decimal Interchange Code.** A code used on IBM *mainframes* and *minicomputers* to assign numerical values to letters, numbers, punctuation marks, and other characters. See also *ASCII, extended ASCII.*

echo check In communications, an error control technique in which the receiving terminal or computer returns the transmitted data to verify correct reception.

edge connector A set of metal contacts on the edge of a printed circuit *expansion board* that fits into an *expansion slot* or a connector on a ribbon cable. See illustration at *printed circuit board.*

editor A program used to create and edit *text files.* Editors typically include features such as deleting, copying, and text blocking, but usually do not have the formatting capabilities of *word processors.* Advanced editor programs also include alternate display modes, comprehensive on-line help utilities, and features that allow the user to edit several files simultaneously, define keyboard *macros*, create *backup* files, and edit such files as the source files for various programming languages. The two basic types of editor are line editors, which only permit one line at a time to be viewed and edited, and full-page or *text editors*, which allow the user to work with an entire page at once.

EEMS Abbreviation of **Enhanced Expanded Memory Specification.** A trademark for a version of the original Expanded Memory Specification (*EMS*) that enabled *DOS* applications to use more than 1MB of *memory*. EEMS provided for up to 64 page frames (memory space reserved for blocks, or *pages* of bytes mapped in from expanded memory) and the storage of executable code in expanded memory. The EEMS was developed by AST, Ashton-Tate, and Quadram in order to improve on the capabilities of EMS, and its provisions were subsequently included in EMS version 4.0.

EEPROM [ee-ee-PROM] Acronym for **electrically erasable programmable read-only memory.** A kind of *PROM* that retains its data even when the power is turned off and that can be erased with an electrical charge and reprogrammed. Most EEPROM can be reprogrammed only with the help of a special peripheral device, but a type of EEPROM called *flash memory* can be reprogrammed while the chip is in the computer. EEPROM, like other *ROM*, is slower than *RAM* and usually has less memory than RAM. EEPROM chips can wear out if they are reprogrammed too many times.

EGA Abbreviation of **Enhanced Graphics Adapter.** A *video adapter* and *video standard* developed by IBM and introduced in 1984. EGA can display 43 lines in *character mode*, and in *graphics mode* it is capable of displaying 16 colors from a *palette* of 64 with a *resolution* of 640 horizontal *pixels* by 350 vertical pixels. See table at *video standard*.

8088 Short for the Intel 8088 *microprocessor*. See also *Intel microprocessors*.

8086 Short for the Intel 8086 *microprocessor*. See also *Intel microprocessors*.

8514/A A *video adapter* and *video standard* developed for IBM Personal System/2 computers. 8514/A has a graphics *resolution* of up to 1,024 horizontal *pixels* by 768 vertical pixels and the ability to display 256 colors at a time from a palette of about 262,000. The original version made use of *interlacing* to reduce cost, but subsequent versions have produced *noninterlaced* 8514/A versions to avoid the flicker inherent in interlaced displays. For IBM PC-compatible computers, similar video performance is available through the use of *VGA* and *SVGA* adapters. See table at *video standard.*

EISA Abbreviation of **Extended Industry Standard Architecture.** A trademark for a standard for *bus architecture* in IBM PC-compatible computers that takes advantage of the 32-bit data path and *multiprocessing* capabilities of the Intel 80386 and 80486 processors. The EISA standard was developed by a group of nine competitors of IBM to compete with the IBM *Micro Channel Architecture* (MCA). In contrast to the MCA bus, the EISA architecture is *backward compatible* with the earlier *ISA* bus, so that 16-bit ISA cards can be used in an EISA machine. See table at *bus.*

ELD Abbreviation of **electroluminescent display.**

electrically erasable programmable read-only memory See **EEPROM.**

electroluminescent display Abbreviated **ELD** A type of *flat-panel display* frequently used in laptop, notebook, and portable computers. A phosphorescent substance is enclosed between two flat panels. Vertical wires run along one panel and horizontal wires along the other so that together they form a grid. When electric voltage is applied to one horizontal wire and one vertical, the point of intersection is changed so that the phosphorescent substance lights up at that point, creating a *pixel.*

electronic mail A feature that lets a computer user send a message to someone at another computer or terminal. The message can be typed directly from the *console* or *uploaded* as a file from a disk. Electronic mail, commonly called *E-mail*, can duplicate most of the features of paper mail, such as storing messages in in boxes and out boxes, message forwarding, pro-

viding delivery receipts, and sending multiple copies, and has
the advantage of speed and convenience. Its primary drawback
is its lack of security compared with paper documents. Most
network systems provide E-mail facilities, as do many *BBS*
systems and the larger *on-line services*. E-mail services are
also offered for an annual fee plus a per-message charge by
public communications carriers, the most notable being MCI
Mail. Once the issue of the legal status of electronic documents is resolved, the technical advantages of electronic mail
are likely to lead to its assuming a dominant role in everyday
communications.

E-mail   See **electronic mail.**

embedded command   In *word processing* programs, a string of
characters that is placed directly into a document file and
controls the formatting or appearance of the text when it is
printed. Entering the command to center a line of text, for
instance, usually inserts a code like [Center] or <CTR>
in the text. These codes are different for each word processing
program, and may appear as uninterpretable characters when
a file is viewed or printed using a program different from the
one it was created in. Embedded commands are usually invisi-
ble in the normal editing mode, but many programs allow you
to view them by switching to a separate viewing mode. In
WordPerfect, for example, the command is called "Reveal
Codes." When a word processing program exhibits erratic or
confusing behavior, the problem can often be solved by
switching to the "reveal" mode to search for and remove
unnecessary embedded commands. See also *ASCII file, format, text file, WYSIWYG.*

EMS   Abbreviation of **Expanded Memory Specification.**   A set
of documents issued by a collaboration of the Lotus, Intel, and
Microsoft corporations (LIM) to standardize the method that
programs would use to access *expanded memory*. The original LIM EMS specification, version 3.0, provided for only 4
page frames and allowed only data to be stored in expanded
memory. To incorporate the advances made by the *EEMS*,

made by the *EEMS*, version 4.0 of the LIM EMS was issued, allowing up to 64 page frames and permitting executable code to be placed in EMS memory. See also *XMS*.

emulate   To behave in the same way as another device or program, usually a widely used one. Some word processors and text editors, for example, can be set to use the same commands as WordPerfect or Microsoft Word. Many printers are able to emulate the popular Epson dot-matrix printers, so that any software written for the Epson will work with them as well. Most communications programs permit the user to choose from a number of different *terminal* emulations, allowing the computer to access mainframes that expect to see such terminal configurations as the DEC vt-52, vt-100, or vt-200. Software or *coprocessor* boards that enable one type of computer to emulate another also exist. For example, a Macintosh computer can emulate an IBM PC computer, enabling it to run *DOS* and *Windows* applications and even to plug into a standard PC network.

Encapsulated PostScript   Abbreviated **EPS**   A standard file *format* for printing high-resolution *graphics* images stored in the PostScript *page description language*. EPS images can be created in such graphics programs as Adobe Illustrator or Aldus Freehand. The instructions for printing them on PostScript-compatible printers are stored in a text file. A description of the image is also stored as a *bit map* for optional screen display. EPS files can also be read by other programs and printed on non-PostScript printers. See table at *graphics file format*.

encryption   The process of enciphering or encoding data so that it is inaccessible to unauthorized users. See also *decryption*.

End key   A key on IBM PC and compatible keyboards that moves the *cursor* to the end of a line, page, or document, depending on which application is running. See also *Home key*.

Enhanced Expanded Memory Specification   See **EEMS**.

Enhanced Graphics Adapter   See **EGA.**

enhanced keyboard   A 101-key keyboard having a row of function keys at the top rather than on the left side and an extra set of cursor control keys between the main typing keys and the *numeric keypad.*

Enhanced Small Device Interface   See **ESDI.**

Enter key   See **Return key.**

environment   **1.** The entire set of conditions under which one operates a computer. The term can refer to a number of different aspects of computer operation. In terms of *hardware* and operating *platform*, one can work in a *mainframe* or a *microcomputer* environment, or a *networking* environment. With reference to *operating systems*, one can be in the DOS, UNIX, OS/2, Macintosh, multitasking, or other environment. It also describes different types of *user interface*, such as *graphics* or *windowing* environments.   **2.** An area of a computer's memory that is used by the operating system and some programs to store certain variables that they need frequent access to, such as the command search *path*, locations of various types of files, and other data. In DOS, the contents of the environment can be viewed with the command SET.

EO   See **erasable optical disk.**

EPROM   [EE-prom]   Acronym for **erasable programmable read-only memory.**   A type of *ROM* (read-only memory) chip that can be erased by exposure to ultraviolet light and then reprogrammed. A special device called a *PROM* burner or PROM programmer is used to erase and write to an EPROM. EPROMs are useful when developing prototype systems for which the large-scale production of PROM chips is not practical, and in systems where frequent changes are expected to be made in the instructions encoded in ROM. See also *EEPROM.* See table at *access time.*

EPS   See **Encapsulated PostScript.**

erasable optical disk   Abbreviated **EO**   A type of *optical disk* that can be erased and have new data recorded on it. Like *CD-ROM* and *WORM* disks, erasable optical disks can store much larger amounts of information than magnetic hard disks, but their *access times* are considerably slower and they are more expensive. See table at *access time.*

erasable programmable read-only memory   See **EPROM.**

erase   To remove recorded material from a magnetic tape or other storage medium. Floppy disks containing unnecessary material can be erased and used again.

error message   A message that is displayed on the screen to warn the user that the system is unable to carry out an operation.

ESC   Abbreviation of **Escape key.**

escape character   An *ASCII* character (ASCII 27), generated by pressing the *Escape key,* that can have different functions depending on which program is running and is often used to cancel the current command or to back up one level in a *menu* structure. The escape character can be combined with other characters to form an *escape sequence.*

Escape key   Abbreviated **ESC**   A key on IBM PC and compatible keyboards that when pressed generates an *escape character.* On some Macintosh computer keyboards, an Escape key is included for compatibility with IBM PC computers, as when a Macintosh computer is *emulating* an IBM PC.

escape sequence   A string of characters, typically beginning with an *escape character,* used to send instructions to a device such as a printer or monitor.

ESDI   Abbreviation of **Enhanced Small Device Interface.**   An *interface* standard for connecting hard disk, floppy disk, and tape drives to IBM PC and compatible computers. The ESDI standard allows disk and tape drives to transfer data to the computer more than twice as fast as the earlier ST-506 standard, in the range of 10 to 20 megabits per second. See also *IDE, SCSI.*

Ethernet [EE-ther-net] A trademark for a widely used *local area network protocol* developed by Xerox, DEC, and Intel. Ethernet uses a *bus topology* and provides for raw data transfer rates of 10 megabits per second.

even footer In word processing, a *footer* that appears on even-numbered pages.

even header In word processing, a *header* that appears on even-numbered pages.

exclusive OR See **XOR.**

executable file A program that has been *compiled* and can be run by the computer when its name is entered as a command. See table at *file.*

execute To run a program, carry out a command, or perform a function.

EXE file [ec-eks-EE] In DOS, an *executable file* with the *extension* .EXE. See table at *extension.*

expanded memory In IBM PC and compatible computers using DOS, memory added to the computer by means of an *expansion board* to supplement *main memory*. Computers based on the Intel 8086 and 8088 microprocessors are unable to make use of more than 1 *megabyte* (1,024 *kilobytes*) of memory. Expanded memory cannot be accessed directly, so it is accessed through the technique of *mapping* blocks of expanded memory, called *pages*, one at a time into an area of the CPU's usable *address space* called the *page frame*. When the computer needs to access data in expanded memory, the desired page is found and inserted into the page frame so that it can be read. This gives programs access to much more RAM for accommodating large documents and spreadsheets, and also allows multiple programs to run simultaneously without exhausting the computer's resources. In order for programs to use this extra memory, it must be configured according to the *EMS* specification, and so is often called EMS memory.

The Intel 80286 microprocessor can address up to 16MB, and the 80386 and later chips can directly address up to 4 *gigabytes*. Computers using these processors can run in either *protected mode*, which configures all memory above 1MB as *extended memory*, or *real mode*, which *emulates* the 8086 and configures all memory above 1MB as expanded memory. The software needed for this configuration is called an EMS driver and is built into DOS 4.0 and later versions. Many programs continue to be written to take advantage of expanded memory. See also *EEMS, XMS*.

Expanded Memory Specification   See **EMS.**

expanded type   A type style that spaces characters farther apart than in ordinary type. Expanded type decreases the number of characters that can fit into a single line.

expansion board   A *printed circuit board* that can be installed in a computer to provide it with additional features, such as extra memory, better graphics capabilities, or more *peripheral* devices. Most IBM PC and compatible computers have *expansion slots* for three to eight expansion boards, one of which is often already filled by a video display *adapter*. Another is sometimes filled by a *disk drive controller*. Other slots are available for *sound boards*, internal *modems*, or other devices. "Full-size" cards take up the full width of a 16-bit slot, and "half-size" cards fit into an 8-bit connector. There are also 32-bit cards for use in machines with *EISA* architecture. See also *accelerator board, adapter, add-in, expansion bus*. See illustration at *printed circuit board*.

expansion bus   The connections between the computer's *motherboard* and all the *peripheral* devices installed in the system. Because it was built around the Intel 8086 micro-processor, whose internal *data bus* could transfer information only 8 bits at a time, the original IBM PC computer had an 8-bit-wide *bus* for interconnecting the system. The IBM Personal Computer AT was based on the 16-bit 80286 processor and so had a 16-bit-wide expansion bus. This became the most widespread industry standard, and is often referred to as the AT bus. Newer processors such as the 80486 can handle data internally over a 32-bit path, but since most peripherals are still 16-bit devices, most systems continue to use a bus of that width. Some, however, do provide one or two 32-bit *expansion slots* for additional memory boards. Systems that use the *EISA* bus architecture have 32-bit slots throughout, and so provide more flexibility for future expansion and use of 32-bit peripherals for faster system performance. See also *architecture, expansion board, ISA, Micro Channel Architecture.*

expansion slot   A long, narrow socket inside a computer cabinet, designed to accept the *edge connector* on an *expansion board.* Most IBM PC-compatible computers provide a number of these slots so that additional devices can be connected to the system's *expansion bus.* Typically the number of expansion slots ranges from three in compact desktop cases to seven or eight in tower-style cases. See also *Apple Desktop Bus.*

expert system   A program designed to help solve problems or make decisions in a particular field by using some of the knowledge that would be used by an expert. This knowledge is stored in a component of the program called the knowledge base, in the form of a large number of IF/THEN statements or rules. In interacting with the system, the user typically provides specific information by filling out a questionnaire or answering a series of questions presented by the program. The system then uses a second component, the inference engine, to process the data in a way analogous to human reasoning and present a conclusion. Some expert systems can also justify their conclusions by explaining their procedures. Although unable to rival the complexity of human reasoning in most areas, expert systems are useful in many limited scientific and financial applications. See also *artificial intelligence, PROLOG.*

exponent **1.** The amount of times a number is to be multiplied by itself; the power to which a number is to be raised. **2.** The digit or digits that indicate the power to which a number is to be raised. In $1,000 = 10^3$, 3 is the exponent of 10.

exponential notation A system of notation in which numbers are expressed as a number between 1 and 10 multiplied by 10 raised to an appropriate power or *exponent.* For example, 8,970 in exponential notation is 8.97×10^3; 0.0026 is 2.6×10^{-3}. In effect, the exponent indicates the number of places the decimal point is to be moved to the right (if the exponent is positive) or left (if the exponent is negative). In computing, exponents are generally not written as superscripts, but rather with the symbol E. 8.97×10^3 becomes 8.97E3, 2.6×10^{-3} becomes 2.6 E–3. See also *floating-point notation.*

export To send data created in one program to a second program. The first program performs whatever *format* conversion is necessary so that the second program can read the data. Many word processing programs can export files created in them to other applications in *ASCII* or other formats. See also *import.*

expression A *string* or combination of symbols that represents some value. An expression can consist of a single value, such as a *variable.* More commonly it consists of two or more values, or *operands*, and one or more *operators*, which specify what actions are to be performed on the operands. Expressions are used in programming, *database management systems*, and *spreadsheets.* See also *arithmetic expression, Boolean expression, query.*

extended ASCII Any of various sets of characters that assign additional *ASCII* values to numbers from 128 through 255.

Extended ASCII uses 8 *bits* for each character, yielding a total of 2^8, or 256, codes, 128 more than are available in the standard ASCII set. The additional codes are used to represent foreign characters, mathematical symbols, and symbols for drawing pictures.

While the basic ASCII character set is standardized for all personal computer hardware and software, various sets of extended character codes are used by different computer manufacturers and software developers. IBM uses a set of extended ASCII characters called the IBM extended character set, which became a de facto standard for IBM PC and compatible computers. Apple uses a somewhat different group of extended ASCII characters for Macintosh computers. See table at *ASCII*.

Extended Binary-Coded Decimal Interchange Code See **EBCDIC.**

Extended Graphics Array See **XGA.**

Extended Industry Standard Architecture See **EISA.**

extended memory In IBM PC and compatible computers based on the Intel 80286 microprocessor and its successors, any system memory or *RAM* that exceeds 1 *megabyte* (1,024 *kilobytes*) and can be accessed directly. The earlier 8086 and 8088, and also the 80286 and later processors running in *real mode*, can directly address only 1MB of RAM. But by operating in *protected mode*, the 80286 can have direct access to 16MB, and the 80386 and later processors can have up to 4 *gigabytes*, without resorting to the page-swapping procedure used by *expanded memory*. This makes extended memory much faster than expanded memory. In the DOS environment, extended memory is commonly used for print *spooling* and *RAM disks*.

Just as the *EMS* specification allows applications to use expanded memory, extended memory can be used by programs that adhere to the Extended Memory Specification, or *XMS*. These programs can gain access to extended memory through an extended memory manager device *driver*. The OS/2 and UNIX operating systems can access extended memory directly.

Extended Memory Specification   See **XMS.**

extension   In DOS file management, an optional set of up to three characters that follow the eight-character file name and are separated from it by a dot. *File name* extensions can be assigned by programs; for example, .COM and .EXE for *executable files*, .BAT for *batch files*, and so on. You can also choose descriptive extensions for your data files, such as .LTR for letters, .MEM for memos, or .JAN for January. Judicious use of file name extensions is a powerful file management tool, as it permits you to copy or delete whole groups of files at once with *wild card* characters. For example, if all your memo files in a current directory called MYDIR are labeled with a .MEM extension, they can all be copied quickly to a floppy disk with the command COPY \MYDIR\ * .MEM A:. Table 10 lists various common DOS file name extensions.

Table 10. Common DOS File Name Extensions

Extension	Meaning
.BAK	Backup file
.BAT	Batch file
.COM	Command file
.EXE	Executable file
.LIB	Library file
.MAP	Map file

external modem   A *modem* that is housed in an individual case and is connected to the computer through a cable attached to a *serial port*. External modems are slightly more expensive than *internal modems*, they have to be plugged into a separate electrical outlet, and they take up space on top of the computer or on a desk. But they can be easily moved from one computer to another and usually provide a set of status indicator lights that can be helpful in monitoring the progress of a communications link.

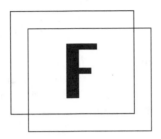

facsimile machine   See **fax machine.**

FAT   [fat]   Acronym for **file allocation table.**

fatal error   An error in program execution that causes the program to *abort*.

fax   [faks]   Short for **facsimile.** *n.*   **1.** The sending and receiving of data or printed pages over telephone lines or radio by converting them into electronic signals and reconverting and reprinting them at the receiving station.   **2.** Material transmitted by fax.   **3.** A fax machine or fax modem.
—*v.* To send data or printed material by fax.

fax board   See **fax modem.**

fax machine   A device that sends and receives printed pages over telephone lines by converting them into electrical signals. The basic components of a fax machine are an *optical scanner* for *digitizing* the page, a telephone line for transmitting the information, and a *printer* for printing received faxes.

Fax machines generally send and receive at a rate of 9,600 *bps*. Most machines use *thermal printers*, but some accept plain bond paper. See also *fax modem*.

fax modem   A *modem* that sends and receives fax transmissions to and from a *fax machine* or another fax modem, rather than another computer, although some fax modems are dual-purpose and can act as regular modems also. Like regular modems, fax modems can be either internal or external. Internal fax modems are called *fax boards* and are *adapters* that fit into an *expansion slot* on a computer. Since fax modems don't have *optical scanners*, documents they transmit must first be stored as disk files in the computer. Likewise, received documents are written to disk files.

FCC   Abbreviation of **Federal Communications Commission.**

FCC certification   A statement that a given make and model of computer falls within the limits set by the *Federal Communications Commission* with regard to radio frequency interference with other devices. *Class A* certification signifies that a computer is suitable for use in commercial and industrial environments. *Class B* certification requires lower levels of radio frequency radiation and is for devices to be used in the home. Class B certification does not guarantee that a computer will not cause interference to nearby radios and television sets, but the levels should be low enough not to be disruptive under normal use for most people.

FDHD   Abbreviation of **Floppy Drive High Density.**   A trademark for a type of *disk drive* used in Macintosh computers that can accept either *double-density* or *high-density* 3.5-inch *floppy disks*. The FDHD, often called *SuperDrive*, can also read and format disks in *DOS* format, enabling Macintosh computers and IBM PC computers to share data.

feathering   In desktop publishing, the process of adding space between the lines of text on a page to force *vertical justification*.

file

Federal Communications Commission Abbreviated **FCC** The
United States government agency that regulates interstate
and international telephone, telegraph, and radio communications.

FEP Abbreviation of **front-end processor.**

FF Abbreviation of **form feed.**

fiber optics A method of transmitting data in the form of laser
light over bundles of glass fibers. This method has numerous
advantages over such traditional techniques as wire cables,
phone lines, and radio waves. Fiber optics offers greater *bandwidth* and is virtually insusceptible to electromagnetic interference. It is also far more suited for use by computers,
because it can transmit *digital* data directly without the need
to convert it into *analog* form through a *modem*. The process
of replacing older cable with smaller, lighter fiber optic cable
is under way, and by the end of the century fiber optics
should be a common method of communications in much of
the world.

field In a *database*, a space for a single item of information
contained in a *record*. For example, in a database containing
records of names, addresses, and account histories for individual clients, one field might hold the ZIP code, another the
telephone number, and another the date of last contact. When
arranged in a table with each record in a single horizontal
row, the fields are displayed in vertical columns. In most
database management systems, each field is assigned a specific length and data type such as text, date, or currency, as
well as other *attributes* such as optional or required, centered,
boldface, and so on.

file A collection of data or information that is stored as a unit
in the computer under a single name, called the *file name*.
Files are the basic units that a computer works with in storing and retrieving data. Although a single file is often scattered across many places on a *hard disk*, the computer
retrieves all the pieces and makes them available as a single

entity. Table 11 lists various common types of files. See also *attribute, directory, file allocation table, fragmentation.*

Table 11. Common File Types

File Type	Contents
Backup file	Duplicate of a program or data
Batch file	Operating system commands
Binary file	Data or instructions in binary format
Command file	Operating system commands
Data file	Data
Executable file	Programs or commands in an executable format
Library file	Programming routines or subroutines
Map file	Map of a program
Text file	Text

file allocation table Acronym **FAT** [fat]. An area on a *hard disk* or *floppy disk* where information is stored about the physical location of each piece of every file on the disk and the location of unusable areas of the disk. In DOS, OS/2, and some UNIX systems, the operating system checks the FAT whenever a request is made to access a file, and uses the information to retrieve the file when reading or to determine where to put it when writing to the disk. If the part of the disk containing the FAT is erased or corrupted, no files on the disk can be read, even though they may be physically intact.

file attribute See **attribute** (sense 2).

file compression See **data compression**.

file compression program A *utility* that compresses files so as to minimize the space they take up on a disk or tape. The files are then decompressed as they are needed. File compression programs are used to compress files for long-term storage, as in an archive, and to decompress files that have been downloaded from a *bulletin board system*. See also *data compression.*

file fragmentation See **fragmentation.**

file locking See **lock.**

file management The placement and organization of *files* and *directories* used by an *operating system.* The operating system has its own file manager, but separate file management programs are also available. These programs provide additional features, such as easier *backup* procedures. See also *directory, file allocation table, hierarchical.*

file name The name given to a file so that it can be distinguished from other files. Different operating systems have different rules for the length and composition of file names. In *DOS,* a file name can be up to eight characters long and must not include these characters:

" ' / \ [ ] , . ? , * < > |

Macintosh file names can be 31 characters long and cannot include a colon (:).

Many operating systems allow you to put a short *extension* on each file name to indicate what type of file it is. The extension usually goes after a period at the end of the file name.

file server See **server.**

file sharing network See **peer-to-peer network.**

file transfer The sending of files from one computer or program to another. For example, if you send a colleague a letter by E-mail and enclose a paper, the file containing the paper is first transferred from your word processing program to your E-mail program, and then transferred to your colleague's computer over a network.

file type A designation for a class of files with the same general structure or function. In DOS, the file type is usually indicated by the *extension.*

fill *v.* In graphics programs, to put a color or pattern into an enclosed shape. When you do this, you fill the shape with a color or design.

—*n.* In spreadsheet programs, a command that allows you to fill a *range* with a series of values once you have provided the starting value, the increment of change between each value, and the ending value.

filter A command that causes the *operating system* to read data, manipulate it in some specified way, and output the manipulated data. In DOS and OS/2, the filter commands are FIND, which searches for text in a file; MORE, which displays a file one screenful at a time; and SORT, which alphabetizes the contents of a file.

Finder A trademark for an interface to the operating system for Apple Macintosh computers. The Finder incorporates *windows, icons,* and other graphics, and it was the first *graphical user interface* to gain wide acceptance. The Finder is the Macintosh computer's disk and *file management* system; it also manages the *clipboard* and *scrapbook.* It is a single-tasking program. *MultiFinder* is the *multitasking* version of the Finder.

firmware Programming instructions that are permanently stored in read-only memory (*ROM*) rather than being implemented through software. ROMs and *PROMs* that have data or programs written on them are examples of firmware.

fixed disk See **hard disk.**

fixed-frequency monitor An *analog monitor* that accepts input signals in only one frequency range. Fixed-frequency monitors come with many inexpensive entry-level computer systems. See also *multifrequency monitor, multiscanning monitor.*

fixed length In database systems, designating a *field* that stays the same size regardless of how much information it contains. The *variable length* field grows or shrinks depending on how much data it holds.

fixed pitch   The allocation of space of the same width to different characters in a font. Fixed pitch contrasts with *proportional pitch*, which gives each character its own particular width. In a fixed pitch font, a narrow letter such as *i* is given the same amount of horizontal space as a wider letter such as *w*, while in a *proportional pitch* font, *i* would be allocated a smaller amount of space. Many computer display screens show text in a fixed pitch font, while books, magazines, and newspapers are printed in *proportional pitch*. Also called *fixed width*. See also *monospace font, pitch*.

fixed-point notation   A format in which numerical values have a set number of digits before and after the decimal point. See also *floating-point notation*.

fixed width   See **fixed pitch.**

Fkey   A *utility* on Macintosh computers that simulates the *function keys* on keyboards for IBM PC and compatible computers. To activate a particular command through the Fkey feature, the user presses the *Command key*, the *Shift key*, and a number key from 0 to 9. The combination Command-Shift-4, for example, prints the text and images currently on the display screen.

flag   A *bit* or series of bits that serve as a signal to a computer. A flag can mark such items as an unusual piece of data, a possible error, or the beginning or end of a message.

flash memory   A type of electronically erasable programmable read-only memory (*EEPROM*) chip whose data can be altered. Flash memory chips are a lightweight, fast data storage medium for portable devices.
      Flash memory chips contrast with *ROM* chips, which are programmed when manufactured and cannot be altered. Flash memory also differs from *PROM*, which is manufactured blank but whose programs, once installed, cannot be erased. *EPROM* chips can be erased through reprogramming, but this process requires a special hardware device. Flash memory

chips can be rewritten without removing them from the computer's circuit board. The data stored in flash memory remain intact even when the power is shut off.

flatbed scanner A type of *optical scanner* that holds a page stationary while the scanning head moves across the page and converts images and text into digital information. Flatbed scanners are able to scan bound documents that cannot be scanned by a *sheet-fed scanner*. See also *hand-held scanner, optical scanner, sheet-fed scanner*.

flat-file database A database that contains all of its information in a single *file*. A flat-file database is less flexible than a *relational database*, which contains a number of different files and can link data from one file to another.

flat-panel display A thin, lightweight *display screen* found in laptop and notebook computers. Flat-panel displays do not use conventional *cathode-ray tubes*. Instead, they use one of the following technologies:

LCD (liquid-crystal display), made of liquid crystals sandwiched between two layers of glass filters. Liquid crystals are rod-shaped molecules that flow like a liquid but have a crystalline order in their arrangement. Electric currents can be used to control the alignment of the molecules and therefore their transmission of light through the filters. Cells of liquid crystals are arranged in an array to form *pixels*, each cell acting as a tiny electronically controlled shutter.

Gas plasma display, made of two sheets of glass each fabricated with rows of conduction film. The sheets are placed on top of each other perpendicularly so that the rows of film intersect. The sheets also enclose a mixture of gases, mostly neon. At each intersection point, a sufficient voltage will ionize the gas, making it glow. In effect, a gas plasma display is like an array of tiny neon lamps.

Electroluminescent display (ELD), constructed similarly to a gas plasma display, except that instead of gas, phosphors (materials that emit light when excited by an electric current) are used.

Thin film transistor (TFT) display, a refinement of LCD technology in which each liquid-crystal cell, or *pixel*, is controlled by three separate transistors, one each for red, blue, and green.

Also called *flat-screen*. See also *active-matrix*, *backlighting*, *passive-matrix*.

flicker   See **screen flicker.**

floating-point coprocessor   See **math coprocessor.**

floating-point notation   A format for representing a number that is not an integer; that is, a number that has some fractional part. Typically, a nonintegral number is represented as a decimal number multiplied by a power of the base 10, but in computer memory it is often represented as a binary number multiplied by a power of the base 2. The number 60⅝ can be expressed in decimal floating-point notation as 60.625 or 6.0625×10^1 or 6.0625E1, or in binary floating-point notation as 111100.101 or 1.111100 (base 2) $\times 2^5$. See also *fixed-point notation*, *scientific notation*.

floppy   See **floppy disk.**

floppy disk   A round, flat piece of Mylar coated with magnetic material and covered by a protective jacket, used as a *storage medium* for personal computers. Originally, floppy disks were the principal storage medium for personal computers, but the development of inexpensive *hard disks* has diminished their role. Floppy *disk drives* are slower, have less storage capacity, and are more easily damaged than hard disks. But floppy disks are more portable, considerably less expensive than hard disks, and essential for loading programs and data into your computer and for *backup*.

Floppy disks for most personal computers come in two sizes: 5.25 and 3.5 inches. The 5.25-inch disks were the more common ones before 1987. They have flimsy sleeves and open access holes, so it's easy to get fingerprints on the disk's surface unless you're careful.

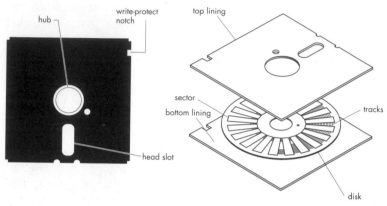

5.25–INCH FLOPPY DISK

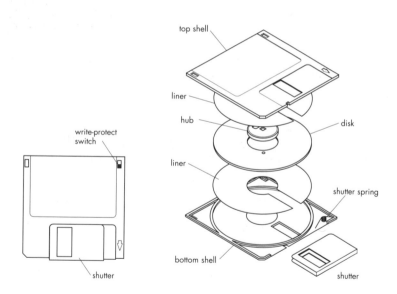

3.5–INCH FLOPPY DISK

floppy disk
Closed and exploded views

The 3.5-inch disk, sometimes called a *microfloppy disk*, is encased in rigid plastic and has a sliding guard that covers the access hole. The drive slides open the guard after you insert the disk. Both 5.25- and 3.5-inch disks are used in IBM PC and compatible computers. Macintosh computers use 3.5-inch disks. The newest floppy, the 2-inch disk, is used in some laptop computers.

Floppy disks can be single-sided or double-sided, which means that data can be recorded on only one side or on both sides. They come in a range of *densities*, including single density, double density, high density, and extra high density. Also called *diskette*. See illustration. See table at *density*.

flowchart   A schematic representation of a sequence of operations, as in a computer program.

flush   Aligned evenly with a margin. "Flush left" means that the text is aligned with the left margin, and "flush right" means that it is aligned with the right margin. See also *justification, ragged*.

Fn   Abbreviation of **function key.**

folder   In *graphical user interfaces*, an organizing structure that contains multiple files and is analogous to a *directory*. A folder is usually represented on the screen by the image of a file folder. Like a directory, a folder may contain other folders. See illustration at *hierarchical*.

folio   A page number. If a folio appears at the bottom of a page it is called a drop folio.

font   1. A complete set of characters of one size and *typeface*. The height of a font is measured in *points* (72 points equal one inch). The most common weights are lightface and *boldface*. Popular styles include *roman* and *italic*. Another font specification is *pitch*, which refers to the number of characters printed per inch. A *fixed pitch* font allocates the same amount of space for every character, while a *proportional* *pitch* font gives each character its own particular amount of space.

Screen fonts are the fonts a program uses to display text on a *display screen*. The screen font usually resembles the *printer font*, but even a "what you see is what you get" (*WYSIWYG*) display does not always correspond exactly to the way a document will look in print.

Printers come equipped with a set of *resident fonts*, also called *internal* or *built-in fonts*. Additional fonts can be added to many printers by inserting a *font cartridge* or by downloading *soft fonts* from software.

Fonts are produced by computers and printers in two ways. *Bit-mapped fonts* use a pattern of bits for each character. Every character has its own map, depending on size, weight, and typeface. *Outline fonts* use *vector graphics* to create a set of mathematical instructions that describe the outline of a font. The same basic set of instructions can produce different sizes of the same typeface. See also *outline font, printer, scalable font*. **2.** See **font family.**

font cartridge   A *ROM* cartridge that plugs into some printers and enables them to print in fonts other than their *resident fonts*. The other way to add fonts to a printer is to download *soft fonts* into the printer's *RAM*.

font family   A set of *fonts* in various sizes and *weights* that share the same *typeface*. For example, Times 10 *point* and Times Italic 14 point are in the same font family. See illustration.

New Caledonia 8 point	New Caledonia 10 point
New Caledonia Italic 8 point	*New Caledonia Italic 10 point*
New Caledonia Boldface 8 point	**New Caledonia Boldface 10 point**

New Caledonia 12 point

New Caledonia Italic 12 point

New Caledonia Boldface 12 point

font family

footer   In *word processing*, printed information, especially a title, page number, or date, placed in the bottom margin of a page and repeated on every page or every other page of the document. A footer that repeats only on odd-numbered pages is an *odd footer*. One that repeats only on even-numbered pages is an *even footer*.

footprint   The amount of space a device occupies on a desk or the floor.

foreground   **1.** In a *multitasking* system, the state of accepting data and commands from an *input device*, such as a keyboard. For example, if your computer is making calculations in a spreadsheet program while you're writing a letter in a word processing program, the word processing program is operating in the foreground.   **2.** On a display screen, the display of characters and graphics, as opposed to the *background*, which is the area of the screen behind the characters and graphics.

format   *n.* An arrangement of data for storage, display, or *hard copy* presentation. Database, spreadsheet, graphics, and word processing programs all have their own formats that can be altered to change the way information is presented.
—*v.*   **1.** To arrange the data in a *document* for display or hard copy presentation. In word processing, for example, setting such *attributes* in a document as the typeface, *point* size, margins, *headers* or *footers*, line spacing, and *justification* is referred to as formatting the document.   **2.** To run an operating system or utility program that prepares a disk for use by organizing its storage space into *addresses* that can be recognized and accessed. Reformatting a disk erases only the address tables on the disk, not the actual data. If you accidentally reformat a disk that contains valuable data, you may be able to recover most of the data with a utility program such as PC Tools or Norton Utilities. You can also hire a specialist to try to recover the data. Also called *initialize*, especially with reference to Macintosh computers.

form feed   Abbreviated **FF**   A command that tells the printer to advance to the top of a new page. Also called *page eject*.

formula An *expression* that instructs an application, such as a *database management system* or a *spreadsheet*, to perform a calculation on one or more values. For example, in a spreadsheet program, a formula plugs in the values of two or more *cells* and performs a calculation on those values.

FORTRAN [FOR-tran] Acronym for **formula translator.** The first *high-level language*, developed in the 1950s by IBM and released in 1957. FORTRAN is designed to handle intensive mathematical calculations and was once used chiefly in mathematics, science, and engineering. Later versions of FORTRAN introduced features that made it useful in other fields as well.

forward compatible Of or relating to a software program designed to run on the present model of a computer as well as on future, more powerful models. For example, all software that runs on IBM PC-compatibles based on the Intel 80286 microprocessor will also run on later models based on the 80386. Software developers strive for forward compatibility because it enables users to upgrade their computer systems without the expense of replacing software and data. New systems can become so technologically advanced, however, that forward compatibility must often be sacrificed. Also called *upward compatible.* See also *backward compatible, compatible.*

486 The Intel486 *microprocessor.* See also *Intel microprocessors.*

4GL Abbreviation of **fourth-generation language.**

fourth-generation language Abbreviated **4GL** A user-oriented *programming language* that is even closer to human language than *high-level languages* are. Fourth-generation languages are often used to structure *queries* in *relational databases.*

fragmentation 1. The condition of having different parts of the same file scattered throughout a disk. Fragmentation occurs when the operating system breaks up a file and fits it into the spaces left vacant by previously deleted files. Fragmentation slows down the operating system by making the *read/write head* search for files over a larger area. Also called *file fragmentation*. See also *defragment*. **2.** A similar scattering in a computer's random-access memory (*RAM*) that takes place when programs and data are repeatedly stored and released.

freeware Computer programs that are given away free of charge, often over a *bulletin board system*. Freeware differs from *public domain software* in that freeware remains copyrighted while public domain software does not. The copyright owner of a freeware program may impose restrictions on its use or distribution. See also *shareware*.

frequency The number of repetitions, expressed in *hertz*, of a complete waveform within a specified period of time. One hertz equals one cycle per second; a *kilohertz* equals 1,000 hertz; and a *megahertz* equals 1,000 kilohertz. See also *hertz, kilohertz, megahertz*.

friction feed A mechanism that draws paper through a *dot-matrix* or *daisy wheel printer* by pinching it between plastic or rubber rollers. In contrast, a *tractor feed* mechanism pulls paper through the printer by using two or more toothed wheels. Tractor feeds are able to use only paper with holes on the edges, while friction feeds can adjust to print envelopes and a variety of cut-sheet paper. Most dot-matrix printers are equipped with both types of feed mechanism.

front-end processor Abbreviated **FEP** A small computer that receives, generates, or handles data before sending it to a larger computer for analysis or further processing. The front-end processor may perform operations such as error checks, *format* conversions, or sorts. A front-end processor may also act as an interface between the user and the larger computer, which is called the "back-end processor."

full backup   A procedure for *backing up* all the files on a *hard disk* by copying them to floppy disks, a *tape*, or another storage medium. It is a good security measure for frequent users to do full backups once a week. See also *incremental backup*.

full duplex   In communications, a mode of transmission in which data can be sent in two directions simultaneously. In the other mode, *half duplex*, data can be transmitted in only one direction at a time. The two senders must alternate their transmissions.

   Modems are equipped with a switch that selects either full duplex or half duplex. Transmission mode is part of the *communications protocol* that must be established for data to be passed smoothly between two or more computers.

function   In programming and in *spreadsheet* applications, a procedure or section within a program that returns a single value. Functions can include calculations in finance, mathematics, trigonometry, and statistics, or involve *lookup* tables or data sorting and comparison. In a spreadsheet, for example, a function may return the amount of compound interest received given the principal, interest rate, and time period.

function key   Abbreviated **Fn**   One of a set of computer keys, located on the top or the left side of the keyboard on an IBM PC or compatible computer that enters specific commands defined by the program you are running. Keyboards are equipped with either 10 or 12 function keys that are labeled F1, F2, F3, and so on. Function keys execute different commands when they are pressed in combination with the *Alt key*, the *Control key*, and or the *Shift key*.

   The equivalent to a function key on a Macintosh computer is the *Fkey* utility, which executes various commands when you push the Shift key, the *Command key*, and a number key from 0 to 9.

G **1.** Abbreviation of **giga-**. **2.** Abbreviation of **gigabyte.**

gas plasma display A type of *flat-panel display* frequently used in *laptop* and *notebook* computers. Neon is enclosed between two flat panels with vertical wires running along one panel and horizontal wires along the other so that together they form a grid. When an electric current is sent along one horizontal wire and one vertical wire, the point of intersection is charged so that the neon glows reddish orange at the point, creating a *pixel.*

gateway A device that connects two *networks* that use different *communications protocols*. A gateway has a *microprocessor* capable of converting information from one network into a readable format for a second network that uses a different protocol. For example, gateways are used to link *AppleTalk* and *Ethernet* networks.

GB Abbreviation of **gigabyte.**

ghosting The permanent "etching" of an image into a *display screen* when the same image has been left on the screen for a long period of time.
     Screen savers prevent ghosting either by dimming the screen brightness or by displaying moving images on a screen that has displayed a fixed image for a specified period of time. Also called *burn-in.*

GIF   A service mark for a bit-mapped color *graphics file format*. GIF is used by many *bulletin board systems* to exchange scanned graphics because it supports efficient *data compression*. See table at *graphics file format*.

giga-   Abbreviated **G**   **1.** A prefix indicating one billion (10^9), as in gigahertz.   **2.** A prefix indicating 1,073,741,824 (2^{30}), as in *gigabyte*. This is the sense in which giga- is generally used in computing, which is based on powers of two.

gigabyte   [JIG-uh-bite or GIG-uh-bite]   Abbreviated **G** or **GB**   A unit of measurement of computer memory or data storage capacity, equal to 1,073,741,824 (2^{30}) *bytes*. One gigabyte equals 1,024 *megabytes*.

global   **1.** Of or relating to an entire program, document, or file. A global format for a spreadsheet, for example, is a format that applies to every cell in that spreadsheet.   **2.** Of or relating to all the users in a computer network.

glossary   In *word processing*, a storage utility for holding text that you would ordinarily have to type over and over again. When you access a glossary it inserts the appropriate text into your document and saves you the trouble of typing it again.

gppm   Abbreviation of **graphics pages per minute.**

graphical user interface   Acronym **GUI**   [GOO-ee].   An *interface* that enables you to choose commands, start programs, and see lists of files and other options by selecting from *windows*, *icons*, and *menus* on the screen. Choices can be made either with keyboard commands or by using the *mouse* to move an on-screen *pointer*.

Graphical user interfaces take full advantage of the bit-mapped graphics displays of personal computers. GUIs are easier for most people to learn to use than *command-driven* interfaces. Also, a GUI uses a standard format for text and graphics, so that different *applications* running under a common GUI can share data.

graphics

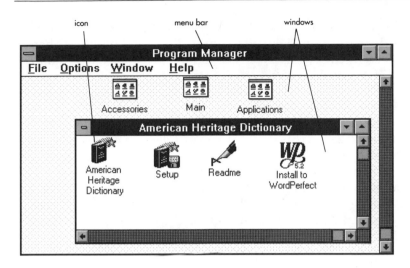

graphical user interface
Microsoft Windows

A graphical user interface is used on all Macintosh computers. Many applications for IBM PC and compatible computers
use GUIs, most of them based either on *Microsoft Windows*
(for *DOS* systems) or *Presentation Manager* (for *OS/2* systems). Many DOS programs include some features of GUIs,
such as menus, but are *character-based*, not *graphics-based*,
and are therefore not true GUIs. See illustration.

graphics   The display and manipulation of pictorial information by computers. The two basic methods of creating computer graphics are *object-oriented graphics* and *bit-mapped
graphics*.

In object-oriented graphics, each pictorial object is represented by a mathematical description. Programs that use
object-oriented graphics, such as *draw programs*, can manipulate one object without affecting surrounding objects. Objects
can be enlarged or reduced without introducing scaling distortions.

In bit-mapped graphics, pictures are represented as patterns
of dots or *pixels*. The patterns are stored in memory as *arrays*

of *bits* called *bit maps*. Bit-mapped graphics cannot be resized easily without distortion. *Paint programs* use bit-mapped graphics.

Many *graphics-based* applications exist, including *desktop publishing* software, *presentation graphics*, and *CAD* (computer-aided design) software.

graphics accelerator An *expansion board* that includes a graphics *coprocessor*. The coprocessor is a *microprocessor* specially designed for fast graphics processing. The graphics accelerator frees the *CPU* (central processing unit) from graphics processing, resulting in significant improvement in a system's ability to run *graphical user interfaces*, such as *Microsoft Windows*, and their related applications.

graphics-based Of or relating to programs and hardware that display images as *bit maps* or geometrical objects, as opposed to the *ASCII* or *extended ASCII* characters used by *character-based* systems. Examples of graphics-based software include *presentation graphics* and *desktop publishing* programs. All programs that run on a Macintosh computer are graphics-based. Graphics-based applications usually require a large amount of memory, a powerful *CPU*, and a monitor with *graphics* capability, and support a graphics standard such as *VGA*.

graphics file format The way in which a program reads and stores information so as to create and manipulate graphics images. There are numerous *proprietary* graphics file formats, with little standardization among them. Table 12 compares various common graphics file formats.

graphics mode A mode of *resolution* on a *video adapter* that allows the screen to display both text and graphics. In graphics mode, both text and images are treated as illuminated patterns of pixels. Programs that run totally in graphics mode are called *graphics-based* programs. In *character mode*, the screen is split into larger units, or boxes, each one able to hold one *ASCII* character.

Table 12. Common Graphics File Formats

File Format	Data Storage Format	Characteristics
BMP	Bit-mapped	Used by Microsoft Windows
CGM (Computer Graphics Metafile)	Object-oriented	Used by many software and hardware products
EPS (Encapsulated PostScript)	Object-oriented	Used by the PostScript language
GIF	Bit-mapped	Used by CompuServe and many other bulletin board systems
HPGL (Hewlett-Packard Graphics Language)	Bit-mapped	Used by many IBM PC-based graphics products
PCX	Bit-mapped	Used by many graphics programs, optical scanners, and fax modems
PIC (Lotus Picture File)	Bit-mapped	Used by the Lotus 1-2-3 spreadsheet and many other IBM PC applications
PICT	Object-oriented	Used by almost all Macintosh graphics programs
TIFF (Tagged Image File Format)	Bit-mapped	Used for storing scanned images
WMF (Windows Metafile Format)	Object-oriented	Used for transferring graphics between Microsoft Windows applications

graphics pages per minute   Abbreviated **gppm**   The speed at which a printer, especially a *laser printer*, can print pages of graphics images, as opposed to *pages per minute* (ppm), the speed at which a printer prints pages of text. Given the relative complexity of graphics versus text, a printer's graphics pages per minute rating is always considerably slower than its pages per minute rating.

graphics tablet See **digitizer** (sense 2).

gray scale A series of shades from pure white to pure black. In computer graphics, the number of gradations within this scale varies depending on the number of *bits* used to store the shading information for each *pixel*. Typically, current hardware and software can represent from 16 to 256 different shades of gray. See illustration at *halftone*.

gray scaling A computer's use of shades of gray to represent a graphics image. Gray scaling usually involves converting a *continuous tone* image—an image with thousands of different shades of gray, such as a black and white photograph—into an image with a much smaller number of gray shades that can be stored and manipulated by a computer. Gray scaling differs from *dithering* in that dithering creates the illusion of shades of gray by alternating black and white dots. In gray scaling, each dot is a particular shade of gray.

greeking In *desktop publishing*, the use of gray bars or garbled text to simulate how text will appear on a page. Greeking is used when one is evaluating the *layout* and design of a document rather than its content. See also *preview, thumbnail*.

groupware Software that helps organize the activities of users in a *network*. Examples of groupware include *schedulers* that help employees plan meetings; electronic newsletters; and software designed to make collaborative writing projects easier.

GUI [GOO-ee] Acronym for **graphical user interface.**

gutter In a bound document, the blank space formed by the inner margins of two facing pages. In *desktop publishing* and *word processing*, you should allow for additional margin space on the side of a page that will be bound in order to accommodate the gutter. Also called *offset*.

GW-BASIC A trademark for a version of the *BASIC* programming language that often comes with IBM PC-compatible computers.

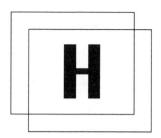

hacker **1.** A person who is proficient at using or programming a computer; a computer buff. **2.** A person who breaks into a computer system to view, alter, or steal restricted data and programs. Some former hackers have become professional designers of sophisticated computer security systems.

half duplex A mode of transmission in which data can be sent in only one direction at a time. The two senders must alternate their transmissions. See also *communications protocol, full duplex.*

half-height drive A disk drive for IBM PC and compatible computers that is roughly half as tall as older drives, which were about three inches high. Half-height drives have become standard for IBM PC and compatible computers.

halftone A photograph or other *continuous tone* image in which the gradation of tones is simulated by the relative darkness and density of tiny dots. In traditional printing, halftones are created by photographing an image through a fine screen. In *desktop publishing*, photographs are scanned and then converted electronically into patterns of black and white dots. Dark shades are reproduced by dense patterns of large dots, and lighter shades by less dense patterns of smaller dots. See illustration. See also *dithering.*

hand-held Of or relating to a computer or device small enough to be held in one hand and operated with the other. A number

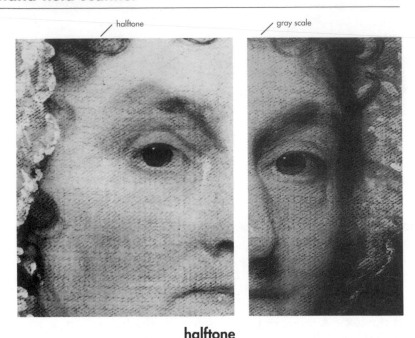

halftone / gray scale

halftone

of manufacturers are developing hand-held devices that read and display information from *CD-ROMs*.

hand-held scanner A compact, portable scanner that relies on the human hand to move the scan head. Most software for hand-held scanners automatically combines two half-page scans into a single image. The hand-held scanner, dependent on the steadiness of your hand to accurately render an image, is generally less expensive because it doesn't require a mechanism to move the scan head or paper.

handle In *object-oriented graphics* programs, one of the squares that appears around an object that you have selected. You use the handle to *drag*, enlarge, reduce, or reshape the selected object. See illustration at *Bézier curve*.

handshaking An exchange that takes place between two devices so that communications can begin. Hardware handshaking occurs over a special communications line between a computer and a *peripheral*, such as a *serial* printer, before a transfer of data takes place. In software handshaking, codes are exchanged through modems to establish a *communications protocol* for the exchange of information.

hang   To halt operations in such a way that the computer system does not respond to any input devices, such as the keyboard or mouse. A hung system usually requires *rebooting*. See also *crash*.

hanging indent   In *word processing*, an indentation of every line in a paragraph except the first. Also called *hanging paragraph*, *outdent*. See illustration.

A paragraph that has all lines except for
the first indented is called a hanging
indent. A hanging indent is also
known as a hanging paragraph or an
outdent.

hanging indent

hard   **1.** Existing physically as opposed to intangibly. For example, a *hard copy* is printed output that exists physically on paper, as opposed to existing electronically in a disk file. **2.** Permanently wired or fixed, as a *hard disk*, which is usually permanently installed in a computer. See also *soft*.

hard card   An *expansion card* containing a hard disk drive. The hard card fits into an *expansion slot* instead of a disk drive bay. Hard cards are easy to install and often faster than conventional *disk drives*, but may have less storage capacity.

hard copy   A printed version of data stored on a disk or in memory.

hard disk   A rigid magnetic disk fixed within a *disk drive* and used for storing computer data. Hard disks offer considerably more storage and quicker access to data than *floppy disks* do. Hard disks for most personal computers have storage capacities ranging from 80 to 512 *megabytes* (MB) and have *access times* of less than 30 milliseconds. Although most hard disks are permanently installed, it is possible to buy removable hard disks in the form of *disk packs* or *removable cartridges*.

A single hard disk consists of several disk *platters*. Each platter has two read/write *heads*, one for each side of the platter, that float on a thin sheet of air just above a magnetized surface. All the read/write heads are attached to a single head arm so that they don't move independently. Each platter has the same number of *tracks*, and the group of tracks in corresponding locations on all the platters is called a *cylinder*.

There are several *interface* standards for connecting hard disks to computers. These include ST-506, *SCSI* (Small Computer System Interface), *SCSI-2*, *ESDI* (Enhanced Small Device Interface), and *IDE interface*. Also called *fixed disk*. See illustration. See table at *access time*.

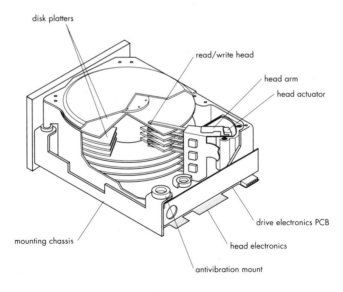

hard disk

hard hyphen In programs with *hyphenation*, a hyphen that you manually add to a word, as in "user-friendly" or a hyphenated last name. *Soft hyphens* are added automatically by the program to break words that would otherwise extend too far into the right margin. The computer will not break a line at a hard hyphen, since hard hyphens are considered part of the spelling of a word.

hard return An instruction that moves the cursor or printer to the beginning of the next line. Since many word processing programs have *word wrap*, *soft returns* are automatically inserted at the end of each line. A hard return is inserted not by the program but by the user, typically to end a paragraph. See also *carriage return*.

hardware A computer, its components, its *peripherals*, and other associated equipment. Hardware includes *chips*, *disk drives*, *display screens*, cables, *expansion boards*, *modems*, and *printers*—in short, any physical object that is part of a computer system. *Software* consists of the programs and data that control the functioning of the hardware. See also *firmware*.

Hayes compatibility The ability of a modem to use a standardized set of *commands* developed by Hayes Microcomputer Products. Most modems are Hayes compatible, as are many popular *communications software* programs. Hayes is a trademark of Hayes Microcomputer Products.

head The *device* in a magnetic *disk* or *tape drive* that enables it to *read* data from and *write* data to the disk or tape. Inside the head are one or two small coils through which electric current can pass. When the head writes data to the disk or tape, current passes through the coils toward the magnetic fields on the disk or tape and causes the magnetic particles directly beneath the head to align either north-south or south-north. When the head reads the data, the magnetic particles directly beneath the head send a current back through the coils to be translated into *binary* code. The direction in which the particles are aligned determines whether the bit will be 0 or 1. Also called *read/write head*. See illustration at *hard disk*.

head crash   The sudden dropping of the *read/write head* onto the surface or *platter* of a *hard disk* or, more rarely, onto a *floppy disk*. When this happens, the oxide coating on the disk or platter is scratched off or burned, and the *data* stored on that part of the disk is destroyed. If this occurs, both the disk and the head will probably have to be replaced. A head crash can be caused by rough handling of the drive, by dirt particles in the drive, or by mechanical failure. It can be prevented by a program that goes into effect whenever the computer is turned off and stations the head over a part of the disk where there is no data. Many new computers come with such programs, but they can also be purchased as part of certain *utility* packages. Also called *disk crash*.

header   1. In *word processing*, printed information, such as a title or name, placed in the top margin of a *page* and usually repeated on every page or every other page of the document. **2.** *Data stored* at the beginning of a *file* or other unit of *memory* to provide information about a given file, *program*, or *device* or about the memory. Headers usually contain information for use by the *operating system* or the *program* the information concerns, and therefore you usually cannot access this information very easily.

Help   Information about an *application* that can be accessed from within the application. Help is generally a shortened version of the information in a *program* manual. On some applications, the information called up on the *screen* varies according to where you are in the program. For example, Help in a *database management system* might explain one set of *commands* when you are *inputting data* and a different set of commands when you are requesting a *report*.

Help key   A *key* that calls up *Help* from within a program. Some keyboards have a special Help key, but each individual program must designate this or a *function key* as its Help key.

Hercules Graphics   An *adapter* developed in the early 1980s for displaying *graphics* on *monochrome monitors* of IBM PC and compatible computers that can otherwise display only *text*. The graphics are displayed with a *resolution* of 720 by 348 *pixels*. If you use Hercules Graphics, you will have to make sure that any graphics *software* you get comes with a Hercules *driver*. Hercules is a trademark of Hercules Computer Technology. See table at *video standard*.

hertz   Abbreviated **Hz**   A unit of frequency equal to one cycle per second.

hex   Short for **hexadecimal.**

hexadecimal   Of, relating to, or based on the number 16. The hexadecimal system uses the digits 0 through 9, and then the letters *A* through *F* to represent the decimal numbers 10 through 15. *Programmers* often use the hexadecimal system instead of the *binary* system that computers use because binary numbers can be overly long, requiring four digits for every hexadecimal digit. For example, hexadecimal *C* is *12* in decimal numbers and *1100* in binary. The term hexadecimal was coined in the early 1960s to replace the earlier "sexadecimal." See table at *binary*.

hidden file   A *file* that is not ordinarily shown in a *directory* listing. In *DOS*, for example, the *system* files IO.SYS and MSDOS.SYS are hidden so that you won't accidentally *delete* or corrupt them. See also *attribute*.

hierarchical   Being organized pyramidally into general groups that divide into more specific subgroups. *Folders* on *Macintosh* computers and *directories* on *IBM PC* and compatible computers are organized hierarchically, so that at the top level there is a small number of folders or *root directories* and at the bottom level there is a large number of *files*. See illustration. See also *directory*, *folder*.

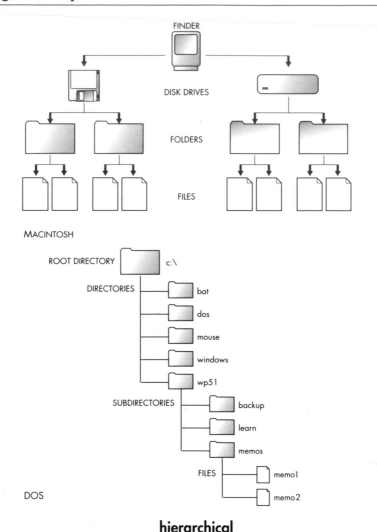

FINDER

DISK DRIVES

FOLDERS

FILES

MACINTOSH

ROOT DIRECTORY   c:\

DIRECTORIES

bat
dos
mouse
windows
wp51

SUBDIRECTORIES

backup
learn
memos

FILES

memo1
memo2

DOS

hierarchical
Hierarchical file management under Macintosh and DOS

high-density disk   A *floppy disk* with more memory than a *double-density disk*. High-density 5.25-inch disks for IBM PC and compatible computers can store up to 1.2 megabytes of data, and 3.5-inch high-density disks can store 1.44MB. See also *density*. See table at *density*.

high-level language   A programming language, such as C or Pascal, that uses words and some form of syntax, bringing it much closer to natural language than *assembly language* or *machine language,* and in which each instruction or statement corresponds to several instructions in machine language. High-level languages are much easier for people to learn and faster to use than assembly language. A high-level language must be translated into machine language by a *compiler* or an *interpreter.* See also *assembly language, low-level language.* See illustration at *programming language.*

high resolution   See **resolution.**

Hobbit   A trademark for a *microprocessor* chip set developed by AT&T to allow pen-based *personal communicators* to access a wide range of both wired and wireless networks and devices for sending and receiving messages.

Home key   The *key* that moves the *cursor* to the beginning of the line, the *screen,* or the *file.*

host   A *computer* containing *data* or *programs* that another computer can access over a *network* or by *modem.* For example, if your computer is part of a network, the computer it connects to when you *log on* is the host. See also *server.*

hot key   A *key* or sequence of keys that accesses a *memory resident program,* such as a *calculator* or a *notepad.* Some programs or applications let you choose your own hot keys and select the features they will access.

hot link   A connection between two *files* that allows one to be updated automatically every time you update the other. For example, you may have a graph illustrating information in a *database.* If you establish a hot link between them, every time you make a change in the database the graph will change accordingly. See also *Dynamic Data Exchange.*

HP-compatible printer   A *laser printer* for IBM PC and compatible computers that understands the *language* developed by Hewlett-Packard for its laser printer *drivers.*

HyperCard   A tradmark for a *hypertext* program for *Macintosh* computers that features *cards* organized into *stacks* and uses *buttons* to allow interaction. A card may have both *text* and *graphics*. You can scroll back and forth through the cards in a stack much the same way you can with a card file. If you press a particular button on a card, you may be shown another card, or an animated graphics display, or you may hear music. HyperCard comes with several stacks, but it also lets you make your own. You can use *HyperTalk* to create *scripts* that determine what will happen when you *click* on any of the buttons. HyperCard can be used to form *databases*, educational programs, and games, among other things. HyperCard can also be used to customize the *desktop*. See also *HyperTalk, hypertext*.

hypermedia   Information that is presented via computer-controlled displays so that readers can navigate easily and quickly between the distinct but integrative components or elements of text, graphics, video, and sound. See also *hypertext*.

HyperTalk   A trademark for the programming language for *HyperCard* that lets you write a *script* to go with any object, such as a *button* or a *field*, on your card. HyperTalk is a *high-level language* designed to be easy even for nonprogrammers. See also *HyperCard*.

hypertext   A computer-based navigation system that allows you to browse texts and graphics in a nonlinear fashion, encouraging you to explore a subject dynamically by creating your own associations and links to other texts and graphics. You can read the text of a book on a computer screen and use a *mouse* to click on words or sections to access more detailed information about the subject. See also *HyperCard, hypermedia*.

hyphenation   A *program* to insert hyphens into a *document* to keep the right margin relatively even and keep the lines as long as possible. Many *word processing* programs include hyphenation. Hyphenation programs may use an internal dictionary, a set of rules, or both to determine where hyphens can be inserted. Whichever process they are using, however, they tend to make mistakes, for you are bound to use a word that their dictionary does not include and that does not follow the rules. Most hyphenation programs allow you to override their decisions as necessary.

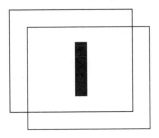

IBM PC   **1.** A trademark for the first *personal computer* made by International Business Machines in 1981, using the *Intel microprocessor* 8088 and having 16 *kilobytes* of *RAM* but expandable to 64KB.   **2.** A trademark for any of the personal computers made by IBM, including the original IBM PC, the IBM PC/AT, the IBM PC/XT, the IBM PS/1 and the IBM PS/2. All IBM PC computers use Intel microprocessors, and for the most part they use the same *software*, allowing them to share files. They all use DOS, but some of the PS/2 computers can also use OS/2. See also *Intel microprocessor, PS/2.*

IBM PC-compatible   A *computer* that can run all or most of the *software* and use many of the *peripheral devices*, such as *printers* and *keyboards*, designed to run on an *IBM PC.*

icon   In *graphical user interfaces*, a picture on the *screen* that represents a specific *file, directory, window,* or *program.* By *clicking* on the icon, you can open the file, directory, or window, or start the program. For example, if you have a *folder* called "word processing," you can click on it to see what *word processing* programs you have on your *disk*, and then click on the icon for *word* to start up that program. See illustrations at *desktop, graphical user interface.*

IDE interface Abbreviation of **Integrated Drive Electronics interface.** A *hard disk interface* located on the *motherboard* of certain IBM PC and compatible computers. Hard disks that use the IDE interface have internal *controllers*, so that they do not need a separate *adapter.* An IDE interface can transfer 7.5 megabits of data a second.

identifier A *character* or *string* of characters that identifies a *file, record, variable*, or other *data.* A *file name*, for example, is the identifier for a file.

illegal character A *character* that your *computer* won't accept in a particular *command* or *statement*, usually because it is reserved for another use. For example, in *DOS file names*, "." always separates the name of the *file* from the *extension*, and for this reason you cannot have a file called "ETC...."

ImageWriter A trademark for any of the *dot-matrix printers* made by Apple for *Macintosh* computers. These include some *letter-quality* printers. See also *laser printer, LaserWriter.*

impact printer A *printer* that prints by striking a *pin* or a *character* against an ink ribbon, which in turn hits the paper, leaving a mark. *Dot-matrix* and *daisy wheel printers* are impact printers. See table at *printer.*

import To bring *data* or a *file* from one *program* or *system* to another. The *format* of the *data* or *file* you wish to import must be *compatible* with the program you are importing it into. Otherwise, you will have to use a *conversion* program. Many programs are designed to be compatible with each other in order to allow importing and *exporting.* For example, a graphics file in *PICT* of *TIFF* formats can be imported into most *desktop publishing* programs. See also *export.*

inclusion   A logical operation that assumes the second statement of a pair is true if the first one is true.

inclusive OR   See **OR.**

increment   *v.* To increase a number by a given amount, usually repeatedly. For example, if you increment 7 by 4, you get 11, then 15, then 19, then 23, and so forth.
—*n.* The amount added each time a number is increased in this way. In the example above, 4 would be termed the increment. See also *decrement.*

incremental backup   A procedure for *backing up* only the *files* that you have changed or added since doing your last *backup.* It is good practice to do an incremental backup from your *hard disk* onto a *floppy disk* or a *tape* whenever you finish working at your computer. See also *full backup.*

Industry Standard Architecture   See **ISA.**

information   Facts, such as figures, words, or graphs, especially when *output* by the *computer* into a form that conveys meaning to you and other humans. For example, when you type a *document* into the computer, the computer stores your document as *data* in *machine language,* but when you call up your document on the *screen,* your computer returns it to you as information. See also *data.*

INIT   [IN-it]   A *utility* program for *Macintosh* computers that is executed whenever you start or restart your computer. INITs sometimes cause *crashes* by interfering with the *memory* for another *program.* See also *terminate and stay resident.*

initialize   **1.** To prepare a *disk* or *printer* for use. See also *format.*   **2.** In programming, to set a variable to a starting value.

ink-jet printer   A *nonimpact printer* that prints by spraying ink onto paper. Ink-jet printers can print with a *resolution* of 300 *dots per inch* (dpi). Work printed on an ink-jet printer looks very similar to that printed by a *laser printer*, but the ink from an ink-jet printer can smear if liquid spills on it or if you touch it too soon after it prints. Ink-jet printers are usually much slower than laser printers, but usually cost significantly less. See table at *printer*.

input   *n.* Information put into a computer for processing, such as *commands* typed from a *keyboard*, a *data file* read from a *disk*, or a *bit map* of a *scanned* image.
   —*v.* To enter data or a program into a computer. See also *output*.

input device   A machine that enables you to put information into a computer. *Keyboards, modems, mice,* and *scanners* are examples of input devices. See also *output device*.

input/output   See **I/O**.

Ins   Abbreviation of **Insert key**.

insertion point   1. In some *graphical user interfaces*, such as those on *Macintosh* computers, the *cursor* appearing as a blinking vertical bar to show the point where *characters* that you insert will go.   2. The point so indicated by the cursor.

Insert key   Abbreviated **Ins**   A *key* that you press to switch between *insert mode* and *overwrite mode*.

insert mode   In *word processing*, a mode in which you can insert new *characters* without deleting what you have already typed in. For example, if you had just entered the sentence "Back up your files to a floppy disk" into your computer and you wanted to change it to "Back up your files from the hard disk to a floppy disk," you would select insert mode, put the *cursor* in front of the word "to," and begin typing. See also *overwrite mode*.

instruction A *command*, especially one in *assembly language* or *machine language*. See also *statement*.

integer A member of the set of positive whole numbers (1, 2, 3, ...), negative whole numbers (–1, –2, –3,...), and zero (0). Integers have no decimal points. They are used in many *programming languages*.

integrated Combining two or more tasks into one *program*, especially offering *word processing*, *spreadsheets*, communications, and database management in one program.

integrated circuit 1. An electronic circuit whose components, such as transistors and resistors, are etched or imprinted on a single slice of *semiconductor* material. Integrated circuits are categorized by the number of electronic components they contain per chip. Table 13 lists various types of integrated circuits. Also called *microchip*. **2.** See **chip**.

Table 13. Types of Integrated Circuits

Type	Electronic Components per Chip
Small-scale integration (SSI)	<100
Medium-scale integration (MSI)	100–3,000
Large-scale integration (LSI)	3,000–100,000
Very large-scale integration (VLSI)	100,000–1,000,000
Ultra large-scale integration (ULSI)	>1,000,000

Integrated Drive Electronics interface See **IDE interface**.

Intel microprocessors A trademark for a group of *microprocessors* made by Intel and used in *IBM PC* computers. The 8086 has a 16-*bit register*, a 16-bit *data bus*, one *megabyte* of *memory*, and a *clock speed* of up to 10 *megahertz*. An 8MHz model is used in the *PS/2* models 25 and 30. The 8088 differs from the 8086 in that it has an 8-bit data bus and originally had a clock speed of only 4.77MHz. A later version has a clock speed of 8MHz. The 8088 was used in the first IBM PC computers, the PC/XT, the Portable PC, the PCjr, and their *clones*. The 80286 differs from the 8086 in that it has a clock speed of up to 12.5MHz and uses *virtual memory*. In *real mode* it can use only 1MB of *RAM*, but in *protected mode* it can use up to 16MB. The 80386, also referred to as 80386DX, features a 32-bit data bus, a 32-bit register, a clock speed of up to 33MHz, virtual memory, the ability to address up to 4GB (*gigabytes*) of memory, and the capacity for *multitasking*. The 80386SX differs from the 80386 in having a 16-bit data bus and a maximum clock speed of 25MHz. The 80486 differs from the 80386 in having a *math coprocessor*, a *memory cache*, and a clock speed of up to 50MHz. The 80486SX is identical to the 80486 except that it has no coprocessor. The 80860 features a 64-bit register, a 64-bit data bus, *RISC architecture*, and a clock speed of up to 50MHz. The Pentium, released in 1993, has a 32-bit register, a 64-bit data bus, and a clock speed of up to 66 MHz. With an improved math coprocessor and twice the number of caches, the Pentium can run up to five times faster than the 80486. All Intel microprocessors except the 80860 are designed so that they can run programs developed for the 8086 and the 8088. See also *CPU, microprocessor, Motorola microprocessors, Pentium.*

intelligent terminal   A *terminal* with more *memory* and greater processing capabilities than a *smart terminal*. For example, many intelligent terminals can send *data* to a *printer*. See also *dumb terminal.*

interactive   Being a *program* or a kind of processing in which you interact directly with the *computer*. For example, if you are running an interactive program, you enter a *command* and the *display* indicates a result. If the result is not what you wanted, you can enter a different command to obtain a different result. Computer games are interactive; you make a move, the computer responds, and you make your next move based on the response. Most processing is now interactive, but *batch processing* used to predominate.

interface   **1.** The *devices, graphics, commands,* and *prompts* that enable a *computer* to communicate with any other entity, such as a *printer* or the user. For example, the *ports* and *connector* are the interface between a computer and a printer. The interface that lets a user communicate with the computer is called a user interface. See also *user interface.* **2.** See **port.**

interlacing   A method of increasing a monitor's resolution by having the *cathode-ray tube* send electrons across every other line of the *screen* each time it *refreshes* the screen. This allows for greater resolution than would otherwise be possible at a comparable cost, but the lines sometimes flicker while they are waiting to be refreshed.

interleaving   **1.** A method of letting the disk drive access the sectors on a *disk* faster. The disk or *platters* spin around so rapidly that the head cannot read every *sector* on each round. If *data* is stored contiguously so that each chunk of data is physically right next to the data it should follow, the head may miss a chunk of data and have to wait a round to catch it. You can figure out how many sectors go by while the head is still reading the first one, and then *format* your disk drive so that it will skip that many sectors when writing data to the disk. That way, the head will be able to read an entire sequence of data on each round without missing any sectors. **2.** A similar method of speeding up access to *RAM.* Ordinarily, the rows of *chips* that make up RAM are organized so that odd and even chips follow each other in one row. On any cycle through the row, the *memory* will have time to read only one chip. The *CPU* usually needs access to odd and even chips alternately, and it can read them much more quickly than the memory. Interleaving establishes two or more rows of chips that alternate all odd with all even. The memory then sends data from each one of these alternating rows of chips to the CPU at one time.

internal font   See **resident font.**

internal modem   A *modem* that goes into an *expansion slot* inside the *computer* instead of sitting outside the computer in a separate box. An internal modem requires one cable to connect it to a telephone jack. Also called *on-board modem.*

InterNet A trademark for a matrix of networks that interconnects hundreds of thousands of supercomputers, mainframes, workstations, personal computers, laptops, and even pocket radios, and an estimated 2 million users. The networks that make up the InterNet all use a standard set of communications protocols, thus allowing computers with distinctive software and hardware to communicate. Some of the most popular features of the InterNet are *electronic mail, file transfer,* and remote log in.

interpreter A program that directly carries out the instructions in a source program without translating it to a different ("object") language. An interpreter is slower than a *compiler.* An interpreter ultimately carries out the program in the computer's native language or in machine language, but an interpreter must decide which machine language instructions to execute for a given source language instruction each time that instruction is evaluated. In a compiled language that translation process happens only once, producing an object program that requires no further translation while it's running. See also *compiler.*

interrupt A signal to a *program* that demands an immediate response. The program may stop temporarily so that another action can be performed. It may also decide to ignore the interrupt. If it stops running, it saves its current work before executing whatever *instructions* are interrupting it. As soon as this is over, the program resumes. Interrupts may come from the *hardware* or the *software.*

inverse video See **reverse video.**

I/O Abbreviation of **input/output.** Designating a *program* or *device,* such as a *mouse* or *printer,* that is used to *input* or *output data* rather than to process it. A *modem,* for example, both inputs and outputs data but does not process it.

IRMA board [UR-muh] An *expansion board* for *Macintosh* computers and IBM PC and compatible computers that lets

them *emulate terminals*. This means that if you have an
IRMA board, you can connect your computer to a *mainframe*
for certain tasks while still using it as a *personal computer* for
others.

ISA   Abbreviation of **Industry Standard Architecture.**   The *bus*
architecture used for IBM PC/XT computers and IBM PC/AT
computers. The ISA bus was originally created for the IBM
PC/XT and had an 8-bit data path. The version created for the
IBM PC/AT, known as the "AT bus," has a 16-bit data path
but remains downward compatible with the older version.
The AT bus has become the industry standard because of the
large number of peripherals and expansion boards designed to
connect to it. See also *EISA, Micro Channel Architecture.* See
table at *bus.*

italic   A *font* style in which *characters* slant to the right. Italic
is based on a Renaissance script. See illustration at *font
family.*

iteration   The act of reprocessing one or more *statements* or
instructions in a *loop* until a given condition is true. See also
loop.

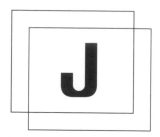

jaggies In computer graphics, jagged distortions that appear where there should be smooth curves or diagonals. See also *aliasing*. See illustration at *antialiasing*.

job A specified action or group of actions that the *computer* carries out as a single unit. For example, when an IBM PC or compatible computer prints a *document*, the process is considered a "print job."

join A procedure used in a *relational database* to extract information from two separate *database files* into a separate file. For example, if you have one database with the phone numbers and addresses of your friends and another with the phone numbers and addresses of your relatives and you're sending a mailing to everyone you know in Wisconsin, you can do a join to get the names and addresses of all your friends and relatives in Wisconsin.

joystick A *pointing device* consisting of a long stick attached to a plastic base. When the stick is moved in any direction, the *pointer* on the *screen* will move in the same direction. When the stick is returned to its original vertical position, the pointer on the screen stops moving. A joystick usually comes with two control buttons attached to the base or to the stick itself. The control buttons are set by the program to activate certain *commands* in much the same way *control characters* are. The joystick is a popular user control device for computer games and some *CAD/CAM* systems.

jumper A plug consisting of two or three metal slots, usually enclosed in a small plastic box, and designed to fit over pins in a *circuit board* to close an electric circuit. You can configure your circuit board by selecting which circuits to close and putting jumpers over them.

justification The adjusting of spacing within a *document* so that lines end evenly at a straight margin. Newspaper articles and other typeset copy, for example, are usually justified both left and right, so that both the left and right margins of each column are even. Copy that is printed on a typewriter, on the other hand, is usually justified only at the left, so that the left margin is even but the right margin is uneven, or *ragged*.

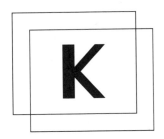

K Abbreviation of **kilobyte.**

KB Abbreviation of **kilobyte.**

Kbyte Abbreviation of **kilobyte.**

Kermit In telecommunications, an *asynchronous protocol* developed at Columbia University to govern the transfer of *files* between *mainframes* and microcomputers or microcomputer terminals. Kermit works by transfering groups of *data* of up to 96 *bytes* at a time and then checking each group for transmission errors. Kermit translates all *control characters* into *ASCII* characters. Because Kermit is known for accuracy, it is used by many *modems* and *communications programs*. Super Kermit is a newer and faster version of Kermit that uses *full duplex* transmission. See also *Xmodem, Ymodem, Zmodem*. See table at *communications protocol*.

kerning   The adjustment of space between pairs of characters, usually in display type, so that the overall spacing of the letters appears even. Kerning makes certain combinations of letters, such as *WA, VA, TA, YA,* and *MW*, look better. Some *page layout programs* have an automatic kerning feature. Manual kerning can be performed with most page layout programs and some word processing programs. See illustration.

WAVY   WAVY

WITHOUT KERNING   WITH KERNING

kerning

key   *n.* A button on a *keyboard* that is pressed to enter *data* or a *command*.
—*v.* To enter *data* into a computer by pressing buttons on the keyboard.

keyboard   A set of keys arranged as on a typewriter that is the principal *input device* for most computers. All keyboards include a set of *alphanumeric* keys, usually in the standard layout of conventional typewriters. Many also have a *numeric keypad* to one side. All keyboards include a number of keys for *special characters*. These special keys include the *Control, Alt,* and *Shift keys* on keyboards for IBM PC and compatible computers and the *Command, Option,* and *Shift keys* on Macintosh keyboards. These keys are used to change the meaning of other keys hit at the same time. Some other spe-

cial keys are the *function keys*, which have different meanings depending on which program is running, and the *Arrow keys*, which enable you to move the *cursor* right, left, up, or down.
Keyboards are not standardized, although many manufacturers imitate the IBM PC keyboards. All Apple Macintosh keyboards are called ADB keyboards because they connect to the *Apple Desktop Bus* (ADB). See also *Backspace key, Break key, Caps Lock key, Delete key, Dvorak keyboard, End key, Enter key, function key, Home key, Insert key, Num Lock key, Page Down key, Page Up key, Pause key, Print Screen key, QWERTY keyboard.*

keypad   See **numeric keypad.**

keystroke   An instance of pressing a *key*. Some *programs* require more keystrokes than others to do the same tasks, so that you have to press more keys to get the same result.

keyword   **1.** In *programming*, a reserved word that is built into the syntax of the programming language.   **2.** In *word processing* programs and *database management systems*, a word, code, or phrase that identifies a *record* or *document* and can be used in *sorting* or *searching.*

kHz   Abbreviation of **kilohertz.**

kilo-   Abbreviated **k, K**   **1.** A prefix indicating 1,000 (10^3), as in *kilohertz.* Many people prefer to abbreviate this *decimal* kilo- with a lowercase *k*, as in *kHz*, to avoid confusion with the binary kilo-, which they abbreviate with an uppercase *K*.   **2.** A prefix indicating 1,024 (2^{10}). This is the sense in which kilo- is generally used in computing, which is based on powers of two. Many people prefer to abbreviate this *binary* kilo- with an uppercase *K*, as in *KB*, to avoid confusion with the *decimal* kilo-, which they abbreviate with a lowercase *k*.

kilobyte   Abbreviated **K, KB,** or **Kbyte**   A unit of measurement of computer memory or data storage capacity, equal to 1,024 (2^{10}) *bytes.*

kilohertz Abbreviated **kHz** A unit of frequency equal to 1,000 *hertz*.

Kittyhawk An extra-small version of a *hard disk* storage device. Developed by Hewlett-Packard, the Kittyhawk drive uses a disk less than 1.5 inches in diameter, making it compact enough to be an alternative to *flash memory* in *handheld* computers.

kludge [klooj] A workable but poorly designed, often makeshift piece of *hardware* or *software*. Kludges are patched together from mismatched elements or elements designed for other uses. A kludge offers a sloppy or inelegant solution to a problem.

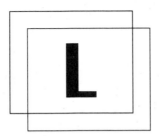

label 1. Generally, a name identifying the contents of *memory* or of a *file, tape, disk,* or *record.* 2. In data storage, one character or a sequence of characters by which the *operating system* identifies a floppy disk, tape, or part of a hard disk, such as the name of a *volume.* Each operating system has its own restrictions on labels, typically limiting the number or kinds of characters allowed. 3. In *spreadsheets,* descriptive text or a heading, such as "Net Income," that is placed in a *cell.* 4. In *programming,* a name identifying a section of a program, such as a particular *routine* or line of *code.* 5. A small piece of paper with an adhesive backing that can be written on and attached to a floppy disk or piece of equipment to identify it.

LAN [lan] Acronym for **local area network.**

landscape Of or relating to a mode in which a page is oriented so that it is wider than it is tall. *Spreadsheets* are typically in landscape mode. Many word processing and page layout programs can also display or print text in this mode. Not all printers, however, are capable of printing in landscape mode. See illustration. See also *portrait.*

language A system for communicating thoughts and feelings through the use of voice sounds and written symbols representing these sounds in organized combinations and patterns. Each sound or combination of sounds, along with its written

Landscape

Portrait

landscape
Landscape and portrait orientations

representation, that communicates a meaning is called a word. All the words in a language constitute its vocabulary. The language's *semantics* define the meanings of words and word combinations. The language's *syntax* comprises the rules whereby words are combined into grammatical sentences.

In computer science, such human languages are called *natural languages*. We cannot yet communicate efficiently with computers using natural languages, although research in this area is beginning to show promise. Instead, we must use specially constructed computer languages. Such languages, in order of increasing closeness to natural languages, include *machine languages, programming languages*, and *fourth-generation languages*. See also *artificial intelligence, translation software*.

laptop A *portable* computer that is smaller than a *luggable* but larger than a *notebook* computer. A laptop usually weighs between 8 and 14 pounds, and when folded shut is about the size of a small briefcase. Laptops can be plugged in or run on batteries, although the batteries must be recharged every few hours.

Laptop computers use a thin, lightweight display screen called a *flat-panel display*, rather than the *cathode-ray tube* technology of larger personal computers. Laptop displays vary widely in quality. Typically, their display screens show fewer lines than displays on larger computers and can be difficult to read in bright light. Laptops are self-contained units, having their own *CPUs*, *memory*, and *disk drives*. While more expensive than a desktop computer with equivalent computing power, a laptop can be ideal for the on-the-go user who needs a second, portable computer.

large-scale integration   Abbreviated **LSI**   The technology for placing up to 100,000 electronic components on a single *integrated circuit*. See table at *integrated circuit*.

laser font   See **outline font.**

LaserJet   A trademark of Hewlett-Packard for a line of *laser printers* used with IBM PC and compatible computers. The *page description language* used by LaserJet printers is Hewlett-Packard's proprietary *PCL* (Printer Control Language). Early versions of PCL used *bit-mapped graphics*, but later versions support Intellifont, Hewlett-Packard's *outline font* technology.

laser printer   A *nonimpact printer* that uses a laser to produce an image on a rotating drum before transferring the image to paper. Signals, in the form of commands in a *page description language*, are sent from the *operating system* or *application* software to control the laser beam, rapidly turning the beam on and off and moving it across the drum. The drum is coated with an electrically charged film. Where each point of light hits the drum, the charge is reversed from negative to positive or from positive to negative, depending on the laser printer's design. As the drum rotates, it comes into contact with a bin of *toner*, a black powder charged oppositely to the charges created by the laser on the drum. Because oppositely charged static particles attract each other, the toner sticks to the drum in a pattern of black dots. Meanwhile, gears and rollers send a sheet of paper past an electrically charged wire, charging the paper, which is then pressed against the drum. The toner is electrostatically transferred to the paper. Finally, heat and pressure fuse the toner to the paper by melting and pressing a wax contained in the toner. Some printers use arrays of *LEDs* (light-emitting diodes) or *LCDs* (liquid-crystal displays) rather than a laser to charge the drum, but otherwise they work like a laser printer.

Two page description languages are de facto standards for laser printers. Hewlett-Packard's *PCL* (Printer Control Language) is the mainstay in IBM PC and compatible computers. *PostScript*, developed by Adobe Systems, is the standard for Macintosh computer printers.

Laser printers transfer the page as a whole to the drum, treating a page and the text it contains as one large graphic image. For this reason, they are sometimes referred to as "page printers." Laser printers are relatively fast and quiet and produce sharp, high-quality text and graphics.

Laser printers come with one or more *fonts* built into their hardware. These are called *resident fonts*, or internal or built-in fonts. You are not limited to your laser printer's resident fonts, however. You can print with a virtually unlimited number of fonts by *downloading* fonts into your laser printer or by inserting *font cartridges*, *ROM* boards hardwired with one or more fonts.

All laser printers contain some *RAM*; often the amount can be increased by adding *memory cards*. Fonts can be downloaded, or copied, from disk to the printer's RAM. The more memory a printer has, the more fonts can be downloaded at one time. A downloaded font is called a *soft font*.

Hard fonts, on the other hand, are built into font cartridges, which are inserted into *slots* in the laser printer. See table at *printer*.

LaserWriter A trademark for a line of *laser printers* used with Macintosh computers. Some less expensive models support *QuickDraw*, the graphics system created by Apple that is used mostly for displaying images on monitors. The other LaserWriters are *PostScript* printers, which are more expensive but have much more sophisticated *font* and graphics capabilities.

LAWN [lon] Acronym for **local area wireless network.**

layout   **1.** In desktop publishing and word processing, the art or process of arranging text and *graphics* on a page. Layout covers the overall design of a page, including elements such as page and type size, *typeface*, and the placement of graphics, titles, and page numbers. See also *page layout program*, *WYSIWYG*. **2.** In *database management systems*, the arrangement of *fields*, *leaders*, and other elements when information is displayed in a *report*. See also *report generator*.

LCD   Abbreviation of **liquid-crystal display.** A low-power *flatpanel display* used in many *laptop* computers and also in devices such as calculators and digital watches. Most LCD displays in laptops are *monochrome*, with blue or dark gray images on a light gray background, and use *backlighting* to enhance image contrast. A technique called "supertwist" yields an especially readable type of backlit LCD display.

There are two basic ways to produce color LCD displays. *Active-matrix* technology produces exceptionally sharp color images but is very expensive. *Passive-matrix* technologies are cheaper but are difficult to read at an angle and produce washed-out color.

leader   A row of dots or sometimes dashes leading the eye across the page, as from an index or table of contents entry to a page number. Most word processing programs allow you to define *tab stops* that automatically insert leaders when you press the *Tab key*.

leading   The vertical spacing between lines of text, measured in *points*. The measure includes the size of the font, so that 12-point type with 2-point spacing between lines is a leading of 14 points. Most word processing and all desktop publishing applications allow you to set the leading. Also called *line spacing*. See also *vertical justification*.

leaf   An element at the lowest level of a *hierarchical tree structure*. Leaves have no other elements branching from them. A file in a hierarchical file system is a leaf; a directory is a node. See also *node*.

LED [EL-ee-DEE] Abbreviation of **light-emitting diode.** An electronic *semiconductor* device that emits light when an electric current passes through it. LEDs need more power than *LCDs* (liquid-crystal displays), and they are not usually used for display screens. They are used for indicator lights, as on the front of a disk drive, and in some printers they serve the same function as a laser beam in a *laser printer.*

left justify To align text so that each line is *flush* against the left margin, but leaving the right margin *ragged,* or uneven.

letter-quality Abbreviated **LQ** Of or producing printed characters similar in clarity to those produced by a conventional typewriter. Computer printers are classified according to those that produce letter-quality type, such as *laser, ink-jet,* and *daisy-wheel printers,* and those that do not, such as most *dot-matrix printers.* Typically, dot-matrix printers produce *near-letter quality* type and *draft-quality* type; that is, type suitable for printing drafts of documents. In reality, laser printers produce type that is significantly better than that produced by typewriters, making the term "letter-quality" a misnomer. See illustration.

DRAFT-QUALITY   NEAR-LETTER QUALITY   LETTER-QUALITY

letter-quality
Common type qualities

lexicographic sort See **dictionary sort.**

LF Abbreviation of **line feed.**

library **1.** In programming, a collection of standard *routines* or *subroutines,* each performing a specific task that a program can use. Libraries save time because a programmer can insert a library routine into a program without rewriting the instructions each time they are needed. Library routines do not have to be explicitly *linked* to every program that uses them. The *linker* automatically checks libraries for routines that it does not find elsewhere. **2.** A collection of information, as in data files.

light-emitting diode   See **LED.**

light pen   A light-sensitive *input device* shaped like a pen, used to select objects on a video display screen. Light pens are used for tasks that involve a lot of updating, such as tracking inventory or filling out forms, since the user can move a light pen quickly and accurately across the screen. Also called *light stylus, stylus.*

line feed   Abbreviated **LF**   **1.** On a display screen, a signal that advances the cursor to the same position one line below. The *Enter* or *Return key*, which moves the cursor to the beginning of the following line, uses both the line feed and *carriage return* signals.   **2.** A signal that tells a printer to advance the paper one line.

line printer   A high-speed *impact printer*, primarily used in data processing, that prints an entire line of type as a unit. The line printer differs from the *dot-matrix printer*, which prints each character individually, and the *laser printer*, which prints each page as a unit. Line printers usually serve more than one user and tend to be fast (up to 3,000 lines per minute) and loud. See table at *printer.*

line spacing   See **leading.**

link   *v.* To connect two files in such a way that a change in the data of one file is reflected in the other. For instance, a customer *database* could be linked to an inventory database so that entering a sale of an item into the customer database would automatically update the inventory database. In some

cases, linked files do not have to be from the same program; a spreadsheet can be linked to a word processing document, and a change in the spreadsheet will then affect the corresponding part of the document. Although they are connected, the two files remain separate entities. A connection between two documents that automatically makes changes is sometimes known as a hot link. A cold link needs to be activated with a command to update. See also *Dynamic Data Exchange.*
—*n.* A connection between computers, devices, programs, or files over which data is transmitted.

linker   An executable program that joins *modules* (small blocks of *code*) so that data can be passed between them. Modules can be added or replaced individually. See also *compile, library.*

liquid-crystal display   See **LCD.**

liquid-crystal shutter printer   A high-quality printer that resembles a *laser printer.* Instead of using a laser to create images on the print drum, it shines a light beam through a liquid-crystal panel. Individual *pixels* in the panel act as tiny shutters, blocking or transmitting the light to form a dot pattern on the drum. See table at *printer.*

LISP   [lisp]   Acronym for **list processor.**   A *programming language* that is widely used in *artificial intelligence* research. Developed in the 1960s by John McCarthy at MIT, LISP is made up of expressions that constitute lists of instructions to the computer. These lists establish relationships between symbolic values, and the computer performs computations based on those relationships. Since each list yields a value that can be used in other lists, there is no distinction between data and instructions within a LISP program.

listing   A printout of a program in *source code.*

list processor   See **LISP.**

load 1. To transfer a program from a storage device into a computer's memory. Before a program on a disk can be executed, it must be loaded into the computer's *RAM* (random-access memory). This process is carried out by the operating system's *loader*. 2. To transfer data into a computer's memory for processing. 3. To mount a disk onto a *disk drive* or a magnetic tape onto a tape drive.

loader A *utility* program in the operating system that transfers programs from a *storage device* into the computer's *RAM* (random-access memory) so that they can be run. Most loaders operate automatically when you run a program.

local area network Acronym **LAN** [lan]. A *network* that uses high-performance cables to link together computers and *peripherals* within a limited area, such as a building or group of buildings. Each computer or device in a LAN is known as a *node*. The computers in a LAN have independent *CPUs* (central processing units), but they are able to exchange data and files with each other and to share such resources as laser printers.

The three principal LAN organizing structures, called *topologies*, are *bus*, *ring*, and *star*. In a bus topology, all computers and other devices are connected to a central cable. In a ring topology, the computers are joined in a loop, so that a message from one passes through each node until it reaches its proper destination. In a star topology, all nodes are connected to one central computer, known as the "hub."

Additionally, LANs are organized as either *peer-to-peer networks*, in which all computers are similarly equipped and communicate directly with one another, or *client/server networks*, in which a central computer, the *server*, provides data and controls communication between all nodes.

Every LAN has a *protocol* that governs the exchange of data between nodes, and a network operating system (NOS), software that allows communication between devices to take place. See also *AppleTalk*, *EtherNet*.

local area wireless network Acronym **LAWN** [lawn]. A *local area network* that uses high-frequency radio waves instead of high-performance cables to link together computers and other devices.

lock **1.** In networking and other *multi-user* systems, to make a file or other unit of data inaccessible. The operating system locks a file or database *record* after one user has begun to work on it so that subsequent users cannot work on it at the same time. A locked file can usually be viewed by other users, but they can not modify it until it is unlocked. **2.** To *write-protect* a *floppy disk*.

logic The nonarithmetic operations performed by a computer — for example, sorting, comparing, and matching — that involve decisions with only one of two possible outcomes, such as yes/no or true/false. See also *CPU*.

logical Of or relating to the way the user perceives the organization of an element such as a database or a file. To the user, a file may be a discrete unit, but it is likely that the file is stored in pieces scattered throughout a computer's memory or a disk. The term *physical* is used when referring to the actual location and structure of an element.

logical operator See **Boolean operator.**

log in See **log on.**

log off See **log out.**

log on To identify yourself to a *multi-user* computer system so that you can begin working on it. Logging on typically consists of giving your *username* and a *password*; it protects a network or system from unauthorized users and allows the network or system to keep track of usage time.

log out To end a session with a *multi-user* computer system. Logging off signals the system that you have finished communicating with it.

look-and-feel   The general appearance and functioning of the *user interface* of a software product. Programs with the same look-and-feel appear essentially the same on-screen, and the user who knows one such program can run the others without learning new commands and menus. The look-and-feel of software, as opposed to its internal structure, has been a consideration in several legal cases concerning software copyright violations.

lookup   In a spreadsheet program, a *function* in which the computer consults a previously assembled table of values until a specified value is found. This table, known as the "lookup table," typically contains a series of values that are frequently needed for calculations. For example, a lookup table may contain the sales tax rates for different cities and states.

loop   In *programming*, a sequence of instructions that repeats either a specified number of times or until a particular condition prevails.

lowercase   Of, related to, or being a noncapitalized letter. See also *case-sensitive*.

low-level language   A computer language, such as an *assembly language* or *machine language*, in which each line of code is an individual instruction that can be directly carried out by the *CPU* (central processing unit). A *high-level language,* on the other hand, often combines several CPU instructions in each statement and is closer to human language.

low-resolution   See **resolution.**

LQ   Abbreviation of **letter-quality.**

LSI   Abbreviation of **large-scale integration.**

luggable   A heavyweight *portable* computer, usually over 14 or 15 pounds, that is bulkier than a *laptop* computer or a *notebook* computer.

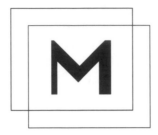

m   Abbreviation of **milli-**.

M   Abbreviation of **mega-**.

Mac   A trademark of Apple Computer, Inc. See **Macintosh.**

machine code   See **machine language.**

machine-dependent   Of or relating to software that can be used only with a particular model of computer. Machine-dependent software often makes optimal use of the special features in a specific piece of hardware.

machine-independent   Of or relating to software that can be used with a variety of computers.

machine language   The language used and understood by the *CPU* (central processing unit) of a computer. Each different type of CPU has its own machine language. Each instruction and piece of data in machine language is made up of a series of 0s and 1s, representing *bits*. Machine language is the lowest-level language, and programs in *high-level languages* must be converted to machine language before thcy can be run or stored by a computer. Such a conversion is made by a *compiler*, which translates the entire program into machine language, or an *interpreter*, which translates and executes each instruction before moving on to the next. Also called *machine code.*

machine-readable In a form that can be fed directly into a computer, as data on a disk. With the development of technology such as *optical character recognition,* even typed documents are machine-readable to a properly equipped computer.

Macintosh A trademark for a popular line of personal computers introduced in 1984. Macintosh computers have a *graphical user interface* (GUI) that employs *windows, icons,* and onscreen *menus.* A *mouse* can be used to control a *pointer* on the screen that chooses commands, selects files, and executes programs. The popularity of Macintosh computers is due in part to this *interface,* which is more intuitive than *command-driven* interfaces.

Since the GUI is built into the *operating system* of Macintosh computers, there is consistency in the look and operation of different Macintosh software applications. Other software companies have developed programs such as *Microsoft Windows* (for *DOS*) and *Presentation Manager* (for *OS/2*) that make the IBM *operating environment* resemble that of the Macintosh, but Macintosh devices and software are generally incompatible with IBM PC and compatible computers. See illustration at *desktop.*

macro A set of stored *commands* that are executed when a simple key combination is pressed. Macros are helpful when you frequently perform a task that requires several commands. For example, a macro can be used to get into a particular file without going through several menus or directories. Macros can also be used as *glossaries,* to record and output a series of frequently used keystrokes, such as a letter heading. Operating systems and many applications allow the user to create personal macros. *Add-in* programs are available for applications without macro capabilities.

magnetic disk See **disk.**

magnetic-ink character recognition Acronym **MICR** [MY-ker]. A technique for making printed characters *machine-readable* by printing with ink containing a magnetic powder. A character-recognition device compares the magnetic pattern produced by a character with patterns produced by known shapes. The matched character is then converted into digital information. MICR differs from *optical character recognition*, in which an *optical scanner* recognizes characters by detecting patterns of light and dark. MICR systems are used by banks to read the codes printed along the bottom edge of checks.

magnetic media Any type of *mass storage* that holds information magnetically. Floppy disks and tapes are magnetic media.

magnetic tape See **tape.**

mail merge A feature in many word processing programs that creates "personalized" form letters. The main document contains the text of the form letter, along with codes or symbols that indicate where personalized information (such as names and addresses) goes. This information is usually contained in a separate *text file* whose *fields* correspond to the codes or symbols in the form letter. Some word processors allow you to uses *Boolean operators*, such as *AND* or *OR*, to specify conditions for merging information. Also called *merge.*

mainframe A large, powerful computer, capable of serving hundreds of connected *terminals* and frequently used for large jobs, such as printing invoices. Mainframes execute many programs simultaneously for multiple users and are used to meet the computing needs of large organizations. See also *supercomputer.*

main memory *Memory* that is internal to the computer and directly accessible to the *CPU* (central processing unit); *RAM* (random-access memory).

map *n.* A representation of the structure or location of something. A *memory* map describes where data and programs are

stored in memory; a *bit map* represents every dot of a graphic image in memory.
—*v.* To translate or be translated from one value or form to another. A *programming language,* such as *C,* maps onto machine language. In computer graphics, a three-dimensional object, such as a sphere, can be mapped onto a plane. The computer maps a *virtual address* onto a *physical address* when it swaps data from disk to *RAM* under a *virtual memory* system.

mass storage   The storage devices and techniques used to supplement the *main memory* of a computer, including *hard disks, floppy disks,* magnetic *tape,* and *optical disks.* Mass storage devices can accommodate larger amounts of data than main memory, and they retain data when power is turned off. Mass storage capacity is expressed in *kilobytes* (1,024 bytes), *megabytes* (1,024 kilobytes), or *gigabytes,* (1,024 megabytes). Also called *secondary storage.*

master page   In desktop publishing, a template used for all the individual pages in a publication.

math coprocessor   A *coprocessor* that performs mathematical operations for the *CPU* (central processing unit). Math coprocessors use floating-point representation to do calculations many times faster than the CPU alone, making them particularly useful with calculation-intensive applications, such as *spreadsheets* and programs that employ *object-oriented graphics.* Most *Motorola* and *Intel microprocessors* have companion math coprocessors, which are built in, or can be added to, computers. Also called *floating-point coprocessor, numeric coprocessor.*

matrix   Plural **matrices.** A rectangular *array* of elements of the same kind, arranged in rows and columns. Matrices are used in a variety of computer operations. A matrix may contain numbers or text in table form, as in *spreadsheets* or *lookup* tables. A *bit map* of a monochromatic image, such as a character on a display screen, is stored in memory as a matrix of

0s and 1s (*bits*). *Dot-matrix printers* produce characters and images as matrices of ink dots.

MB Abbreviation of **megabyte.**

MCA Abbreviation of **Micro Channel Architecture.**

MCGA Abbreviation of **multicolor/graphics array** or **memory controller gate array.** A *video adapter* included in low-end models of the IBM *PS/2*. It has more graphics capabilities than *CGA* but is not as powerful as *EGA* or *VGA*. See also *video standard.*

mean time between failures See **MTBF.**

meg Abbreviation of **megabyte.**

mega- Abbreviated **M** **1.** A prefix indicating 1 million (10⁶), as in *megahertz.* **2.** A prefix indicating 1,048,576 (2²⁰), as in *megabyte.* This is the sense in which mega- is generally used in computing, which is based on powers of two.

megabyte Abbreviated **MB, meg** A unit of measurement of computer memory or data storage capacity, equal to 1,048,576 (2²⁰) *bytes.* One megabyte equals 1,024 *kilobytes.*

megaflop Acronym **MFLOP** [EM-flop]. A measure of computing speed, equal to one million *floating-point notation* calculations per second. *Workstations, minicomputers,* and *mainframes* are rated in megaflops.

megahertz Abbreviated **MHz** A unit of *frequency* equal to 1,000,000 *hertz.*

memory **1.** See **RAM.** **2.** The capacity of a computer, chips, and *storage devices* to preserve data and programs for retrieval. Memory is measured in bytes. **3.** A system for preserving data and programs for retrieval. *Volatile memory,* or RAM, stores information only until the power is turned off. *Nonvolatile memory* stores memory even when the power is off. Nonvolatile memory includes *ROM, PROM, EPROM,* and

EEPROM, as well as such external devices as *disk drives* and *tape drives.* See also *expanded memory, extended memory, flash memory, main memory,* and *virtual memory.*

memory cache   See **RAM cache.**

memory caching   See **RAM caching.**

memory card   A storage device that uses *flash memory* chips. Since the data stored in a memory card remains intact even when the power is turned off and you can rewrite data without removing the card from the computer's circuit board, the memory card functions as a substitute for a *hard disk.*

memory controller gate array   See **MCGA.**

memory-resident   Designating a program that remains permanently in a computer's *RAM* (random-access memory). The *CPU* must load a file or program into RAM before it can be processed. Other data or programs are copied or *swapped* from RAM onto disk to make room for the program that you are running, but a *memory-resident* program will not be moved from RAM. Central parts of the *operating system* are memory-resident, as are *utilities* or accessory programs such as *calendars, calculators,* and *spell checkers.* These memory-resident programs are activated when you press a simple key sequence known as a *hot key.*

In *DOS,* memory-resident programs are called *pop-up utilities* or *terminate and stay residents* (TSRs). On Macintosh computers, they are called *desk accessories* (DAs). Also called *RAM-resident.*

menu   An on-screen list of available options or commands. Usually the options are highlighted by a bar that you can move from one item to another. You can choose a menu item by keying in its code or by pointing to the item with the *mouse* and clicking a mouse button. Choosing often leads to a *submenu,* called a *cascading menu,* or to a *dialog box* containing options that further refine the original menu selection. See illustration. See also *menu bar, pull-down menu, tear-off menu.*

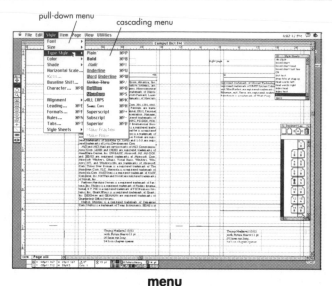

pull-down menu

cascading menu

menu
On a Macintosh computer

menu bar   A horizontal bar that runs across the top of the screen or of a *window* and holds the names of available menu options. When you choose an option from the menu bar, another list of commands or options drops down below the bar. See also *menu*. See illustrations at *desktop, graphical user interface.*

menu-driven   Of or relating to a type of *user interface* in which the user issues commands by making selections from on-screen *menus*. Menu-driven programs are more intuitive than *command-driven* programs, which require you to learn and type in commands.

merge   *v.*   **1.** To combine two files into one so that the resulting file has the same structure as each of its components. If you merge two files, each containing an alphabetically arranged list of names, the resulting file will contain all of the names from the two files in alphabetical order. In contrast, if you were to *append* the same files, the first list of names would simply be followed by the second. **2.** To generate form letters by doing a *mail merge.*
—*n.* See **mail merge.**

message box   See **alert box.**

metaphor   An *interface* technique of expressing abstract or *soft* entities, such as computer functions, programs, or data, as everyday objects such as desktops, paintbrushes, file folders, or trash cans. *Graphical user interfaces*, such as the one used by the Macintosh computer, are based on these metaphors.

MFLOP   [EM-flop]   Acronym for **megaflop.**

MHz   Abbreviation of **megahertz.**

MICR   [MY-ker]   Acronym for **magnetic-ink character recognition.**

micro   Short for **microcomputer** or **microprocessor.**

micro-   **1.** A prefix indicating something very small.   **2.** A prefix indicating one millionth (10^{-6}), as in *microsecond.*

Micro Channel Architecture   Abbreviated **MCA**   The *bus* architecture used in high-end IBM *PS/2* computers, characterized by a 32-bit data *path*. Although many computers use a 32-bit bus structure on the *motherboard* to connect the *RAM* and the *microprocessor*, the 16-bit *ISA* bus has been the standard for *expansion boards*. MCA's 32-bit expansion slots do not accommodate the many *peripherals* and *adapters* that were designed for the ISA bus, so it has not been universally accepted as the new standard for expansion bus architecture.

Other hardware and software companies have developed EISA (Extended Industry Standard Architecture), a competing bus architecture that is compatible with boards that were designed for the ISA bus as well as with 32-bit boards. See table at *bus.*

microchip   See **integrated circuit.**

microcomputer   See **personal computer.**

microfloppy disk   A *floppy disk* 3.5 inches in diameter and encased in a hard protective covering, used as a *storage* medium for Macintosh and IBM PC and compatible computers. Microfloppy disks have greater storage capacity than 5.25-inch floppy disks. See table at *density*.

microprocessor An *integrated circuit* that contains the entire *CPU* (central processing unit) of a computer on a single chip. When referring to personal computers, the terms "microprocessor" and "central processing unit" are often used synonymously. Microprocessors manufactured by Intel are generally used in *IBM PC* and compatible computers. Motorola microprocessors are used in Macintosh and Amiga computers and in Hewlett-Packard *workstations*.

Microprocessors are distinguished on the basis of power and speed. Power is measured by data width; that is, the number of *bits* of data the microprocessor can process at one time. Often, it is useful to distinguish between *register* width, or the number of bits of data the computer can process within its CPU at one time, and *bus* width, the number of bits of data than can be transferred between the CPU and other components, such as *expansion boards*, *printers*, or *disk drives*, at one time. Speed is specified by the *clock speed* given in *megahertz* (MHz). A microprocessor that runs at 25MHz executes 25 million cycles per second. A cycle is the shortest time during which any operation can happen in a computer, so clock speed determines how fast a computer can execute instruc-

Table 14. Widely Used Microprocessors

Microprocessor	Register Width (bits)	Data Bus Width (bits)	Maximum Clock Speed (MHz)	Characteristics
Zilog Z80	8	8	2	• Used in Kaypro systems
MOS Technology 6502	8	8	1	• Used in Apple II computers
MOS Technology 6502A	8	8	2	• Used in Commodore VIC-20 computers
Intel 8080	8	8	2	• Forerunner of current Intel line
Intel 8088	16	8	8	• Used in the original IBM PC
Intel 8086	16	16	10	• 8MHz version used in IBM PS/2 Models 25 and 30

Table 14. Widely Used Microprocessors (continued)

Microprocessor	Register Width (bits)	Data Bus Width (bits)	Maximum Clock Speed (MHz)	Characteristics
Intel 80286	16	16	12.5	• Real mode (compatible with MS-DOS; limited to 640KB of memory) • Protected mode (can accesss up to 16MB of memory; protects from crashes caused by program errors) • Used in IBM PC/AT, AT&T PC 6300, Hewlett-Packard Vectra PC, and Tandy 3000 computers
Intel 80386	32	32	33	• Can access up to 4GB of memory in protected mode • Supports multitasking • "Virtual 8086 mode": can be divided into the equivalent of several 8086 microprocessors, each capable of running a separate program • Used in Compaq Deskpro 386 computers
Intel 80386SX	32	16	33	• Lower-cost alternative to the faster 80386 • Compatible with both the 80286 and the 80386
Intel 80486	32	32	50	• Built-in math coprocessor • Built-in memory cache • Faster than 80386
Intel 80860	64	64	50	• RISC architecture
Pentium	32	64	66	• Up to five times faster than the 80486 microprocessor • Suitable for processor-intensive applications, such as spreadsheets, CAD, and multimedia
Motorola 68000	32	16	8	• Can access up to 16MB of memory • Used in the original Macintosh computer and certain laser printers
Motorola 68020	32	32	33	• Can access up to 4GB of memory • Used in Macintosh II and LC computers
Motorola 68030	32	32	40	• Can access up to 4GB of memory • Used in certain Macintosh II and SE/30 computers
Motorola 68040	32	32	50	• Built-in math coprocessor • Used in Macintosh Quadra and Centris computers

tions. The higher the clock speed and the bigger the data width, the more powerful the microprocessor. Table 14 compares the features of various microprocessors. See also *CISC, Intel microprocessors, Motorola microprocessors, RISC.*

microsecond   A unit of time equal to one millionth (10^{-6}) of a second.

Microsoft Windows   A trademark for software that provides a *graphical user interface* for computers running under DOS. Like *DESQview*, Microsoft Windows furnishes an alternative *operating environment* for DOS-based computers. Application programs, however, must be written to run specifically under Windows. This results in a consistent *look-and-feel* for all programs, based on *pull-down menus*, *icons*, and (of course) *windows*. All programs are able to use the tools and common file *formats* provided by Windows, which allows data and graphics to be easily transferred from one program to another. Windows supports *multitasking*, the running of more than one program at the same time. Windows also takes full advantage of the *protected mode* offered by the *Intel* 80286 and 80386 microprocessors, using *extended memory* to run more powerful applications.

Microsoft Windows has enabled IBM PC and compatible computers to tap into some of the most successful features of Macintosh computers, including its graphical user interface and a consistency in the look and operation of different programs. The latest version of Microsoft Windows features improved speed and graphics capabilities and *multimedia* extensions that directly challenge the traditional dominance of the Macintosh in *desktop publishing* and multimedia. See illustration at *graphical user interface.*

microspacing   The insertion of spaces of various sizes between characters to achieve *justification*, the alignment of text with respect to left and right margins.

MIDI   [MID-ee]   Acronym for **Musical Instrument Digital Interface.**   A *protocol* for the exchange of information between computers and musical devices such as synthesizers. Computers with a MIDI interface can read encoded data representing sounds and can manipulate it in many different ways, as by changing pitch, tempo, or volume. These computers can also translate data representing sounds into a musical score.

milli- Abbreviated **m** A prefix indicating one thousandth (10^{-3}), as in *millisecond*.

million instructions per second See **MIPS.**

millisecond Abbreviated **ms** A unit of time equal to one thousandth (10^{-3}) of a second.

mini Short for **minicomputer.**

minicomputer A computer, usually fitting within a single cabinet, that has more memory and a higher execution speed than a *personal computer*, but is less powerful than a *mainframe*. A minicomputer can process input and output from many *terminals* simultaneously. A minicomputer is often used as the *server* in a *client/server network*.

minifloppy disk A 5.25-inch *floppy disk* with a flexible protective sleeve and a hole in the middle, used as a *storage* medium for IBM PC and compatible computers. See table at *density*.

MIPS [mips] Acronym for **million instructions per second.** A measure of computing speed. MIPS refers to the number of *instructions* a computer's *CPU* (central processing unit) can carry out in one second. For example, a computer rated at 0.5 MIPS executes, on the average, 500,000 instructions per second.

MIPS is not the only variable to consider when judging a computer's speed. Other factors include the rate of data transfer between *memory* and the CPU and the speed of *peripherals* such as disk drives. See also *throughput*.

mode   An operating state for a program or device, especially one that can be selected by the user. In many word processing programs, you can choose between the *insert mode*, which inserts whatever you are typing without deleting text, and the *overwrite mode*, which replaces existing text with whatever you are typing. In some programs the actions carried out by the *function keys* change if you change modes.

modem   [MOE-dem]   Acronym   for   **modulator/demodulator.** A device that converts data from *digital* signals to *analog* signals and vice versa, so that computers can communicate over telephone lines. Telephone lines are designed to carry the human voice, and thus they transmit analog waves. A modem must encode digital information as electromagnetic waves in order to transmit it. At the other end, a modem must change analog waves back into digital code so that they can be understood by the receiving computer.

Modems are *serial* devices; that is, they transmit data one bit at a time rather than sending several bits simultaneously. The speed at which modems transmit data is measured in *bps* (bits per second), although the *baud rate* is also used. The format for the exchange of data between modems is called the *communications protocol*, and the process of setting this protocol is called *handshaking*. There are several widely used communications protocols, including *Kermit, Xmodem, Ymodem*, and *Zmodem. Communications software* controls handshaking, automates log-on procedures, allows access to on-line services, and performs other functions to make data transmission via modem easy and efficient. Internal modems are on an *expansion board* that is plugged into a computer; external modems are connected by cable to a computer's *serial port*. See table at *communications protocol*.

modular architecture   A hardware or software system in which each component, or *module*, can be replaced independently of all the other modules. The opposite of modular is integrated; in a system with integrated architecture, no clear distinction exists between components. See also *integrated circuit*.

module   **1.** In software, a portion of a program that carries out a specific function and may be used alone or combined with other modules to compose a program. Modules can be copied and used in many programs, and new programs can be created by combining existing modules in different ways with a *linker.* **2.** In hardware, a self-contained component that is installed as a unit.

monitor   The *display screen* of a computer and the case in which it is contained. Monitors come in a variety of screen sizes. A typical monitor has a screen that measures 14 inches diagonally, but larger screens that can display full pages at their actual size are also available.
   Monochrome monitors are able to display only one color against a background, while color monitors are capable of displaying many colors. The more *bits* a monitor uses to represent each pixel, the greater the number of colors the monitor can display. *Analog monitors* accept a continuous, or *analog,* signal that allows them to display an infinite variety of colors, while *digital monitors* can display only a fixed number of colors. Some monitors can accept either analog or digital signals.
   The *video adapter* sends signals to the monitor and determines, within the limits imposed by the monitor's structure, what the display will look like. The *video standard* supported by a video adapter determines the *resolution* and colors that a monitor can display. Also called *video display terminal.* See also *fixed-frequency monitor, multifrequency monitor, multiscanning monitor.*

monochrome   Of, relating to, or being a computer screen capable of displaying only one color on a dark or light background.

monospace font   A font in which each character is given the same *pitch,* or width. See also *fixed pitch, proportional font.*

motherboard   The main *printed circuit board* in a personal computer. It contains the *CPU,* main system *memory, controllers* for disk drives and other devices, *serial* and *parallel ports,* and sometimes *expansion slots.* The motherboard is easy to recognize because it is typically the largest printed circuit card inside the computer's case, and the large CPU chip is usually clearly labeled. An effective way to *upgrade* the performance of an older computer is to replace the motherboard.

By replacing the CPU, *ROM*, memory, and support circuits all at once, this method ensures that these key components of the system will continue to work together, and in effect creates a new computer in the old case. Also called *system board*, especially on an IBM PC.

Motorola microprocessors [mo-ter-OH-luh] A family of *microprocessors* made by Motorola Corporation and used in Macintosh computers and in Hewlett-Packard *workstations*. The early, 8-bit 6800 model was succeeded by the 68000, which had a 16-bit *data bus* and was the basis for the original Macintosh computer. Later models include the 32-bit 68020 with a *clock speed* of 16MHz used in the original Macintosh II, the 68030, versions of which had clock speeds of 16, 20, 25, 33, 40, and 50 megahertz, and the 68040, which achieves higher component density than previous models and includes a *math coprocessor* and a *RAM cache*. The 68060, due out next year, will have three times the speed of a 25 MHz 68040. See also *Intel microprocessors*. See table at *microprocessor*.

mouse Plural **mice** or **mouses**. A hand-held, button-activated *input device* that when rolled along a flat surface controls the movement of a *cursor* or *pointer* on a display screen. A mouse frees the user from the keyboard. With *menu-driven* applications the user simply points to a command choice and clicks a button on the mouse. With *draw* or *paint programs* the mouse can be used like a pen or brush. Mice are distinguished by the way they work internally and by how they connect to the computer.

A mechanical mouse has a rubber-coated ball on its underside that rotates as you move the mouse. Optical sensors detect the motion and move the screen pointer correspondingly. You can roll the mouse over almost any surface, but using a *mousepad* gives the best results.

An *optical mouse* uses reflections from an *LED* (light-emitting diode) to track the mouse's movement. An optical mouse requires a special mat to reflect the light properly. The mat is marked with a grid that acts as a frame of reference for the optical device.

Most mice connect to the computer through a special

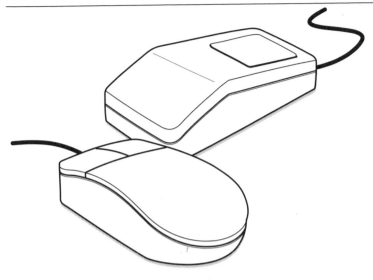

mouse
Two types of mouse

mouse *port*. A *serial mouse*, however, connects to a standard *serial port*. A *bus mouse* connects to the *bus* through an interface *card*. This is more of a job because you need to configure and install an *expansion board*. Obviously, if you have a free serial port, it is easier to connect a serial mouse. See illustration.

mousepad   A flat piece of material, such as specially coated foam rubber, designed to provide an optimum surface on which to use a *mouse*.

ms   Abbreviation of **millisecond.**

MS-DOS   [em-ess-DOSS]   A trademark for the *DOS* operating system.

MS-Windows   See **Microsoft Windows.**

MTBF   Abbreviation of **mean time between failures.**   A measure of the reliability of electronic and mechanical devices. The MTBF for a component reports its average working life, as tested under ideal conditions, before its first failure requiring service. MTBFs for electromechanical components such as disk drives are usually expressed in thousands or tens of thousands of hours.

multicolor/graphics array   See **MCGA.**

MultiFinder   A trademark for a version of the Macintosh computer *Finder* that allows more than one program to be loaded into memory at a time so that the user can switch quickly from one program to another. It differs from a true *multitasking* system in that it uses the technique known as context switching or *task switching*, in which all *background* applications are halted and only the one in the *foreground* runs.

multifrequency monitor   A *monitor* that can respond to a fixed number of different video signal frequency ranges. This allows it to support different resolutions and video standards, such as *CGA, EGA,* and *VGA.* See also *multiscanning monitor.*

multimedia   Designating a type of computer *application* that can combine text, graphics, full-motion video, and sound into an integrated package. For example, a multimedia encyclopedia can allow you to look up the entry for "Mozart," *click* on a *button,* and hear a selection from a Mozart symphony while looking at the score, or to view a moving animated diagram of a jet engine at "jet." Because graphics and sound files require large amounts of storage space, multimedia applications have only become practical with the development of sufficiently fast microprocessors and *CD-ROM* technology. Minimum requirements for a personal computer to run multimedia applications include an 80386 processor running at 20MHz or faster, 2MB–4MB of *RAM, VGA* graphics, a mouse, a *sound board,* and a multimedia-compatible CD-ROM drive.

multiprocessing   A method of computing in which different parts of a task are distributed between two or more similar *CPUs,* allowing the computer to complete operations more quickly and to handle larger, more complex procedures. See also *coprocessor, multitasking, parallel processing.*

multiscanning monitor A monitor that can automatically detect and respond to a signal from a *video adapter* at any frequency within a wide range. This allows it to work with adapters for any video standard from *monochrome* to *SVGA*. See also *multifrequency monitor*.

multitasking A mode of operation in which a single *CPU* works on more than one task simultaneously. Multitasking differs from *task switching* in that a program can continue to run in the *background* while the user's attention is on another process in the *foreground*. This can be done either by having the *operating system* parcel out fixed slices of CPU time to each program in succession or by allowing the programs themselves to turn over control of the CPU to other programs in the intervals when they do not need it. Although the processor can only perform one operation at a time, it switches from one to the other so quickly that it seems to the user as if all the programs are running together. Popular operating systems and environments that offer multitasking for personal computers include *DESQview*, *OS/2*, *Microsoft Windows*, and Windows NT. See also *multiprocessing*, *operating environment*, *parallel processing*.

multi-user Of, relating to, or being a computer system intended to be used by more than one person at a time. Multi-user systems differ from *local area networks* in that the processing power is centralized in a single location and access to it is provided by *dumb terminals* rather than through personal computers or *workstations*. Most multi-user systems are built around *mainframes* or *minicomputers*, typically using an *operating system* such as *UNIX* that is designed for this purpose.

Musical Instrument Digital Interface See **MIDI.**

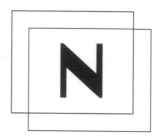

n   Abbreviation of **nano-**.

nano-   Abbreviated **n**   A prefix indicating one billionth (10^{-9}), as in *nanoseconds*.

nanosecond   [NAN-uh-sek-und]   Abbreviated **ns**   A unit of time equal to one billionth (10^{-9}) of a second.

natural language   In computer science, human language as opposed to a *programming language* or *machine language*. One of the long-standing goals of computer science, particularly in the field of *artificial intelligence*, has been to develop computer systems that can interact with human beings in natural language. Computers work well with programming languages such as BASIC or C because their *syntax* is finite, well-defined, and relatively small, but natural language presents problems because it is exactly the opposite. Human language is such a complex phenomenon that linguists have found it impossible even to agree on a theory that adequately explains what language is, much less a comprehensive description of the rules that make it work. See also *language*.

near-letter quality   Abbreviated **NLQ**   Of, related to, or being a print mode of *dot-matrix printers* that is better than *draft-quality* mode but not as good as *letter-quality* mode. See illustration at *letter-quality*.

nest   To embed one subroutine, set of data, or word processing *document* sequentially within another. In a database, for example, a nested *record* is a record containing a *field* that is itself a record. A nested table is a table within another table.

network   A system of computers, and often *peripherals* such as printers, linked together. The smallest networks are *local area networks* (LANs), in which as few as 2 or as many as 500 computers are connected by cables within a small geographic area, often within the same building. Larger networks, called *wide area networks* (WANs), use telephone lines or radio

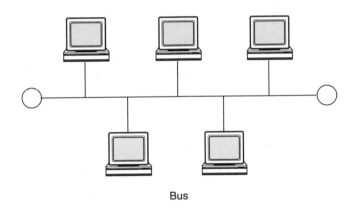

Bus

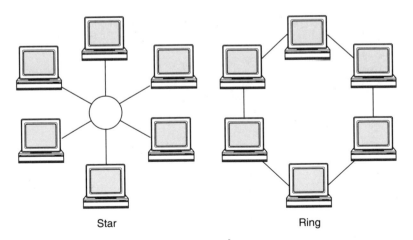

Star   Ring

network
Three common network configurations

waves to link computers that can be thousands of miles apart. The geometric arrangement of the computers is called the *topology* of the network. Common topologies include the *star, bus,* and *ring.* The *protocol* standardizes the rules and signals that computers on a network use to communicate. *AppleTalk,* a protocol suitable for small networks, is built into all Macintosh computers and laser printers. Popular protocols for LANs include *Ethernet,* and, specifically for IBM PC computers, the IBM *token-ring network.* See illustration. See also *client/server network, peer-to-peer network.*

network interface card Abbreviated **NIC** A *printed circuit board* or an *adapter* that allows a computer to be connected to a *network.* Network interface cards permit the network connection to be made directly to the computer's internal *bus,* rather than through the much slower *serial port.* Interface cards are usually made for a single type of network.

neural network A computing system modeled after a biological nervous system that attempts to approximate the workings of the human brain. Interconnected "processing elements" play the role of neurons (nerve cells). Each processing element has a limited number of inputs, corresponding to the impulses a neuron receives. Its inputs determine each element's output, which corresponds to the nerve impulse that travels to the next neuron. Rather than being programmed, the processing elements "learn" from the kinds and patterns of input they receive.

Neural networks are either built from *hardware* circuits or simulated on a computer through *software.* Although commercial applications of neural networks are limited at this point, they are beginning to be used in areas such as voice and pattern recognition and speech synthesis. See also *artificial intelligence.*

Newton A trademark for a hand-held *pen computer* that contains a *PIM* (personal information manager), sends *faxes,* and responds to commands written on its screen in plain English.

NIC Abbreviation of **network interface card.**

NiCad battery [NYE-cad] A type of rechargeable battery widely used with portable electronic equipment, including *portable* computers. NiCad batteries are made up of cells containing nickel and cadmium and can be recharged up to about 1,000 times under ideal conditions. The most significant characteristic of NiCad batteries is the so-called memory effect, in which a battery that is recharged after being only partially drained soon loses its ability to hold a full charge.

nickel-metal-hydride battery Abbreviated **NiMH** A type of rechargeable battery similar to a *NiCad battery* but using nickel metal hydride rather than cadmium. Besides avoiding the problems of using and disposing of cadmium, which is toxic, NiMH cells provide higher power density than NiCads, allowing batteries to be much smaller for a given storage capacity or to last longer for a given size.

NLQ Abbreviation of **near-letter quality.**

node 1. In a *local area network*, a *workstation, server, printer,* or another device that is connected to the network and able to process data. 2. In a *tree structure* as used in *directory* or *database* management and programming, a point where two or more lines or branches of the tree meet.

noise A random electrical signal on a communications channel that interferes with the desired signal or data. Noise can either be generated by the circuitry of the communications device itself or come from one of a variety of external sources, including radio and TV signals, lightning, and nearby transmission lines.

nonimpact printer A printer that does not rely on mechanical force to transfer ink or wax to the page, such as a *laser printer,* an *ink-jet printer,* or a *thermal printer.* Nonimpact printers are considerably quieter than *impact printers,* but they cannot be used for printing multipart forms. See table at *printer.*

noninterlaced Designating a type of monitor that does not use the technique of *interlacing* when scanning the display screen, but instead scans every line on every *refresh* cycle. Although noninterlaced displays are more expensive than interlaced ones for the same level of resolution, they allow the screen to be redrawn faster for graphics and video images and avoid the *flickering* of interlaced displays. See also *interlacing.* See also *raster scanning.*

nonvolatile memory Memory whose contents are not lost when the system power is shut off. Nonvolatile memory is used in calculators, printers, and other devices whose programming does not need to be changed, and in personal computers for the *BIOS* and other instructions the computer needs to read during the *boot* sequence. Disk storage and *ROM* are both nonvolatile memory, as opposed to the *volatile memory* held in *RAM.*

NOR [nor] A *Boolean operator* that returns the value TRUE if and only if both of its operands are FALSE. Table 15 shows the results of the NOR operator.

Table 15. Results of NOR Operator

a	b	a NOR b
FALSE	FALSE	TRUE
FALSE	TRUE	FALSE
TRUE	FALSE	FALSE
TRUE	TRUE	FALSE

NOT [not] A *Boolean operator* that returns the value TRUE if its operand is FALSE, and FALSE if its operand is TRUE. Table 16 shows the results of the NOT operator.

Table 16. Results of NOT Operator

a	b	NOT a
FALSE	FALSE	TRUE
FALSE	TRUE	TRUE
TRUE	FALSE	FALSE
TRUE	TRUE	FALSE

notebook   A *portable* computer that is smaller than a *laptop*. Typical notebook computers are about one foot wide, weigh up to 6 or 7 pounds, and are powered by rechargeable batteries. They usually contain a single 3.5-inch *floppy disk* drive. Despite their small size, many notebook computers offer nearly the same capabilities as desktop models, but they are more expensive.

notepad   A *desk accessory* in the *Microsoft Windows* operating environment. Notepad is a text *editor* that allows the user to jot down notes, write short memos, and create and edit batch files.

ns   Abbreviation of **nanosecond.**

NuBus   [NOO-bus or NYOO-bus]   A trademark for a high-speed *expansion bus* used in Macintosh II computers. NuBus expansion slots accept 96-pin expansion boards.

null character   A data control character that fills computer time by adding nonsignificant zeros to a data sequence. The null character can be used, for example, to pad data fields, terminate character *strings*, or separate blocks of data. In the *ASCII* character set, the null character is symbolized by NUL and represented by the character code 0.

null-modem cable   A cable that allows two computers to be connected directly together through their *serial ports* without using a *modem*. A null-modem cable is used, for example, to connect a portable computer with a larger computer so that they can exchange data.

number cruncher   A program or computer, such as a *supercomputer*, that is able to perform complex, lengthy calculations.

numeric coprocessor   See **math coprocessor.**

numeric keypad   A group of keys, separate from and usually to the right of the typing area on a keyboard, that consists of the numbers 0–9, a decimal point, and mathematical operators, arranged as on an adding machine. Numeric keypads are designed for entering large amounts of numeric data. A numeric keypad may also have function keys and an Enter key.

Often, as on keyboards for IBM PC and compatible computers, the keys on the keypad do double duty. In numeric mode, the keys represent numbers. In cursor control mode, they function as *arrow keys*. The *Num Lock key* is pressed to toggle between modes.

Num Lock key A key on IBM PC and compatible computers that *toggles* the *numeric keypad* between numeric mode and cursor control mode.

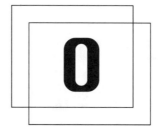

object code The *code* that is produced by a *compiler* from the *source code*. Source code consists of the instructions written by the programmer in a high-level *programming language* such as *C* or *FORTRAN*. The object code is most often in the form of *machine language* that can be directly executed by a computer. It may, however, be in *assembly language*, an intermediate code that is then translated into machine language by an *assembler* or a *linker*.

object-oriented Describing and handling data as a set of discrete units known as "objects" rather than as a collection of elements, *bits,* or points. This approach allows a single entity to be manipulated with one operation rather than one element at a time. For example, the user can move, rotate, enlarge, or reduce a figure in a drawing without having to redraw every point, or move or copy a file directory by *dragging* an *icon* without having to select and copy each file individually. See also *object-oriented graphics, object-oriented interface, object-oriented programming.*

object-oriented graphics   A method of representing *graphics* images by mathematical description rather than as a series of points. This allows the user to move, resize, rotate, stretch, or copy an element in a design in one operation without having to redraw all the points on the figure that are to be changed, as must be done with a *bit-mapped graphic.* Even overlapping objects can be handled in this way without being confused or interfering with other objects. Also in contrast with bit-mapped graphics, an object-oriented image can be viewed or printed at whatever *resolution* is available to the monitor or printer. Also called *vector graphics.* See also *page description language, PostScript, raster graphics.*

object-oriented interface   A *user interface* in which actions are performed by manipulating symbols on the screen. These symbols are typically *icons* and *folders* that represent files, programs, directories, drives, and devices and are arranged in groups and *windows* that reflect the logical structure of the system. Rather than typing commands to move a file to another directory, for example, you simply *drag* the file's icon and drop it into the folder for the new directory. The actual commands and processes that complete the operation are carried out automatically and hidden from view. This type of interface also allows files created in one program to be made into objects and embedded in or linked to files created in another, where they can then be edited or automatically updated. See also *Dynamic Data Exchange, Finder, graphical user interface, Microsoft Windows, OS/2.*

object-oriented programming   Abbreviated **OOP**   A paradigm for programming that is schematic rather than linear. In conventional programming, the programmer lists the procedures to be performed on the data in order to accomplish a task. In object-oriented programming, the concepts of procedure and data are replaced by the concepts of "objects" and "messages." An object includes both a package of data and a description of the operations that can be performed on the data. A message specifies one of the operations but, unlike a procedure, does not describe how the operation should be carried out. *C++* is an example of an OOP language.

Programmers can send messages to objects and create relationships between objects. New objects can take on all relevant features of existing objects. Since objects are self-contained, they function as *modules* and can be copied and combined to create new programs. Object-oriented programming meshes naturally with *graphical user interfaces*. An object can be represented on-screen by an *icon*, and the user can copy or reposition the object by *dragging* its icon around the screen with a mouse. The internal complexity of the object is completely hidden from the user.

oblique   A simulated *italic* type style created by slanting the *roman* characters of a *font*. Oblique letters lack the cursive appearance of italic letters.

OCR   Abbreviation of **optical character recognition.**

octal   Of or relating to a number system with a base of 8. In contrast with the *decimal* (base 10) system most of us use everyday, in which each place in a number represents a successive power of 10, each place in an octal number represents a power of 8. Thus the decimal number 1,165 is written in octal notation as 2215, which stands for $(2 \times 8^3) + (2 \times 8^2) + (1 \times 8) + (5 \times 1)$ or $1,024 + 128 + 8 + 5$. Octal notation is used in computer programming because three-digit *binary* numbers are readily converted into one-digit octal numbers from 0 to 7. See also *binary, hexadecimal.*

odd footer   In word processing, a *footer* that appears on odd-numbered pages.

odd header In word processing, a *header* that appears on odd-numbered pages.

OEM Abbreviation of **original equipment manufacturer.** The company that actually manufactures a piece of computer equipment, which is then modified or repackaged and sold to the consumer. The term is often applied to value-added resellers (VARs), who purchase separate components in bulk from large manufacturers and package them as complete computer systems. Although technically not OEMs, these VARs are the first to create a working computer out of separate parts and therefore they are sometimes considered to be entitled to the designation.

off-line Not connected to a computer or computer network.

offset 1. A value that specifies the distance of an address from a reference point known as the *base address*. If A is the address 100, then A + 7, where 7 is the offset, specifies the address 107. **2.** See **gutter.**

on-board modem See **internal modem.**

on-line Connected to or accessible by means of a computer or computer network.

on-line service A commercial service that makes one or more large *databases* available over telephone lines for a subscription fee. To access an on-line service, you must have a *modem* connected to your computer. On-line services may provide electronic searching and reporting for researchers in various fields. Some also offer *electronic mail*, conferencing, file *libraries*, and other facilities of a *bulletin board system*, as well as *gateways* to other services. On-line services vary in their focus from personal and hobby-oriented ones such as CompuServe to professional research and financial data services such as LEXIS, NEXIS, and the Dow Jones News/Retrieval Service.

OOP Abbreviation of **object-oriented programming.**

open 1. To make a *file* ready for reading or writing. 2. In a *graphical user interface*, to expand an *icon* into a *window*.

open architecture 1. A system design whose specifications are publicly available. Open architecture is exemplified by the IBM PC computer design, which can be copied by anyone and for which any third party is free to design and distribute *add-on* products. This approach allows for more flexibility in the design of new devices and techniques, but risks incompatibility. See also *closed architecture, proprietary*. 2. A computer design that includes *expansion slots* for additional *printed circuit boards* to enhance or customize a system.

operand 1. A number or *variable* on which a mathematical *operation* is performed. In the *expression* 8 + x, 8 and x are the operands, and the operation is addition. 2. In programming, the data on which a single instruction acts.

operating environment The type of *interface* and *command* structure under which one operates a computer. For example, the *Macintosh* computer environment is a *graphical user interface* that uses *icons* and *menus*. The term is often used to make a distinction between a true *operating system* such as *OS/2* or Windows NT and a program such as *Microsoft Windows* or *DESQview*, which seem to function as operating systems but in fact rely on *DOS*. See also *environment*.

operating system *Software* designed to control the *hardware* of a specific computer system in order to allow users and *application* programs to employ it easily. The operating system mediates between hardware and applications programs. It handles the details of sending instructions to the hardware and allocating system resources in case of conflicts, thus relieving applications developers of this burden and providing a standard *platform* for new programs. The most common operating systems for personal computers are *DOS*, the Macintosh *System*, *OS/2*, *UNIX*, and Windows NT. See Table 17 for features of various operating systems.

Table 17. Widely Used Operating Systems

Operating System	Characteristics
MS-DOS	• Does not support multitasking or multiple users • Limited to 1MB of memory • Nearly identical to PC-DOS
OS/2	• Relatively powerful • Requires Intel 80286 or later microprocessor • Supports multitasking • Supports virtual memory • Supports a graphical user interface (Presentation Manager) • Networking capability (LAN Manager) • Compatible with MS-DOS
System	• Designed for use on Macintosh computers • Uses a graphical user interface • Supports multitasking (MultiFinder) • Networking capability (AppleTalk)
UNIX	• Powerful • De facto standard operating system for workstations • Supports multiprocessing • Supports multiple users • More portable than other operating systems
XENIX	• A version of UNIX designed for use on IBM PC and compatible computers

operation **1.** An action performed on one or more numbers or *variables*. Addition, subtraction, multiplication, and division are common arithmetic operations. See also *operand*, *operator*. **2.** In programming, an action resulting from a single instruction.

operator A symbol or character that represents an *operation*. In computing, the following symbols are used as common mathematical operators: + (addition), − (subtraction), * (multiplication), / (division), and ^ (exponentiation). In programming, spreadsheets, and database *query* languages, one encounters *Boolean operators* such as *AND*, *OR*, and *NOT*, and *relational operators*, such as > (greater than) and < (less than).

optical character recognition   Abbreviated **OCR**   The use of a light-sensitive device, such as an *optical scanner* or reader, to identify and encode printed or handwritten characters. The scanner matches the patterns of light and dark on a printed page against patterns stored in memory and then generates output to the computer or performs some other operation, such as sorting or searching. A page that is scanned into the computer or received over a *fax modem* can be converted into a computer file and then edited or retransmitted.

optical disk   A plastic-coated disk that stores digital data, such as music or text, as tiny pits etched into the surface to be read by a laser. Optical disks provide much higher storage density than magnetic disks, but the data may take longer to retrieve and optical disk technology is still expensive. Most current optical disks are used for *read-only* data storage, although *erasable optical disks* are becoming more available. See also *CD-ROM, WORM.*

optical fiber   See **fiber optics.**

optical mouse   A *mouse* that senses motion by reflecting the light from a pair of *LEDs* (light-emitting diodes) off a special pad marked with a grid of colored lines. Optical mice are more precise than mechanical ones but are also more expensive. The optomechanical mouse is a hybrid that uses a rolling ball as in a mechanical mouse but replaces the mechanical motion-encoder wheels with optical encoders. The optical encoders consist of a pair of slotted wheels that periodically interrupt the signals sent from two LEDs to a pair of light-sensitive transistors. The optomechanical mouse provides some of the precision of the optical mouse but does not require a special pad.

optical scanner   A device that converts images and text printed on paper into digital information that can be stored as a computer file and processed by *graphics* software. Optical scanners work by sensing the light and dark areas on a page and *digitizing* the lightness values, converting them into numerical values that are recorded in electronic form as a *bit-mapped graphic*.

There are three main types of optical scanners. *Sheet-fed scanners* operate much like *fax machines*, with single sheets of paper being inserted manually. A *flatbed scanner* works like an office copying machine and can scan books and other printed material. *Hand-held* scanners are relatively inexpensive and can also be used on books but can only scan part of a page at a time. Scanning a whole page requires multiple passes and a steady hand. Scanners also vary in their *resolution*, which ranges from 75 to 300 or more dots per inch, and in their ability to perform *gray scale* scanning. Gray scale scanners can register from 16 to 256 shades of gray, providing better results with *halftone* images, photographs, and materials in color.

Scanners are often used to insert graphics or text copied from other sources into a document. Because all images are stored in bit-map form, however, it is important to remember that text copied by a scanner cannot be edited in a word processing program; this can only be done if the text is read and converted to *ASCII* characters by an *optical character recognition* program.

option   1. A character or *string* that may be added to a *command* at the user's discretion to change the way the command works, but is not required. For example, the DOS command DIR, issued by itself, brings to the screen a list of files in the current directory, in their order on the disk and with *subdirectory* names first. The use of *command line* options, however, lets you issue a command such as DIR /P /A:-R, which yields a directory with pauses when the screen is full (/P) and does not list any files marked with the *attribute* read-only (/A:-R). In DOS, command options are usually preceded by a forward slash or a hyphen. Also called *switch*. See also *argument.* **2.** In *graphical user interfaces,* a choice that can be made within a *dialog box.*

Option key A key on *Macintosh* computer keyboards that when pressed in combination with another key generates a number of special characters or alternate commands.

OR [or] A *Boolean operator* that returns the value TRUE if either or both of its *operands* are TRUE. Table 18 shows the results of the OR operator. Also called *inclusive OR.*

Table 18. Results of OR Operator

a	b	a OR a
FALSE	FALSE	FALSE
FALSE	TRUE	TRUE
TRUE	FALSE	TRUE
TRUE	TRUE	TRUE

original equipment manufacturer See **OEM.**

orphan In word processing, a first line of a paragraph that appears as the last line on a page. See also *widow.*

OS/2 [oh-ess-TOO] A trademark for an *operating system* for personal computers. OS/2 was originally developed by IBM and Microsoft to be the successor to *DOS.* OS/2 requires an Intel 80286 or later microprocessor, and unlike DOS it can use *protected mode.* This allows it to offer such features as *virtual memory* and *multitasking.* Versions of OS/2 after version 1.0 provided a *graphical user interface* called *Presentation Manager.* Version 2.0, developed by IBM alone, was a major advance that made full use of the 32-bit *architecture* of the 80386 and later processors. See table at *operating system.*

outdent See **hanging indent.**

outline font   A *printer font* or *screen font* in which the outlines of each character are defined by a mathematical formula. The printer then fills in the outlines at its maximum resolution. The most popular *page description language* for defining outline fonts is *PostScript*.

Unlike *bit-mapped fonts*, outline fonts are scalable; that is, they can be scaled up and down in size without becoming distorted. Because mathematical formulas adjust the lines and arcs of the outline, you need only one font in the printer's memory to print or display any type size from 2 to 127 *points*. Also called *scalable font*, *vector font*. See illustration.

outline font
Bit-mapped and outline fonts

output   *n.* Information produced by a computer, such as the results of processing data input to the computer. Output can be printed, displayed on a screen, written to *disk*, or transferred via *networks* to other computers.
—*v.* To send output to a printer, display screen, storage device, modem, or other output device. See also *input*.

output device   A machine that enables you to get information out of a computer. *Printers, display screens,* speakers, and *CD-ROM* drives are examples of output devices. See also *input device*.

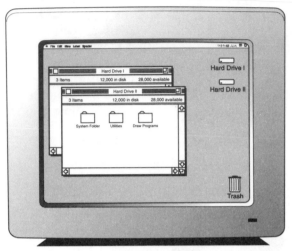

OVERLAID WINDOWS

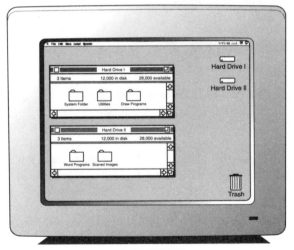

TILED WINDOWS

overlaid windows
On a Macintosh computer

overflow error   An error that results when a calculation produces a unit of data too large to be stored in the memory location allotted to it.

overlaid windows   A display *mode* in which *windows* overlap each other, with only the topmost window displayed in full. Overlaid windows are also called *cascading windows,* especially if the windows overlap in such a way that the *title bar* remains visible in each window. See illustration. See also *pop, tiled windows, zoom.*

overstrike mode   **1.** In word processing, a mode in which you can type two characters in the same position so as to create or simulate another character that may not be available, such as o and / for the character ø.   **2.** See **overwrite mode** (sense 1).

overwrite   To record new data on a disk where other data is already stored, thus destroying the old data.

overwrite mode   In word processing, a mode in which you can type over an existing character and replace it with a new character. Most word processors allow you to select either overwrite mode or *insert mode.* In insert mode, typing inserts new characters but does not delete old ones. Also called *overstrike mode, typeover mode.*

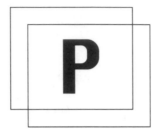

p   Abbreviation of **pico-**.

pack   To store data in compressed form by either compressing a *file* or eliminating the space between files on a disk. A *packed file* is a file in a compressed format. Some *modems* pack data before transmission. Since fewer bytes need to be sent, the data can be transmitted in less time. The receiving modem must then be able to *unpack* the data. See also *data compression*.

packaged software   Software not designed for a specific client but written for mass use and commercially distributed through dealers and other channels.

packed file   A *file* that has undergone *data compression* so as to take up less *memory*. There are various programs available for packing files, and each employs its own set of *codes* to represent data. This means that you need a copy of the program used to pack a file in order to *unpack* it. Most files available for *downloading* from *bulletin board systems* have been packed. Many people pack all files they don't need on a regular basis.

page   A fixed quantity of *memory*. In *word processing*, a page of memory corresponds to a page of printed text. For example, you can set different margins for each page of a *document* and have a page number appear at the top or bottom of the page.

In *graphics* programs, a page of memory corresponds to one screen's worth of images. In *virtual memory*, a page is a set amount of memory, usually 256, 512, or 1,024 *bytes*, that can be moved as a block between *RAM* and a *disk*.

page break   In *word processing*, a separation between pages of text. Most word processing programs create a page break automatically when you have entered enough text to fill a page. If, however, you want a page break before one would otherwise appear, you can insert a *hard* page break into the text by using a special command.

page description language   Abbreviated **PDL**   A *programming language* for controlling the *layout* and contents of printed pages with instructions indicating, for example, what *fonts* and margins are to be used. A page description language gives descriptions of *characters* and *graphics* that a *printer* can process according to its own capabilities, so that the same page description language description will yield different results from printers with different resolutions. This means that although you don't have to change the printing codes in your *document* every time you use a different printer, you can use only a printer with some processing capabilities of its own. Two popular *laser printer* page description languages are Adobe *PostScript* and Hewlett-Packard *PCL* (Printer Control Language).

Page Down key   Abbreviated **PgDn**   A *key* that moves the *cursor* down a screenful of lines in most word processing programs but may have other uses in other *applications*.

page eject   See **form feed.**

page frame   An area of the *CPU*'s usable *address space* to which a *page* of *virtual memory* may be *mapped* from disk.

page layout program   An *application* that allows you to arrange text and *graphics* from various files together on a page. Page layout programs let you change *fonts*, crop graphics, create text columns, and adjust the size of text and images. The page design you are creating is displayed as a graphics image on-screen. Two popular page layout programs are PageMaker from Aldus Corporation and QuarkXPress, developed by Quark, Inc. See also *desktop publishing*.

page preview   See **preview.**

pages per minute   Abbreviated **ppm**   A measure of the speed of certain printers, especially *laser printers*. A printer's ppm rating is calculated by its manufacturer and is usually based on how fast it can print a page that has text in a single *typeface* and no *graphics* or other special elements. Therefore, this rating is not a reliable measure if you use many typefaces or lots of graphics. In the latter case, the *graphics pages per minute* (gppm) rating is more meaningful. See also *characters per second*.

Page Up key   Abbreviated **PgUp**   A *key* that moves the *cursor* up a screenful of lines in most word processing programs but may have other uses in other *applications*.

pagination   **1.** The dividing of a *document* into pages, as in word processing. Most programs do this automatically. **2.** The numbering of the pages of a document at the top or bottom of each page.

paging   In *virtual memory* systems, the transfer of *pages* of data between *RAM* and an auxiliary memory device, such as a *hard disk* or, in DOS systems, expanded memory. Paging allows virtual memory to seem larger than actual *physical* memory. When you ask the computer for a page of data not on hand in RAM, the operating system exchanges a page of data in RAM for the requested data residing elsewhere. This can greatly increase the apparent amount of RAM available. See also *page, virtual memory*.

paint program   A *graphics* application whose images are stored as *bit maps*. A paint program lets you select a *tool*, such as a paintbrush or a can of spray paint, from a group of *icons* and paint with that tool in the shape and width it permits. Whatever area you cover with that tool will be shaded with the solid or patterned background you have chosen. You can also select an icon that guides you in drawing circles, curves, or straight lines. Table 19 shows some common paint program tools. See also *draw program*.

Table 19. **Common Paint Program Tools**

Tool	Function
Pencil	Draws a line one pixel thick
Eraser	Erases black or colored areas
Paintbrush	Paints areas with the selected fill pattern
Paint Bucket	Pours the selected fill pattern into an enclosed area
Airbrush	Sprays the selected fill pattern with adjustable rates of flow, spray area, and dot size
Freehand	Paints freeform shapes
Grabber	Moves the document in the window
Text	Enters text

palette   **1.** The group of colors that a given monitor is capable of displaying.   **2.** The selection of colors available in a given *graphics* program. In general, fewer colors can be displayed on-screen at one time than are available in the palette overall. **3.** The group of patterns, widths, and drawing *tools*, such as paintbrushes and pencils, available in a *paint* or *draw program*.

palmtop   A computer that is small enough to fit in the palm of your hand and usually features a *PIM* (personal information manager). See also *PDA*.

Pantone Matching System   Abbreviated **PMS**   A trademark for a standard system for identifying approximately 500 ink colors, each assigned a specific number. PMS also allows you to mix colors. Many *graphics* and *desktop publishing* programs use PMS, as do traditional print shops.

paper feed   The mechanism that feeds paper through a printer. For example, some *dot-matrix printers* use a *tractor feed*. See also *friction feed, pin feed*.

paper-white display   A *monochrome monitor* that displays characters and graphics in black against a white background.

parallel   **1.** Using or used in the simultaneous transmission of several *bits* of data over separate wires within a cable or over separate communications lines. See also *parallel interface, parallel port, serial*.   **2.** Of, relating to, or carrying out the simultaneous performance of separate tasks. See also *parallel processing*.

parallel interface   A system for the transmission of data along several parallel wires. The *interface* itself consists of these wires, their *connectors*, and the *parallel ports* in each of the devices being connected. Each wire transmits one bit at a time so that together they transmit several bits simultaneously. In a *Centronics interface*, there are eight of these wires, so that data is transmited in *bytes*. The remaining wires send information telling one device that the other is ready to receive or send data. A printer is usually connected to a personal computer by a parallel interface. See also *serial interface*.

parallel port   A *port* with multiple *pin* holes for use in a *parallel interface*. Each pin in the input/output *connector* connects to a parallel wire. Most computers have at least one parallel port, usually used by a *printer*. See also *Centronics interface, parallel, serial port*.

parallel processing   The simultaneous *processing* of different tasks in a program by two or more *microprocessors*. Parallel processing is usually carried out by a single computer with more than one *CPU* (central processing unit), but it can also be carried out by several computers (each with a single CPU) connected together in a *network*. Sophisticated software is required to distribute tasks among the microprocessors. In *multiprocessing*, a program is broken down into sequential tasks so that, for example, one microprocessor sorts data, another analyzes it, and a third sends the results to a display screen. In *multitasking*, on the other hand, one CPU runs several programs at once.

parameter   **1.** One of a group of adjustable factors that distinguish an *environment* or determine how a *system* will work. For example, when you determine what color will represent what on your *display screen*, or when you set the margins and page length in a word processing *document*, you are setting parameters.   **2.** A specification that you add or change in giving the computer a *command*. For example, if you give the *DOS* command COPY, you must specify what you want copied and where you want the copy to go. If you enter COPY A:\DFILE.RUR, the file name "DFILE.RUR" is a parameter that tells the computer what to copy.   **3.** In programming, a value that is passed to a *function* or *routine* so that it can be operated on to produce a result. See also *argument*.

parent directory   A *directory* in which a *subdirectory* is located. For example, if you work in a directory called MYSTUFF and have a subdirectory called MEMOS, then MYSTUFF is the parent directory of MEMOS. Each directory except the *root directory* has a parent directory. See illustration at *hierarchical*.

parity   The even or odd quality of the number of 1s or 0s in a group of seven bits, often marked by an added *parity bit* and used to determine the integrity of data especially after transmission.

parity bit   A bit added to a group of seven bits to indicate *parity* so that the data can be checked for integrity.

park To lock the *head* of a hard *disk drive* above a part of the disk that contains no data. If you handle your disk drive too roughly, the head could fall, causing a *head crash*. If you park the disk before moving it, even if the head falls it won't cause a crash. Some hard disks park themselves automatically whenever the power is turned off, and many disk *utility* packages have parking programs.

partition *n.* A section of a *hard disk* that functions as an independent hard disk. An entire disk may consist of only one partition, or it may have several. Partitions must be created before the disk can be formatted and used by an *operating system*. Different operating systems can be used on each partition. Early versions of *DOS* required any disk drive larger than 32MB to be divided into two or more partitions. On Macintosh computers, *hard* partitions are fixed and cannot be changed without reformatting. *Soft* partitions can be made without affecting the data or disk. The *Finder* acts as if the disk is physically partitioned.
—*v.* To separate a hard disk into partitions.

Pascal [pass-KAL] A *high-level language* designed by Nicklaus Wirth in the early 1970s. Pascal is a highly structured language with a relatively simple *syntax*. Because Pascal insists on careful organization, it is popular for teaching programming and widely used in colleges and universities. Pascal is named after Blaise Pascal, a 17th-century French mathematician and religious philosopher who developed one of the first mechanical adding machines.

passive-matrix A type of *LCD* (liquid-crystal display) that controls an entire row of *pixels* in the liquid-crystal layer with a single transistor. Passive-matrix displays tend to be less bright and clear than *active-matrix* displays, but they also cost less. See also *flat-panel display*.

password A secret sequence of *characters* that is used as an *access code* for a *file, program, computer,* or *network*. All authorized users have a password; no one else can gain access to the file, program, computer, or network in question. To maintain security, some systems ask users to change their passwords on a regular basis.

paste   To insert text or graphics into a document from a *buffer.* See also *clipboard, copy, cut.*

path   A sequence of *commands* or a link between points that is needed to reach a particular goal. Every programming *routine,* for example, has a path leading through a number of commands. A *modem* establishes a path for communication between a computer and a *network* or another computer. You can create a path in a *graphics* program and insert text along it so that the text appears as a curved line. The *Macintosh* computer sets up a path to every *file* that you open and identifies each path internally with a distinct number. In *DOS,* a path is the list of *directories* leading from the *root directory* to any given file; the PATH command reveals this list.

pathname   In a *hierarchical* file system, the name of the *file* you are accessing, together with the names of all the *folders* or *directories* that you have to go through to reach it from the drive and folder or directory you are in now. For example, if you are working in *DOS* in the C: drive (the primary hard disk drive) in a directory called \WORK, and you want to reach the file QUERIES.DOC, which is in a subdirectory LEFTOVER, then the pathname would be LEFTOVER\ QUERIES.DOC. If you had to get to QUERIES.DOC from the A: drive (a floppy disk drive), the pathname would be C:\WORK\LEFTOVER\QUERIES.DOC.

Pause key   A *key* that interrupts a command, a program, or the on-screen display of data when pressed. Keyboards for *IBM PC* and compatible computers have a Pause key that stops the display of data when you are *scrolling* through several *screens.* Many games have Pause keys so that you can interrupt the game and come back to it later.

PC   Abbreviation of **personal computer.**

PCB Abbreviation of **printed circuit board.**

PC-DOS [pee-see-DOSS] A trademark for the *DOS* operating system.

PCL Abbreviation of **Printer Control Language.** A trademark of Hewlett-Packard for the set of *commands* used to control its printers and also used by all *HP-compatible printers.* Recent versions of PCL support a *scalable font* technology, Intellifont.

PDA Abbreviation of **personal digital assistant. 1.** A lightweight, hand-held computer developed by Apple Computer, Inc. and released in 1993. See also *Newton, palmtop.* **2.** A lightweight, hand-held computer, often featuring an internal *modem* and cellular phone to be used as a link to a larger computer. A growing number of PDAs are *pen computers.* See also *palmtop, pen computer.*

PDL Abbreviation of **page description language.**

peer-to-peer network A *network* of *personal computers,* each of which acts as both client and *server,* so that each computer can exchange *files* and *electronic mail* directly with every other computer on the network. Each computer can tap into any of the others, although *access* can be restricted to those files a computer's user chooses to make public. Peer-to-peer networks are connected by cables. They are cheaper than *client/server networks* but less efficient when large amounts of data need to be exchanged. Peer-to-peer networks work best with 20–25 users. Also called *file sharing network.*

pel [pel] See **pixel.**

pen computer A computer, especially a *PDA,* that lets you *input* and retrieve *data* by writing with a *light pen* directly on a *display screen.* The screen turns black wherever you touch it with the light pen, so that it looks as if you were writing with ink on paper. Pen computers can recognize handwritten characters, so you can write words as well as draw graphics with the light pen. Pen computers come with *modems* and built-in cellular phones to connect users to larger, less mobile computers and *databases*.

Pentium   A trademark for a *microprocessor* designed by Intel for personal computers and *workstations* and introduced in March 1993. Pentium is so named because it represents the fifth generation of microprocessors from Intel, succeeding the popular 80486 series. Pentium can perform calculations up to five times faster than the 486 microprocessor and is fast enough to support such CPU-intensive applications as speech recognition and high-bandwidth video.

peripheral   A *device*, such as a *printer, modem, keyboard, monitor,* or *hard disk*, perceived as distinct from and external to a computer's *CPU* (central processing unit). Some people call *monitors* and *keyboards* peripherals, but since a computer might be unusable without these devices, some others would not consider them truly peripheral.

personal communicator   A lightweight, hand-held *pen computer* that can access a *PIM*, fax, modem, voice mail, electronic mail, and telephone. Personal communicators are designed to allow people who work away from their desks to use their electronic equipment from a distance. See also *palmtop, PDA.*

personal computer   Abbreviated **PC**   A computer built around a single *microprocessor* and designed to be independent of a *mainframe* or any other computer. Personal computers have their own *operating systems, software,* and *peripherals* so that they can be set up and run without any additional equipment. Personal computers can be linked to *networks* by *modems* or by *cables.* Personal computers tend to be less costly and less powerful than *workstations,* but at the high end of the market personal computers can and often do substitute for workstations. Also called *desktop computer, microcomputer.*

personal digital assistant   See **PDA.**

personal information manager   See **PIM.**

PgDn   Abbreviation of **Page Down key.**

PgUp   Abbreviation of **Page Up key.**

physical   Of, relating to, or being *hardware.* A physical hard disk, for example, is a piece of hardware that you can see and feel. It may be *partitioned* into a number of *logical* drives that function as if they were physically separate, so that you could have several logical drives but only one physical drive. Physical memory is the *RAM* chip installed in the computer. *Virtual memory* mimics RAM but is actually located on a hard disk and swapped into RAM. See also *virtual.*

physical address   An *address* for data located in *physical* memory. Programs that use *virtual memory* must swap *virtual addresses* for *physical addresses.*

PIC   [pik]   A trademark for the *graphics file format* used with the *spreadsheet* program Lotus 1-2-3. See table at *graphics file format.*

pica   In typesetting, *word processing,* and *desktop publishing,* a unit of measurement equal to twelve *points* or approximately $\frac{1}{6}$ of an inch.

pico-   Abbreviated **p**   A prefix indicating one trillionth (10^{-12}), as in *picosecond.*

picosecond   Abbreviated **psec**   A unit of time equal to one trillionth of a second (10^{-12}).

PICT   [pikt]   A *graphics file format* that supports both *object-oriented* and *bit-mapped graphics.* PICT was developed by Apple and is used by almost all Macintosh graphics programs to store and exchange graphics documents. The original PICT format supported 8 colors along with black-and-white images. An updated version, PICT2, supports 256 colors. See table at *graphics file format*.

PIM Abbreviation of **personal information manager.** A *database management system* geared to personal information, such as notes, appointments, and addresses. PIMs often come with calculators, calendars, and schedulers.

pin **1.** One of the small metal prongs at the end of a *connector* that fit into the holes in a *port*. **2.** One of the wires attached to a magnet on the head of a *dot-matrix printer*. Each pin is matched to an electromagnet. When the printer sends a current to the electromagnet, it creates an electromagnetic field that repels the magnet on the pin and sends the pin against an inked ribbon to print a dot on the paper. The greater the number of pins in a dot-matrix printer, the higher the *resolution*. **3.** One of the plastic sprockets on a *dot-matrix printer*. The pins fit into the holes along the edges of the paper and hold the paper in place. **4.** One of the prongs at the bottom of a *chip*. The pins connect the chip to the *printed circuit board*.

pin feed A mechanism for advancing continuous-form paper through a printer by means of two *pin*-studded rollers at the ends of the platen. The pins catch matching holes along the edges of the paper.

piracy The copying and distribution of software to unauthorized users. Some software has *copy protection*, which acts as a deterrent but is not foolproof against those with enough skill to circumvent it. Some software companies have responded to piracy with incentives for purchasing, such as documentation, upgrades, and support; and lawsuits against those who deal in large-scale piracy. Still other software developers make shareware.

pitch In word processing, the number of printed *characters* per inch. In *proportional pitch* fonts, pitch is an average. Ten pitch, for example, would mean an average of ten characters per inch in proportional pitch, or precisely ten characters per inch in *fixed pitch*.

pixel [PIK-sel] or **pel** [pel] Acronyms for **picture element.** The smallest image-forming unit of a display screen. A display screen is divided into millions of tiny dots of light called pixels, arranged in rows and columns. When you type a character or draw a line on-screen, the computer turns the pixels on in a specific pattern to render the image. If a pixel has only two color values (for example, black and white) it can be encoded by one *bit* of information. Colors or shades of gray can be displayed by increasing the number of bits used to represent each pixel. An 8-bit color *monitor*, for instance, uses 8 bits for each pixel, making it possible to display 256 different colors or shades of gray. Technically, an image of 2 colors is called a *bit map*, and an image of more than 2 colors is called a pixel map. See illustration. See also *convergence, resolution.*

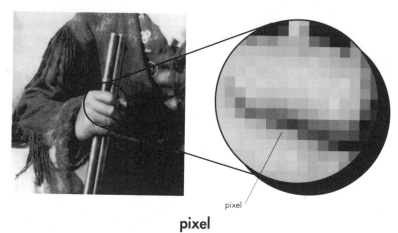

pixel

pixel

plasma display A kind of *flat-panel display* used in some *laptop* computers. Most plasma displays produce orange images on a black background. Research is being conducted on ways to make color plasma displays, which, if they prove practical, might be used in high-definition television screens.

platform   The part of a computer system that is perceived as most fundamental and with which any additional hardware and software must be compatible. Thus, one could refer to a Macintosh or IBM PC platform, but one might also consider an *operating system* to be part of the platform.

platter   One of the round metal plates inside a *hard disk*. The platters are coated with a magnetic film containing scattered iron particles. Data is encoded by the alignment of the iron particles in a magnetic field. Each platter has two *read/write heads*, one on each side. See illustration at *hard disk*.

plot   To draw an image mapped onto a grid so that each point in the image can be located in relation to the *x-axes, y-axes,* and sometimes *z-axes.*

plotter   An output *device* that physically draws by moving a pen. The computer tells the plotter how the graphics *map* on to *x-axes* and *y-axes.* In many plotters, the paper moves along one axis while the pen moves along the other.

plug   A *connector* linking two *devices.*

plug-compatible   Being a hardware device that can connect without modification to a computer or device made by a different company. For example, a plug-compatible modem can be plugged into a computer without the cables having to be rewired.

PMS   See **Pantone Matching System.**

point   *v.* In a *graphical user interface,* to move a *pointer* to an item you plan to select.
—*n.*   **1.** In typography, *word processing,* and *desktop publishing,* approximately $\frac{1}{72}$ of an inch, used to measure *character* height and *leading* between lines of text.   **2.** In *graphics,* a *pixel.*   **3.** In *graphics,* a unique location where two axes meet in a geometric figure. For example, you can identify the center of a circle as a point.

pointer 1. In a *graphical user interface,* a symbol appearing on a *display screen* to show where *input* will appear next. A pointer also lets the user *select* a *command* by *clicking* with a *mouse* or pressing the *Enter key* when the pointer is on the appropriate *button* or *option.* You can move the pointer with a *mouse.* Pointers often have the form of arrows. See illustration at *graphical user interface.* **2.** In *programming* and *database management systems,* a variable that gives the memory *address* of a piece of data.

pointing device An *input device* with which you can move a *cursor* or a *pointer.* Common pointing devices are *mice, joysticks, light pens,* and *trackballs.*

pop 1. In *programming,* to access an item from a *stack* and so remove it from the *stack.* See also *push.* **2.** To select one of two or more overlapping *windows* so that it becomes the uppermost window on the screen.

pop-up utility A *memory resident* program that can be accessed from within any *application* by pressing a *hot key.* See also *desk accessory, terminate and stay resident.*

pop-up window A *window* that appears on the screen and offers a *menu* when you select a particular *option* or press a particular *function key.* As soon as you choose one of the *commands* from the menu, the pop-up window vanishes. See also *pull-down menu.*

port A place where *data* can pass into or out of a *CPU* (central processing unit), computer, or *peripheral.* In the case of computers and peripherals, a port is generally a socket into which a *connector* can be plugged. In the case of microprocessors, a port is a particular point in *memory* reserved for incoming and outgoing data. See also *parallel port, SCSI, serial port.*

portable 1. Designating *software* that is capable of running on two or more kinds of computers or with two or more kinds of *operating systems; machine-independent.* **2.** Designating *hardware* that is capable of being carried around. The first computers termed portable weighed more than 25 pounds. Today most people would not consider anything heavier than a *laptop* truly portable.

portrait   Of or relating to a mode in which a page is oriented so that it is taller than it is wide. Most *documents* are printed in portrait mode. See also *landscape*.

POST   [post]   Acronym for **power-on self-test.** A set of operations stored in *ROM* (read-only memory) that tests each of a computer's components every time it is turned on. If the POST detects a problem, it will display an error message on the screen (if possible) and issue a beep or series of beeps as a warning in case the problem is in the monitor. If the POST does not detect any problems, the computer begins to *boot*, or load the *operating system*.

posterize   In *graphics* and *desktop publishing*, to transform an image into a starker version by rounding all tonal values to a smaller number of possible values. An example is printing an image in black and white only, eliminating any shades of gray.

PostScript   A trademark for a high-level, object-oriented *page description language* used to print high-resolution text and graphics. PostScript is used most often with *laser printers*, but it can be adapted to run on any kind of printer. PostScript uses *outline fonts* that are considerably smoother and better-looking than *bit-mapped fonts*. PostScript fonts are *scalable*; that is, they can be scaled to any desired size without distortions. PostScript fonts will also print at the full resolution offered by the printer. See illustration at *outline font*.

PowerBook   A trademark for any of a group of Macintosh laptop computers first released in 1992. All PowerBook computers have a built-in *trackball*, and later versions come with an *internal modem* and an internal audio recorder.

power down   To turn a computer or other device off.

power supply   The electrical device that converts the alternating current (AC) of standard U.S. outlets to the lower-voltage direct current (DC) a computer requires. Most computer power supplies provide between 5 and 12 volts and anywhere from 90 to 250 watts. The higher the wattage, the more powerful the computer and the more *peripherals* it can support. Most modern computers that support peripherals require a power supply of at least 200 watts.

power up   To turn a computer or other device on.

power user   An experienced computer user who feels comfortable with the most complicated features of *applications* and learns new applications relatively quickly, but who is not necessarily a programmer.

ppm   Abbreviation of **pages per minute.**

precision   The exactness with which a number is represented in *memory*. Precision depends on the number of *bits* allotted to a number; the more bits are allotted, the more digits can be used to represent a fraction. Some systems for representing floating-point numbers distinguish between "double precision" and "single precision." Double precision allots twice as many bits to a number as single precision.

presentation graphics   A kind of *graphics* geared to business presentations of statistical information and featuring a wide variety of graphs and charts including pie charts, flow charts, and bar graphs. Presentation graphics lets you insert titles, labels, text, and *clip art* to make a graph or chart clearer and more interesting. Presentation graphics programs come with decorative *fonts* and usually have a clip art *library*. They often take advantage of color graphics. You can usually *import* data from *spreadsheets* and *databases*, and also *export* charts and graphs into *documents* created with other applications. Once you have made a set of charts and graphs, you can print them, present them on a *display screen,* or send them by *modem* or *floppy disk* to a company that will make slides or a film from them.

Presentation Manager   A trademark for a *graphical user interface* (GUI) that provides a windowing *environment* for the *OS/2* operating system. Presentation Manager is distinct from *Microsoft Windows,* the graphical user interface that runs under the *DOS* operating system. Presentation Manager has many of the same features as the GUI on Macintosh computers, such as *pull-down menus,* multiple on-screen *windows,* and *desk accessories.*

preview   In word processing, a feature that allows the user to format a *document* for the printer and then view it on the display screen instead of printing it. The user can check to see if the appearance of the printed document will be satisfactory or not and can reset margins, spacing, and so on before printing. If the word processor is a *WYSIWYG* (what you see is what you get), the display screen always shows the document as it will appear printed, and previewing is unnecessary. Also . called *page preview.* See also *greeking, thumbnail.*

primary storage   The computer's *RAM* (random-access memory). Primary storage is directly accessible to the computer's *CPU,* unlike *mass storage* devices such as disk drives and tapes, which are sometimes referred to as *secondary storage.*

print   To send a *document* to the printer in order to obtain a *hard copy;* to route *output* to a printer rather than to a disk file.

printed circuit board   Abbreviated **PCB**   A flat plastic or fiberglass board on which electrically conductive circuits have been etched or laminated. *Chips* and other electronic components are mounted on the circuits. Computers consist of one or more printed circuit boards, usually called *cards* or *adapters.* The board that contains the *CPU* is typically called the *motherboard.* See illustration.

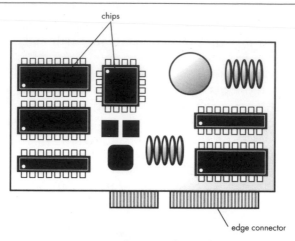

chips

edge connector

printed circuit board

printer A device for printing text and graphics, especially onto paper. Table 20 compares features of various kinds of printers. See also *daisy wheel printer, dot-matrix printer, impact printer, ink-jet printer, laser printer, line printer, liquid-crystal shutter printer, nonimpact printer, thermal printer, thermal wax printer*. See illustration at *computer*.

Table 20. Common Printer Types

Type	Letter-Quality?	Relative Speed	Other Characteristics
Dot-matrix printer	No	Usually has three speeds (higher speed means lower quality)	• Can print on multilayer forms • Limited font availability
Daisy wheel printer	Yes	Slow	• Can print on multilayer forms • Daisy wheel must be changed manually to change fonts • No graphics capability
Line printer	No	Very fast	• Usually used in business offices to serve many computers • Extremely noisy
Laser printer; Liquid-crystal shutter printer	Yes	Fast	• Unlimited font availability

Table 20. Common Printer Types (continued)

Type	Letter-Quality?	Relative Speed	Other Characteristics
Ink-jet printer	Yes	Slow (often has faster draft-quality speed)	• Fonts readily available • Some models are portable • Some models can print in several colors • Ink can smear or bleed
Thermal printer	No	Moderate	• Often comes built into many fax machines and adding machines; also sold separately as a label printer • Paper is slippery and tends to discolor over time
Thermal wax printer	No	Slow	• Usually can print in several colors fairly high quality • Black-and-white portable models available

Printer Control Language   See **PCL.**

printer driver   A program that enables a computer to work and communicate with a particular brand and model of printer. See also *Chooser, driver.*

printer font   A *font* that is only available for use by a printer and cannot be displayed on-screen. If text is formatted with a printer font, it is displayed on-screen using a default *screen font.* You must wait until you print to see what the printer fonts used in a document look like. Printer fonts can be built into the printer (*resident fonts*), *downloaded* from disk into the printer's memory, or stored in a *font cartridge.* Users of Macintosh computers or Microsoft Windows who may wish to avoid the discrepancy between screen and printer fonts can buy Adobe Type Manager (ATM) or Apple's TrueType *outline fonts,* which look the same on-screen as when printed.

printout   Printed output of text or data; *hard copy.*

Print Screen key   Abbreviated **Prt Sc**   A key on many IBM PC and compatible computer keyboards that when pressed sends whatever text and graphics are currently on the display screen to the printer. It works under *DOS* but may not be supported in all applications. It can be a handy feature. For example, you can list all the files in a *directory* on the screen with the DOS command DIR and then obtain a *hard copy* of the list by pressing the Print Screen key.

print server   See **server.**

print spooler   See **spooler.**

process   *n.*   **1.** A program.   **2.** A part of a program that does a single task.
   —*v.* To perform an operation, such as sorting or calculating, on data.

processor   **1.** See **microprocessor.**   **2.** See **CPU.**

program   *v.* To write a set of instructions that a computer can execute.
   —*n.* A set of instructions that a computer can execute. A program is a sequence of directions, called *statements*, that specify exactly what the computer needs to do to accomplish a predetermined task. A program is written in a *programming language*, a specially constructed vocabulary and set of rules for instructing a computer. Generally, one programs in a *high-level language*, such as *Pascal, C, BASIC,* or *FORTRAN.* Programs can also be written in *assembly language*, a *low-level language* one step removed from the *machine language* understood by the computer.
   Programming instructions are often referred to as *code.* The program as written by the programmer is called the *source code.* A program that has been translated into machine language and is ready to run is known as an "executable program" or "executable code." *Software* that you purchase consists of one or more executable programs.

program file   A file that contains an *application* or program. A *data file* contains work created with an application or program.

programmable read-only memory   See **PROM.**

programmer   One who writes computer *programs.*

programming language   An artificial *language* consisting of a
vocabulary along with grammatical rules used to write a set
of instructions that can be translated into *machine language*
and then executed by a computer. Machine language is the
language the computer actually understands. Each different
type of *CPU* has its own unique machine language. English
and other *natural languages* are not programming languages
because they cannot be translated into machine language.

The term programming language usually refers to *high-
level languages,* such as *FORTRAN, C, COBOL, Pascal,* or
BASIC. Lying below high-level languages are *assembly languages,* which are similar to machine languages. Programmers
can also program in assembly languages.

Lying above high-level languages are *fourth-generation lan-*

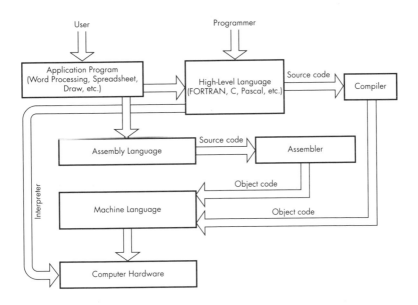

programming language

guages, usually called 4GLs. 4GLs are the closest to natural languages.

Regardless of the language in which it's written, the program must be translated into machine language. This is done by either *compiling* the program or interpreting the program. See illustration.

PROLOG [PRO-log] Acronym for **programming in logic.** A *high-level language* widely used for programming in the field of *artificial intelligence*, especially *expert systems*. It was developed in the early 1970s by Alain Colmerauer and Philippe Roussel. PROLOG works with the logical relationships between pieces of data rather than with their mathematical relationships. A program is constructed as a set of facts and a set of rules for deriving new facts.

PROM [prom] Acronym for **programmable read-only memory.** A type of *ROM* (read-only memory) chip onto which data can be written, or programmed, only once. PROMs retain the contents of their memory even when the computer is turned off. PROMs are programmed at the factory for use with a particular computer. Unlike ROMs, PROMs can also be manufactured as blank memory, and data can be programmed onto the chip by the user with a special device called a "PROM programmer" or "PROM burner." Programming a PROM chip is often referred to as "burning" the PROM. An *EPROM* (erasable programmable read-only memory) is a type of PROM that can be erased and reprogrammed.

prompt A symbol, or sometimes a phrase, that appears on a display screen to indicate that the computer is ready to receive input. Depending on which program is running, the symbol could be a colon (:), a backslash (\), a greater than sign (>), or one of various others. Some programs will wait indefinitely for input; others will resume execution after a *timeout*, a set interval that passes without user input.

proportional font A *font* in which the characters have varying *pitches*, or widths. See also *fixed pitch, monospace font.*

proportional pitch   The allocation of space of varying widths to different characters in a font. Proportional pitch contrasts with *fixed pitch*, in which each character is given a space of the same width. In a proportional pitch font, a narrow letter such as *i* is given a smaller width than a wide letter such as *m*. Also called *proportional spacing*.

proprietary   Privately owned, especially by an individual or corporation under a trademark or patent. A proprietary product, program, or technology cannot be duplicated unless an explicit license is purchased from its owner. In order to legally use proprietary software, for example, one must either purchase it or obtain permission from the owner.

Apple maintains a proprietary *architecture* for its *Macintosh* computers. No Macintosh *clones* are possible without a license from Apple. IBM, on the other hand, chose an *open architecture* for its *IBM PC* computers, a decision that spawned the huge industry of *IBM PC-compatible* computing.

protected mode   An operating mode available on the Intel 80286 and later *microprocessors*. It supports more advanced features than *real mode*, the *default* operating mode of *Intel microprocessors* (including the earlier 8088 and 8086). Protected mode supports *multitasking* by allocating each program a certain area of memory that other programs cannot access. Each program is thus protected from interference from other programs running simultaneously. Such interference can cause a computer to *crash* in real mode.

Protected mode also provides for *extended memory*—the 80286 can access up to 16MB (megabytes), and the 80386 and later microprocessors can have up to 4GB (*gigabytes*). This contrasts with real mode, which can directly access only 1MB of *RAM*. Protected mode also features over 1GB of *virtual memory*.

The *DOS* operating system cannot take advantage of protected mode. The *OS/2* operating system runs in protected mode, as does *UNIX* and the operating environment *Microsoft Windows*.

protocol   A standard procedure for regulating data transmission between computers or between devices such as *modems*. See also *communications protocol*.

Prt Sc   Abbreviation of **Print Screen key.**

psec   Abbreviation of **picosecond.**

PS/2   A trademark for the second generation of IBM personal computers. The first PS/2 appeared in 1987 and was based on the Intel 8086 *microprocessor*. Recent models that use the Intel 80486 microprocessor and the *OS/2* operating system support *multitasking* and can run DOS, *Microsoft Windows*, and OS/2 applications. See also *IBM PC, Micro Channel Architecture*.

public domain software   Software that is not copyrighted and is available to users without charge or restriction. Public domain software is not the same as *shareware* or *freeware*. Shareware is copyrighted and users are asked to pay a fee to the author. Freeware is also copyrighted but is given away for free.

puck   An *input device* that resembles a *mouse* but has a clear plastic section that is marked with cross hairs. It is used on a *digitizer* to trace accurately a hard copy of a graphical image into a form that can be used by the computer. Pucks are often used in architectural and engineering applications.

pull-down menu   A *pop-up window* that appears directly beneath the item selected on a *menu bar*. Also called *drop-down menu*. See illustration at *menu*.

push   In programming, to add an item to a stack. See also *pop, stack*.

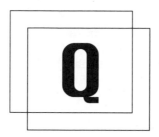

QBE   Abbreviation of **query by example.**

QIC   [kwik]   Acronym for **quarter-inch cartridge.**   A *tape* cartridge in which the magnetic tape is $^1/_4$ inch wide, used especially for *backups*. Such cartridges may be the same size as standard cassette tapes or they may be miniature. The manufacturers of these tapes have established a set of standards for identifying and distinguishing their different sizes. See table at *access time.*

query   A request to a *database* for *information*. For example, if you have a database with the prices of widgets from every company in the United States and China for every month from 1993 to 2003, you might send a query asking for a list of companies selling widgets in a certain price range in January 1994.

query by example   Abbreviated **QBE**   A form of sending *queries* to a *database* in which the *database management system* gives a template with all the *fields* for the database. You then enter any restrictions under the field to which they apply. For example, if your database has names, addresses, telephone numbers, and birthdays of your friends, you could type in "March" under the field "birthday" to elicit a list of the names, addresses, telephone numbers, and birthdays of all your friends with birthdays in March.

query language The *language* used by a *database management system* for *queries*. For example, if you want a list of the names, addresses, telephone numbers, and birthdays of friends with birthdays in March or April from a *database* called B-DAYS & ADDRESSES, you may have to type SELECT ALL FROM B-DAYS & ADDRESSES WHERE B-DAY = MARCH OR B-DAY = APRIL.

queue *n.* **1.** In programming, a place in which *data* items can be stored and from which they can be removed only in the same order in which they were placed there. See also *stack*. **2.** A *buffer* that stores *commands* waiting for the computer or device to attend to them. For example, if you tell the computer to print several documents, it will begin printing one document and put the commands to print each of the others in the queue until it can get to them.
—*v.* To place *commands* in a *buffer* until the computer or device can attend to them. For example, if you tell the computer to print several documents, the operating system will queue the commands to print each document until it can carry them out.

QuickDraw A trademark for an *object-oriented* system for displaying graphics and text that is used by all *Macintosh* computers and programs and by some printers. QuickDraw enables applications for Macintosh computers to create *dialog boxes*, icons, menus, and the other features that distinguish the Macintosh *graphical user interface*. Different versions of QuickDraw have different color capabilities.

QuickTime A trademark for an extension of Apple's System 7 operating system that incorporates digital video and other time-based data. QuickTime is often used in *multimedia* applications.

quit To turn off a program with the appropriate command, usually QUIT or EXIT, so as to save all your data and *configuration* choices. While you work, many programs store your data in temporary *buffers* that may get lost if you turn off the computer without quitting. When you quit, the computer asks you to save anything that hasn't yet been saved on your hard disk, floppy disk, or other storage device. It then erases any extra copies from the buffer so as not to waste memory with unnecessary copies.

QWERTY keyboard [KWUR-tee] A keyboard having the traditional arrangement of keys on a standard English *keyboard* or typewriter. The name comes from the letters of the first six keys on the left side at the top row of the keyboard. Several alternative keyboards have been designed to facilitate faster typing, of which the best known is the *Dvorak keyboard*. See illustration.

QWERTY keyboard

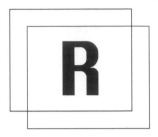

radio button   In a *graphical user interface*, a *button* representing one of a group of mutually exclusive options. For example, a *menu* may have radio buttons for various fonts. Since only one font can be selected at a time, *clicking* on a particular radio button selects that font and rejects all the others.

radix   The base number of a number system. For example, the radix is ten in the decimal system and two in the binary system.

radix point   A character that separates the integer in a mixed number from the fraction. In the number 3.14, for example, the decimal point is the radix point.

ragged   Not aligned evenly with a margin. "Ragged right" refers to text that is not aligned, or justified, along the right margin. See also *flush, justification.*

RAID   [rayd]   Acronym for **redundant array of inexpensive disks.**   A group of *disk drives* over which *data* is distributed. The disk drives are used together to facilitate faster *storage* and *retrieval* and greater data security than would be possible with a single disk drive.

RAM   [ram]   Acronym for **random-access memory.**   The main *memory* of a computer. Because RAM allows *random access*, the *central processing unit* can access the data it needs in RAM without having to go through other data first, making RAM faster than memory that offers *sequential access*. When a computer is turned on, the information from the *startup disk* is immediately loaded into RAM. Next, the operating system is loaded into RAM. Any program instructions or data to be worked with must first be moved to RAM. Any new or changed data will be stored in RAM until it can be written to a hard disk or a similar storage device. The *microprocessor* can also *write* data to RAM. Most RAM consists of *semiconductors* that provide *volatile memory*. This memory is destroyed every time the computer is turned off or experiences a power outage. See also *ROM, SIMM*.

RAM cache   A part of *RAM* set aside to facilitate access to the data that is needed most often. The RAM cache uses faster, more expensive *static RAM chips*. Every time a request for data is sent to RAM, the RAM cache intercepts the request. If the data is already in the cache, it can be sent immediately. Otherwise, the RAM cache accesses the data from the slower chips in RAM and sends it to the *microprocessor*, but also keeps a copy in case it is needed again soon. When no requests are made, the RAM cache copies and stores data from RAM *addresses* near the data most recently needed on the theory that they may be needed next. When the RAM cache is full, it erases the data that has waited the longest without being needed. Also called *memory cache*.

RAM caching   The process by which a *RAM cache* works. Also called *memory caching*.

RAM disk   A part of *RAM* configured so as to be treated as a *peripheral disk* by the *operating system*. RAM works much faster than a disk, so using a RAM disk can speed a computer up considerably. However, a RAM disk uses the same RAM that serves as the computer's *main memory*, so before setting up a RAM disk you need to be sure that you will have enough RAM left to run the software. Because RAM is *volatile memory*, anything left on a RAM disk when you turn your computer off will be lost unless you have copied it to a hard disk or some other storage device. Also called *virtual disk*.

RAM-resident   See **memory-resident**.

random access   Immediate *access* to *data* items from their *addresses*. When a data *record* that is stored in *RAM* is retrieved, for example, an electrical pulse goes directly to the address of the data requested. If the record is on a hard disk, the *head* will be positioned directly above the first *sector* with data from the record. The computer won't have to sift through extra data on the way to the record it is looking for. Also called *direct access*. See also *sequential access*.

range   In a *spreadsheet*, a set of one or more contiguous *cells* that form a rectangle and have been selected so that an operation can be performed on all of them at once. For example, if you use a spreadsheet to keep track of the prices of merchandise in a store and the price of plastic widgets has just increased by ten percent, you could select the range that gives

	A	B	C	D
1	YEAR	CANADA	FRANCE	JAPAN
2	1970	1.0103	5.5200	357.60
3	1980	1.1693	7.2250	226.63
4	1983	1.2325	7.6203	237.55
5	1985	1.3658	8.9799	238.47
6	1988	1.2306	5.9594	128.17
7	1989	1.1842	6.3802	138.07
8	1990	1.1668	5.4467	145.00
9	1991	1.1460	5.6468	134.59

range
Valid ranges

the current price of all plastic widgets and add ten percent to each cell.

One usually identifies a range by the *address* of the cells in the upper left and lower right corners. For example, B2..P7 would define a rectangle border by the cells from B2 to B7, from B7 to P7, from P2 to P7, and from B2 to P2. Also called *cell block*. See illustration.

raster graphics   The use of *bit maps* by software or hardware to create, display, or store graphics.

raster scanning   A process for creating and refreshing an image on a *display screen*. In raster scanning, the *cathode-ray tube* sends electrons across the top of the screen from the left edge to the right edge. The cathode-ray tube then begins again from the left edge, but this time it directs the electron path to begin each line slightly below the line just covered. When the electon beams reach the bottom right corner, the process begins again.

read   To get *data*, as from a *hard disk* or other *storage device*. When a computer reads a hard disk, it copies the data it needs into *RAM*. When it reads RAM, it accesses the data from RAM and proceeds to process it.

readme file   A *text file* in many programs that provides useful information not given in the manuals that come with the program. A readme file may, for example, explain how to install the program and warn about *bugs* recently discovered in the program and provide tips on how to deal with them.

read-only   Designating information that is permanently stored and can be read but not changed or deleted. It is impossible to alter the content of a read-only file, and the instructions and information contained in read-only memory (*ROM*) are also unalterable. See also *RAM, ROM*.

read/write head   See **head.**

real mode The *default* operating *mode* for IBM PC and compatible computers that uses *conventional memory* only, allows only one *program* to run at a time, and allots that program 640 *kilobytes* of *RAM*. See also *conventional memory, protected mode*.

real time **1.** The *processing* of *data* by a *computer* as rapidly as the data is input or within some small upper limit of response time, typically milliseconds or microseconds. For example, an automatic pilot must respond to data on changing flight conditions or the position of other aircraft immediately. Accordingly, automatic aircraft guidance systems must use real time. **2.** Animated *computer graphics* or *multimedia applications* in which real-life situations are simulated at the speed at which they would normally occur. For example, flight simulation *programs* used to train pilots use real time.

real-time Of or using real time, as in flight simulation or an automatic pilot. See also *real time*.

reboot To restart a *computer*. See also *cold boot, warm boot*.

recalculate To determine the value of cells in a *spreadsheet* again to reflect new data or a change in a *formula*. Some spreadsheet programs recalculate automatically whenever new data is entered or a formula is changed, while other programs have a special recalculation *command* that the user must enter, as by a *function key*.

record **1.** In *database management systems*, a single set of related *data* organized into *fields*. For example, if you have a *database* to help you keep track of personal correspondence, you might keep a record for each letter you receive. Within the record, you might have separate fields telling you when you received the letter, when it was written, what it was about, who sent it, the address of the person who wrote it, and when you replied. See also *field, report*. **2.** In certain *programming languages*, a collection of *data* set up as a unit.

recoverable error   An error that does not cause a *crash* or the loss of *data;* an error that the user, the *computer,* or the *software* can deal with so as to continue working without serious or lasting consequences.

red-green-blue monitor   See **RGB monitor.**

redirect   To direct a program to send *output* to or receive *input* from a *device* that is not the *default.* For example, the default input device is usually the keyboard or the mouse, but you could redirect the program to take input from a stylus. The default output device is the display screen, but when you print, you redirect the program to send output to your printer.

redline   In *word processing,* to mark pages in a text so that they can easily be reviewed by another person. For example, if you are writing an article with a colleague, you may want to redline your proposed changes in order to show them to your colleague later. The redlined text may appear in *boldface* or in a color that you have selected.

refresh   **1.** To renew the image on a *display screen* by renewing the flow of electrons from the *cathode ray tube.* This frequency is measured in *hertz.* **2.** To renew the *data* in *dynamic RAM* by sending a new electric pulse to recharge the *chips.*

refresh rate   The frequency with which the image on a display screen must be renewed by refreshing.

register   A temporary *storage* area in a *microprocessor.* A register holds either *bits* of data that are currently being processed or *addresses* for data that are currently being processed. If you need to add two numbers, for example, each number (or its address) will be placed in a register, and the sum will be placed in a third register. The more registers a microprocessor has, and the more bits those registers can hold, the faster the microprocessor.

relational database A *database management system* in which you enter *data* into tables and use *queries* to elicit new tables. For example, you might draw up a table with a row for every place you would like to visit and columns showing the best time of year to go, friends you hope to see, tourist attractions, and approximate transportation costs. Then you might draw up another table with a row for each of your friends and columns showing their addresses and phone numbers, how many nights they could put you up for, and what kind of gifts they like. If you were planning a vacation for January, you could get a table showing you where to go, transportation costs, friends you could stay with, their phone numbers, and what presents to bring.

relational operator An *operator*, such as =, >, or <, that is used to compare two or more values. Table 21 lists relational operator symbols and their meanings.

Table 21. Relational Operators

Symbol	Meaning
=	Equal to
<>	Not equal to
>	Greater than
>=	Greater than or equal to
<	Less than
<=	Less than or equal to

relative address An *address* expressed as the distance between two locations rather than as a specific point in space. For example, "three cells up and two columns to the left" is a relative address and therefore makes sense only if a starting point has been established, in contrast to "cell 32," which identifies one cell without reference to any other.

release number The number that identifies a new release of a *program*. In general, integers identify versions to which major changes have been made and decimals identify versions to which only minor changes have been made. Thus, the difference between versions 2.5 and 3.0 of a given program would be greater than the difference between versions 3.0 and 3.5.

remote   Controlled, operated, or used from a distance, as by *modem* or over cables.

remote control   The control of a computer, a device, an activity, or a program from a distance. For example, certain gadgets allow you to turn on a light inside your car or house by remote control.

remote control program   A program that provides you with *remote control* over one computer from another computer. For example, a remote control program might let you call up a database in your office from a laptop during a business trip.

removable cartridge   A portable plastic or metal cartridge with 45MB-200MB of memory. Removable cartridges are almost as easy to disconnect, transport, and connect elsewhere as *floppy disks*, but they can store much more *data*.

replace   *n.* See **search and replace**.
—*v.* To do a *search and replace* so as to change a given *string* of *characters*.

report   *Information* that has been output from a *database* in response to a *query* and organized and presented according to particular specifications. For example, if you have a database that gives the dates and costs of home repair projects and specifies the type of repair, you could request a report showing dates and costs of all repairs in the calendar year 1993, arranged alphabetically by the type of repair. See also *database management system, report generator.*

report generator   A program that creates *reports* from a *database* in response to a *query*. Most *database management systems* come with a report generator. The report generator generally lets you specify the form of the report, which may be a table, a graph, or a chart, for example. You can also usually create your own design for the report by selecting a *font*, requesting *pagination*, and writing headers and footers. The report generator lets you save both the report itself and the design, which you may want to use with another report.

report writer   See **report generator.**

reserved word   A word or *string* of *characters* that has been assigned a particular meaning in a program, system, or *programming language* and that therefore cannot be used in other circumstances, as in naming a file in a word processing program. For example, "then" is a reserved word in *BASIC*; you may call a variable "neht" but you cannot call it "then". The file name "PRN" is reserved in *DOS*; you cannot call a file "PRN". Also called *keyword*.

reset button   A button, key, or sequence of keystrokes pressed to restart the *computer*.

resident font   A *font* stored in a printer's *ROM*. All *laser printers* come with one or more resident fonts, but additional fonts can usually be added to a printer's repertoire by downloading *soft fonts*. Also called *built-in font, internal font.* See also *soft font*.

resolution   The clarity or fineness of detail that can be distinguished in an image, especially one produced by a *monitor* or *printer*.
   For printers, resolution is generally measured in dots per inch, or *dpi*. The higher the dpi, the sharper the resolution. A low-quality dot-matrix printer may print at 125 dpi, and a laser printer at 600 dpi, but professional typesetters will print at 1,200 dpi or better.
   For monitors, resolution is measured as the number of *pixels*, or dots, horizontally displayed, and the number of lines vertically displayed on the screen. The denser the pixels, the clearer the image will be. A 640 × 480 pixel screen, typical for

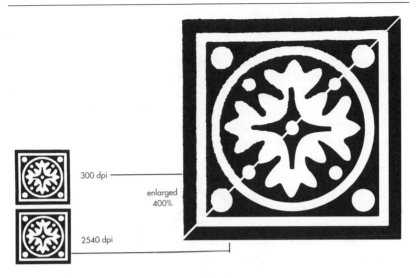

300 dpi

enlarged
400%

2540 dpi

resolution
In dots per inch

a *VGA* monitor in *graphics mode*, displays 640 distinct dots
on each of 480 lines, or about 3 million pixels. A *Super VGA*
monitor has a resolution of 1,024 × 768, or almost 8 million
pixels, more than $2^{1}/_{2}$ times the resolution of the VGA monitor.

The terms *high resolution* and *low resolution* are often
used to describe printers and monitors. The meanings of these
classifications shift as the technology improves. See illustration.

restore **1.** To reverse the *compression* of a *backup file* in order
to work with the file. For example, if your original file
becomes *corrupted*, then you will need to work from your
backup file, but if the file is compressed, you must first
restore it. **2.** In *graphical user interfaces*, to bring back a
window to its previous size after it has been shrunk.

retrieve To access information or a file, as from a database or
storage device. When you sit down at your computer to revise
a document, you begin by retrieving the file containing your
document.

return   1. In *word processing*, a *command* that moves the *cursor* to the next line on the *display screen*. In most programs, *soft returns* are entered automatically whenever you reach the end of the line. If you want an additional line break, however, you must enter a *hard return*.   **2.** A *command* that enters or confirms another command. For example, when you select an *option* from a menu, you first move your cursor to that option and then either *click* or press the *Return key* to enter your selection.

Return key   1. The *key* used to enter or confirm a *command*. The program receives and responds to your command only after you press the Return key.   **2.** In *word processing*, the *key* used to enter a *hard return*. Also called *Enter key*.

reverse video   The reversal of background and foreground colors on a *display screen* to highlight certain *characters*. For example, if your screen normally displays white characters on a blue background, highlighted characters may appear in blue on a white background. Also called *inverse video*.

RGB monitor   Abbreviation of **red-green-blue monitor.** A *monitor* with a *cathode-ray tube* that houses three electron guns directing separate streams of electrons at the screen to represent the colors red, green, and blue. An RGB monitor creates other colors by combining these three.

right justify   To *justify* a text on the right margin, so that the right edge of the text is even. If you write your name and the date in the upper right-hand corner of a paper, for example, you may wish to right justify that part of the text so that the date will line up under your name with the year ending right under your last name. See also *justification*.

ring   One of the three principal *topologies* for a local area network, in which all computers and devices, known as *nodes*, are arranged in a circle and connected by cables. *Data* is passed in one direction along the ring from one computer or device to the next. Each computer or device renews the data with a new electric pulse and sends it on its way. When the data reaches its destination, the computer or device to which it is addressed copies it before sending it to the next *node* in the network. When it returns to the sender, the sender takes it out of circulation. See also *bus, star, token-ring network.* See illustration at *network.*

RISC [risk] Acronym for **reduced instruction set computer.** A design that restricts the number of *instructions* that a *microprocessor* can handle. The more instructions a micro-processor can handle, the slower the execution of each instruction. RISC *architecture* speeds up processing by eliminating the instructions that are needed least often. When they are needed, they must be composed from the smaller group of instructions selected for inclusion. See also *CISC.*

robotics The branch of computer science that applies *artificial intelligence* and engineering to the creation and programming of robots able to detect and react to sensory *input* and designed to perform tasks previously carried out by people. Robots are now being used to perform some manufacturing operations and to carry out certain tasks, such as cleaning toxic waste sites, that would pose serious danger to humans.

ROM [rom] Acronym for **read-only memory.** *Nonvolatile memory* consisting of *chips* that store data that cannot be changed, expanded, or erased and that was installed when the chips were manufactured. ROM stores the *BIOS* and sometimes parts of the *operating system.* See also *EPROM, PROM, RAM.* See table at *access time.*

roman A *font* style marked by upright letters with serifs and in which the vertical lines are thicker than the horizontal lines. See also *italic.* See illustration at *font family.*

root directory The uppermost *directory* in a hierarchy of directories or *folders;* the *directory* from which all other *directo-*

ries or *folders* branch out. For example, when you format a *floppy disk* in *DOS*, DOS sets up a root directory marked by a back slash. You can create folders or other directories and subdirectories within this directory, or you can place your files directly into the root directory. See also *directory*. See illustration at *hierarchical*.

routine A set of programming *instructions* designed to perform a specific, limited task within a larger program. A routine usually has an *identifier* that serves as a *command* to execute the routine. Each *module* in a program may consist of several routines. See also *function, subroutine*.

rule **1.** In *word processing, graphics,* and *desktop publishing* programs, a straight vertical or horizontal line used to set a graphics image or a small section of text, such as a column or a footnote, apart from the rest of the page. **2.** In *expert systems*, a conditional *statement* that tells the program how to respond to particular *input*.

ruler In *word processing, desktop publishing,* and *graphics* programs, a short *window* covering the width of the *display screen* and containing a line with inches, *picas,* or *points* marked off and indicators for margins and tab settings. In many programs, these indicators can be moved to adjust the margins and tab settings.

run **1.** To process or execute a program or an instruction. **2.** To be processed or executed. For example, *multitasking* allows different programs to run at the same time.

runtime error An error that occurs while a *program* is *running*. A runtime error may result from insufficient *memory* or from a *bug* in the program. Runtime errors are generally *recoverable*.

runtime version A limited version of a *program*, usually an *operating environment* or *interpreter*, sold with another *application* for the sole use of that *application*. A particular *graph-*

ics program, for example, may run only in a certain operating system, but naturally its developer would like to be able to sell it to people who do not have that particular operating system. The developer can order a runtime version of the operating system that supports this graphics program only and sell the runtime version together with the graphics program.

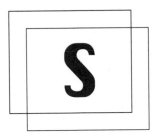

sans serif   Of, relating to, or being a *font* that does not have *serifs*. Helvetica and Geneva are sans serif fonts.

save   To copy a file or files from a *buffer* to a *disk* or other long-term *storage device*. While you work, everything you do stays in a buffer, but since the buffer is *volatile memory*, it can easily be *erased*, as by a power failure. The more often you save, the less work you can lose in case of a *crash*. While floppy and hard disks can also be destroyed, they are *non-volatile* and therefore far more durable than *RAM*. Saving to more than one storage device increases the chances that data will not be lost.

scalable   Designating a computer file, as an audio or a video file, for example, that can be played at varying rates and levels of quality in accordance with the resources of the computer being used.

scalable font   A *font* whose size can be changed freely without changing the proportions of the characters. This means that you do not need a new font for every size you want to use; you can enlarge or reduce the same font and it will look just as good. *PostScript* and *TrueType* are scalable fonts for *printing*. The *screen fonts* for *graphical user interfaces* are also scalable fonts.

scaling   1. The process of adjusting the size of an image or *font* without changing its proportions.   2. The process of adjusting the scale of an image, such as a graph or design, so as to change the perspective from which the image is viewed. Many *presentation graphics programs*, for example, allow scaling of the *y-axis* on bar graphs to highlight certain features.

scanner   See **optical scanner.**

scheduler   1. In an operating system, a program that allocates the use of such resources as the CPU or a printer so that several *tasks* can be handled at the same time without interfering with each other.   2. A program that helps people using a *network* schedule meetings. The scheduler compares the relevant calendars, sends out invitations, and distributes follow-up reminders. Some schedulers can also reserve conference rooms, slide projectors, and similar items.

scientific notation   A way of representing a number, especially a very large or a very small number, by showing it as the product of a power of ten and a number between one and ten. For example, the number 23,456,000,000,000,000 would be written in scientific notation as 2.3456×10^{16} or as 2.3456E16, with "E" standing for "ten to the *exponential* power of." Similarly, .0000007 would be written as 7×10^{-7} or as 7E–7. Scientific notation is widely used in science and engineering because it allows precise calculations with very large or very small numbers. Table 22 lists some example of numbers in scientific notation. See also *floating-point notation*.

Table 22. Examples of Scientific Notation

Scientific Notation	Decimal Expansion
1.2345E4	12,345.0
1.0E–5	0.00001
–6.789E3	–6,789.0
–9.0E–2	–0.09

SCRAM [skram] Acronym for **static random-access memory.** See **static RAM.**

scrapbook A *desk accessory* that allows you to save frequently used pictures or passages of text. The scrapbook can store multiple images. You can cut, copy, or paste images from the scrapbook into documents created with most application programs.

scratch pad A section of *memory*, especially a high-speed memory circuit in a *microprocessor*, used for temporary *storage* of preliminary data during processing. Data held in the scratch pad is erased when the *computer* is turned off.

screen See **display screen.**

screen capture The act or process of sending a copy of whatever is on the *display screen* to the disk for storage or to the printer to print out. A screen capture converts graphics to a *bit map* and text to *ASCII* code. See also *screen dump.*

screen dump The act or process of sending a copy of whatever is on the *display screen* to the printer.

screen flicker The appearance of a flicker or other distortion on the *display screen*. A low *refresh rate* is the most frequent cause of screen flicker. *Monitors* use phosphors of various durations to create the display, and the fading of these phosphors may also give the appearance of screen flicker.

screen font A *bit-mapped font* used to show text on the *dis-*

play screen. Screen fonts are designed to look as similar as possible to the *printer fonts* used by the same program, but printers, especially laser printers, can often achieve higher *resolutions* than monitors.

screen saver   A *utility program* designed to protect *monitors* from *ghosting*. Some screen savers work by substituting animated graphics for whatever was left on the *display screen*. The animation is too fast to give any of the images displayed a chance to become etched into the screen. Other screen savers cause the image on the screen to fade significantly or even entirely, so as to leave the screen blank until it is reactivated by a resumption of processing. A screen saver can be activated manually or automated so that it runs whenever the display is left unchanged for a specified period of time.

script   A series of *instructions* that can be written from within a program in order to accomplish a particular task and that can be launched easily, as by *clicking* on a *button*, and executed without further *input* from the user. Scripts must sometimes be written in a script language, a relatively simple *high-level programming language*, such as *HyperTalk*. See also *HyperTalk, macro.*

scroll   To move a *file* within a *window* so as to change what can be seen in the window. For example, you may originally see only the top half of your page, but if you scroll down, you will see the middle half, losing a quarter at the top and at the bottom. You can also view the bottom part of one page and the top part of the next page together on one *screen*. You can scroll vertically or horizontally by using the *arrow keys* and the *Page Up* and *Page Down keys* or by using the *scroll bar.*

scroll bar   In *graphical user interfaces*, a narrow bar that appears on the side of or beneath a *window* to let you *scroll* by *clicking* or *dragging* with the *mouse*. A scroll bar will generally have arrows at each end, and by clicking on an arrow you can scroll a *document* or *menu* in the direction in which the arrow points. Scroll bars usually also have a box indicating the relative position of the document within the window. You move a document by dragging the box along the scroll bar in the desired direction. See illustration at *desktop*.

Scroll Lock key   A *key* that is pressed to change the effect of the *cursor control keys* as determined by the *application*. In some applications, for example, when the Scroll Lock key is depressed the cursor control keys scroll the document rather than moving the *cursor*.

SCSI   [SKUZ-ee]   Acronym for **small computer systems interface.**   A standard *parallel interface* for rapid *data* transmission. As many as seven *devices* can be connected to one SCSI port. Because only one transmission can be made at a time, each device is assigned an *address* reflecting the priority to be given to transmissions to and from that device relative to transmissions to and from the other devices connected to the same port. The SCSI then dispatches data in priority order. Even though some data must wait to be dispatched, it is still transmitted faster over a SCSI than over most other *interfaces* because a SCSI can handle up to 32 megabits per second. *Hard disks* are the *peripherals* most often connected over a SCSI. *Macintosh* computers, some *IBM PC* and compatible computers, and many *UNIX* systems use SCSI interfaces.

SCSI-2   A version of *SCSI* that can transmit 10MB–20MB of data per second.

scuzzy   See **SCSI.**

search   **1.** In *word processing* and *desktop publishing*, to find and review every occurrence of a *string* of *characters* in a *document*. For example, if you were writing a review of a new book and you wanted to make sure you had underlined the book's title at each occurrence, a search for the title would allow you to underline those occurrences that you had missed the first time.   **2.** A procedure for *searching*.

search and replace   *n.* In *word processing* and *desktop publishing*, a procedure for changing a *string* of *characters* to a different string of characters throughout a document. For example, you might want to *replace* "don't" with "do not" in a letter. In some programs, the search and replace feature comes with an option to review and confirm the change each time. While this obviously takes much longer, it can prevent you from accidentally making a change you don't want to make. For example, if you used the phrase "do's and don'ts" in your letter, you might not want it to become "do's and do nots."

—*v.* To do a *search and replace.*

secondary storage See **mass storage.**

sector An area on a *disk* that contains the smallest addressable unit of information. When a disk is formatted, the *operating system* divides it into sectors and *tracks*. Tracks are concentric circles around the disk; sectors are segments within each circle. Generally, each track contains the same number of sectors. The operating system and disk drive know where information is stored on the disk by noting its track and sector number, or *address*.

Some hard disk drives use *zoned-bit recording*. Here tracks on the outside have more sectors than tracks on the inside. See also *bad sector*. See illustration.

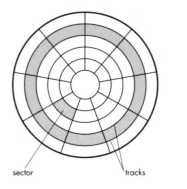
sector   tracks

ZONED-BIT RECORDING

sector
Sectors and tracks

security   The prevention of unauthorized use of a program or device. On *networks* or any other system where more than one user can access programs and data, security usually involves the use of *passwords* to identify authorized users, and *encryption*, which renders data unintelligible to unauthorized users. See also *encryption, password.*

seek time   The amount of time required for a disk drive's read/write *head* to move to a specific location on a disk. Seek time is expressed in milliseconds, or thousandths of a second. It differs from *access time*, the amount of time that elapses before the read/write head locates a piece of data and is ready to transfer it from the disk. See also *access time, disk drive, head.*

select   1. To choose a portion of a document, spreadsheet, or database by highlighting it, as by changing the background color, so that an operation can be performed specifically on that portion. See also *block.*   2. In a *graphical user interface,* to choose a command or action by moving the *mouse* until the *pointer* touches a specific object on the screen, and then *clicking* that object.

semantics   The meaning of a programming instruction as opposed to the *syntax,* or the rules governing its spelling and structure. The semantic rules of a programming language are violated when a command is syntactically correct but makes no sense in the context of its program.

semiconductor   1. A crystalline substance, such as silicon or germanium, having electrical conductivity that is greater than an insulator (such as rubber) but less than a good conductor (copper, for example). Computer *chips* and a variety of other electronic devices are made of semiconductor material. By adding impurities called dopants to semiconductor materials, manufacturers can precisely control the semiconductor's electrical resistance.   2. An *integrated circuit* or another device made up of semiconductor material.

sequential access   A method of storing and retrieving information in sequential order. A sequential access device must search from the beginning of a sequence of locations each time it seeks data. Sequential access contrasts with *random access*, which allows a device to access data directly, without passing through all locations preceding the one where the data is stored. See also *random access*.

serial   Of or relating to the transmission of the bits of a byte over one wire, one bit at a time. Serial communication contrasts with *parallel* communication, in which data is transmitted and received in many bits at once. See also *parallel*, *serial port*.

serial mouse   A *mouse* that is attached to the computer through a *serial port*. A *bus mouse*, on the other hand, is connected to the computer through an *expansion board*. A serial port is adequate for the limited amount of data that is transmitted by a mouse, and a serial mouse is easy to install. See also *mouse*.

serial port   A port at the back of a computer that is used for serial communication. Devices such as *modems* and *serial mice* are connected to a computer's serial port. A serial port transmits data on series—one bit of data at a time. It is often referred to as an RS-232 port. RS-232 is the Electronics Industries Association's designation for a standard for how the various connections in a serial port are to be used. The serial port contains one line for transmitting data, one line to receive data, and several other lines that signal when transmission or reception will occur and generally maintain a smooth flow of data between the computer and whatever device is attached. Also called *serial interface*.

serif   A fine line finishing off the main strokes of a letter. Typefaces without these fine lines are called *sans serif*.

server   In a *client/server network*, a computer that stores files and provides them to individual *workstations*, or clients.

Additionally, the server often controls access to peripherals such as printers and executes complex programs or tasks that the client requests. Also called *file server.*

shadowing   A technique that speeds up a computer by taking certain programs stored in the slower *ROM* (read-only memory) and copying them into the faster *RAM* (random-access memory). Although shadowing improves computer performance, it can cause a shortage of RAM, especially if you are running programs designed to use *extended memory.*

shareware   Copyrighted programs that are made available on a trial basis. Users who like the software and would like to keep using it are asked to pay a small fee to the author and are often registered so that they can receive program updates and assistance. Shareware differs from public domain software, which is not copyrighted. See also *public domain software.*

sheet-fed scanner   An *optical scanner* into which documents can be fed. In a sheet-fed scanner, the document is rolled past the scan head. A *flatbed scanner*, on the other hand, moves the scan head past a stationary page, much in the same way as a photocopier does. A sheet-fed scanner is suited for scanning unbound documents or single pages, while a flatbed scanner can handle bound books. See also *hand-held scanner.*

sheet feeder   A mechanism that feeds paper one sheet at a time. Sheet feeders are standard with laser printers and are also available for some dot-matrix printers and fax machines. Also called *cut-sheet feeder.*

shell   A program that facilitates communication between the user and the operating system, often presenting a *menu-driven* user interface that makes it easier to select files and choose and process commands. See also *DOS, Finder, MultiFinder.*

shift clicking   The act of holding down the Shift key and clicking the mouse button at the same time. Shift clicking can have different effects depending on what application you are using, but on Macintosh computers and in Microsoft Windows, it allows you to select more than one item from a screen.

Shift key A key on a computer keyboard that, when pressed and held down, changes letters from lowercase to uppercase. In many applications, the Shift key changes the meaning of a *function key* when the two keys are pushed at the same time. The Shift key can also change the function of *mouse* button. See also *function key, shift clicking.*

SIG [sig] Acronym for **special interest group.** A group of computer users who share an interest in a specific subject. The members of a SIG can share information and have discussions electronically, usually through a *bulletin board system,* an *on-line service,* or a *dedicated* network.

SIMM [sim] Acronym for **single in-line memory module.** A small *printed circuit board* that contains up to nine memory *chips.* SIMMs plug into sockets inside the computer. Installing them increases the *RAM* (random-access memory) of your computer. Common SIMM capacities are 256KB, 1MB, and 4MB. See illustration at *chip.*

single-density disk A *floppy disk* with 50–75% less storage capacity than a *double-density* or *high-density disk.* Single-density disks are rarely used today. See table at *density.*

single in-line memory module See **SIMM.**

single-sided disk A *floppy disk* that can store data on one side only. *Double-sided disks,* with twice as much storage capacity, are more commonly used in personal computing today. See table at *density.*

size To shrink or enlarge an object. In word processing, text can be sized to fit a new page size; in *graphical user interfaces,* sizing a *window* means enlarging or reducing it on the screen. Sizing a graphical image is accomplished with *object-oriented graphics*, a method of storing and representing images with mathematical descriptions. When an object is sized, its mathematical description is recalculated, yielding a distortion-free enlargement or reduction. See also *object-oriented graphics, window.*

slate PC   A *notebook computer* that has a surface, called a "slate," onto which you can input data and commands by writing with an electronic pen. The slate PC can translate printed words, numbers, and punctuation into ASCII characters.

slot   See **expansion slot.**

small computer systems interface   See **SCSI.**

smart   Designating a program that performs correctly in a wide variety of complicated circumstances without having to be explicitly instructed by the user. A program that is able to anticipate the information that will next be requested from a disk is said to be smart software.

smart terminal   A terminal in a *multi-user* system that has some processing capabilities, such as the ability to run a program supplied by the host computer. The development of *workstations* and *personal computers* has made this term and the product it describes somewhat outdated, but the phrase "like a smart terminal" is sometimes used to describe the behavior of workstations or personal computers with respect to programs that run almost entirely from a remote *server*'s storage. Smart terminals are intermediate between *dumb terminals*, which have no processing power and can only accept data, and *intelligent terminals*, which have more extensive processing capabilities.

smoothing   A technique used by laser printers for eliminating *jaggies*, the jagged distortions that appear on curves. Smoothing usually involves reducing the size or alignment of the dots that make up a curved line. See illustration at *antialiasing*.

soft   **1.** Designating something intangible, such as a program or concept, as opposed to something that exists physically, such as a keyboard or disk drive.   **2.** Designating something that is changeable or impermanent, such as a soft copy, which is a temporary representation of a program or document on a computer's display screen. See also *hard*.

soft font   A font that must be *downloaded* from a disk to a printer. Soft fonts contrast with hard fonts (fonts that are permanently stored in a printer's memory) and fonts contained in a *font cartridge* that is plugged directly into the printer. Also called *downloadable font*. See also *font, font cartridge, laser printer*.

soft hyphen   In word processing and desktop publishing programs with *hyphenation*, a hyphen that is automatically inserted to break a word at the end of a line. Soft hyphens are inserted and deleted by the program as a document is revised. *Hard hyphens*, on the other hand, are added and deleted by the user. See also *hard hyphen, hyphenation*.

soft return   In word processing and desktop publishing programs, a line break that occurs automatically when the cursor reaches the right margin. If the document is changed, the soft returns are moved by the program to the appropriate places at the end of each line. A *hard return* is supplied by the user, and it remains at the same place unless the user deletes it. See also *hard return, word wrap*.

software   The *programs, programming languages*, and *data* that control the functioning of the *hardware* and direct its operations. Software and hardware are integrally connected, and the distinction between them can be subtle. When you buy a word processing program, you are buying software, but the disk on which the program is recorded is hardware.
   Software is usually divided into two categories. *Systems*

software controls the workings of the computer. It includes *operating systems, utilities, compilers, assemblers,* and *file management* tools.

Applications handle the multitude of tasks that users want their computers to perform. Examples are *word processing* programs, *database management systems, spreadsheets,* and games. Applications software is unable to run without the operating system and utilities.

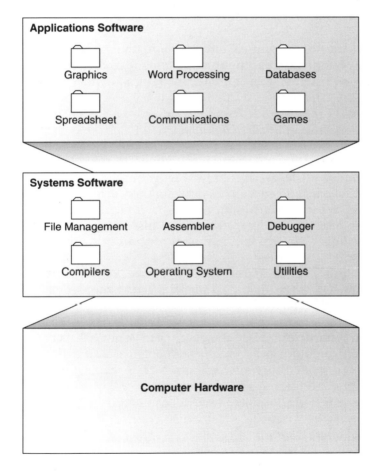

software

Two additional categories that contain elements of systems and applications software are *network* software, which enables computers to communicate, and programming languages, which give programmers the tools to write programs. See illustration.

sort An operation that takes a set of data and arranges it in alphabetical or numerical order. Sorting is a common procedure in word processing, database management, and spreadsheet programs.

sound board A *printed circuit board* that plugs into an IBM PC or compatible computer, enabling it to digitally reproduce a wide range of sounds. Also called *sound card*.

source The place, such as a file, a disk, or a device, from which data is moved. See also *destination*.

source code Programming instructions in their original *high-level language*, as written by a programmer. Before a program can be read and executed by a computer, it must be converted from source code to *object code* or *machine language* by a *compiler* or an *interpreter*. See also *high-level language*, *machine code*. See illustration at *programming language*.

space bar A bar at the bottom of the keyboard that when pressed down introduces a blank space to the right of the preceding character.

special character **1.** A character that is not a letter, number, or space. Punctuation marks, symbols, and *control characters* are considered special characters. **2.** A character that is not a letter, number, space, symbol, or punctuation mark. *Control characters* are considered special characters.

special interest group See **SIG**.

speech recognition The ability of a computer to accept human speech as an *input device*. Just as you can use a keyboard to enter either a command that a given program will recognize or data that the computer can store and sometimes manipulate without necessarily understanding its meaning, so too does speech recognition let you speak words that the computer either understands as commands or stores as data. Speech recognition makes it possible for people who cannot use a mouse or keyboard to input information into their computers.

So far, computers with speech recognition can recognize limited numbers of words, reaching at best into the thousands. Most need to be instructed to recognize each user's voice and pronunciation separately. Some systems do not require this but can recognize a small number of words as spoken by a large number of people. In general, a large vocabulary makes it harder for the computer to learn to understand a particular accent and voice, and would allow only a few speakers to use the system. Furthermore, speakers must not only speak slowly and clearly but must also pause between words. Eventually, speech recognition may allow computers to handle both large vocabularies and large numbers of speakers. The next step will then be to integrate speech recognition with the development of systems that can understand *natural languages*. Also called *voice recognition*.

spell checker   A program that searches a document for misspelled words by comparing each word in the document to a dictionary file of correctly spelled words. The spell checker will stop at an incorrectly spelled word and offer a list of correctly spelled substitute words. A spell checker that has a larger dictionary file will be less likely to stop at uncommon words that are correctly spelled.

Other useful spell checker features include the capacity to add new words to the dictionary file, the ability to stop at a word that occurs twice in a row, and the ability to count the number of words in a document.

split screen   A display screen that is divided in two, allowing you to view two documents at the same time or to view one document in two different ways.

spool Acronym for **simultaneous peripheral operations on-line.** To put commands or requests temporarily into a *buffer*, so that they are carried out when they are able to be processed.

spooler A program that paces print jobs by temporarily storing them in a *buffer* and sending them to the printer when the printer is able to process them. This frees up the CPU, allowing the user to work on something else while a document is printing. Also called *print spooler.*

spreadsheet An on-screen display of a table of values arranged in rows and columns. The intersections of rows and columns are called *cells.* The rows are numbered and the columns are alphabetized, so each cell can be identified by its column letter and row number. B9, for instance, is the cell in column B and row 9.

Spreadsheet applications are accounting and bookkeeping programs that let you create and manipulate spreadsheets electronically. You define what data is in each cell and how different cells depend on each other. The relationships between cells are *formulas*, and the names of the cells are *labels.*

Formulas make spreadsheets powerful by linking data in different cells together. The purpose of a spreadsheet isn't to find just one answer. After you complete a calculation, you can enter new values, *recalculate*, and see how a change in one value affects the results. For example, you may use a spreadsheet to keep track of your annual budget. If your rent goes up, you adjust the value in the cell indicating rent, and the application recalculates your budget.

Many spreadsheet applications exist, but two of the most well-known are Lotus 1-2-3 and Excel. Some spreadsheet applications support graphics, high-quality fonts, and database management. Recent trends include *three-dimensional spreadsheet* programs and Windows spreadsheets. Also called *worksheet.* See illustration.

SRAM [ESS-ram] Acronym for **static random-access memory.** See **static RAM.**

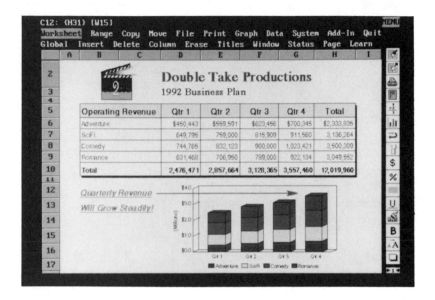

spreadsheet
Lotus 1-2-3

stack **1.** A section of memory used for temporary storage of information in which the item most recently stored is the first to be retrieved, and the first item stored is the last to be retrieved. **2.** In programming, a similar type of data structure.

stand-alone A term describing a self-contained, independently operating computer or device.

standard An agreed-upon procedure or structure for a specific type of communication. There are standard physical structures that enable a device such as a printer to plug into a variety of different computers, and there are standard communications methods, called *protocols*, that make the data in one computer usable by other computers and devices.

Some standards are set by an official organization, such as ANSI (American National Standards Institute), which establishes standards for programming languages. Other standards evolve naturally as hardware and software developers attempt to create products that will be compatible with the more popular computers and devices. Some commonly used standards include the ASCII standard for characters and TCP/IP, a communications protocol. See also *communications protocol*, *compatibility*, *protocol*.

star   One of the three principal *topologies* for a *local area network*, in which all computers and devices, known as *nodes*, are connected to one central computer, known as the hub. All communication between nodes is routed by the hub. See also *bus*, *ring*. See illustration at *network*.

start bit   In *asynchronous* communication, the *bit* that signals the beginning of a *byte* of data. See also *stop bit*.

startup disk   A disk that contains the operating system files that a computer needs to start working. The startup disk is usually a *hard disk*; if a computer does not have a hard startup disk, a floppy startup disk must be inserted into one of the disk drives every time the computer is turned on. Also called *system disk*. See also *operating system*.

statement   An elementary instruction in a *high-level language*. Programs are made up of statements and *expressions*, operations, and values stated in symbolic form.

static   Unchanging or fixed. See also *dynamic*.

static RAM   Acronyms **SCRAM** [skram]   or **SRAM** [ESS-ram]. A type of random-access memory that does not need to be refreshed by the CPU as often as *dynamic RAM*. Substantially faster than dynamic RAM, static RAM chips are used for cache memory, a reserved area of memory that stores frequently used data or instructions for fast access. See table at *access time*.

static random-access memory   See **static RAM.**

stop bit   In *asynchronous* communication, the *bit* that signals the end of a *byte* of data. See also *start bit.*

storage   The places that hold computer information for subsequent use or retrieval. There are two types of storage: *primary storage* consists of a computer's *RAM* (random-access memory); secondary storage, or *mass* storage, refers to the places, such as hard disks or floppy disks, where large amounts of information can be permanently stored.

storage device   Any device used to record and store computer data. Among storage devices are *hard disks, floppy disks,* and *tape.*

store   To copy data onto a *mass storage* device, such as a floppy disk, or into memory from the *CPU.*

string   A set of consecutive characters treated by a computer as a single unit. Computers can perform operations on text by treating words as strings. Also called *character string.*

striping   On an *array* of disk drives, a technique for improving disk drive speed. Each file written into a striped array is spread, or striped, over several drives. See also *array, RAID.*

style sheet   In *word processing* or *desktop publishing,* a file of instructions for the *format* of a *document.* The style sheet gives such specifications as margins, page size, fonts, and line spacing. The style sheet can be easily adjusted to change the format of a document.

stylus   See **light pen.**

subdirectory   A subdivision within a larger computer *directory* that stores related files. All subdirectories are branches of the *root directory*. The directory immediately above the one you are working in is called the *parent directory*. See illustration at *hierarchical*.

submenu A *menu* that appears and presents further options or commands after a selection from a previous menu has been made.

subroutine A sequence of programming statements that perform a specific task within a program.

subscript A letter or number that is printed slightly below the level of other characters on the same line.

supercomputer A computer that is among the fastest and most powerful available at a given time. Supercomputers are designed to execute computation-intensive programs as quickly as possible. They generally handle fewer programs at a time than ordinary mainframes; but the programs they handle are far more complex, and they execute them much faster. Supercomputers are used in scientific research, especially in performing the enormous number of calculations required in modeling complex phenomena such as weather patterns or nuclear explosions.

SuperDrive A trademark for a 3.5-inch floppy disk drive that can read all Macintosh formats (400KB, 800KB, and 1.4MB) and can read and format 720KB and 1.4MB DOS disks. The SuperDrive is now standard on Macintosh computers, and it allows you to move files between IBM and Macintosh systems.

superscript A letter or number that is printed slightly above the level of other characters on the same line.

Super VGA See **SVGA**.

support To have the ability to work in a certain way, to interact with a certain device or program, or to perform a certain task. For example, Adobe Photoshop, a desktop publishing program, supports *TIFF* files.

surge protector   A device that prevents electrical power surges from damaging a computer. Another device, called the uninterruptible power supply (*UPS*), prevents the loss of data from *brownouts*. Also called *surge suppressor*. See also *brownout, UPS*.

SVGA   Abbreviation of **Super Video Graphics Array.**   A display standard for IBM PC and compatible computers that offers better *resolution* than *VGA* (Video Graphics Array). SVGA video adapters and monitors are able to display up to 1,024 pixels by 768 lines. Also called *extended VGA, VGA plus*. See also *monitor, resolution, VGA, video adapter*.

swap   To exchange one segment or *page* of data for another. For example, a *RAM cache* swaps data with the slower *RAM* chips, and in a *disk cache*, RAM swaps data with the disk. In systems using *virtual memory*, pages of data are swapped between RAM and the hard disk. See also *paging*.

switch   See **option** (sense 1).

synchronous   A type of communication in which the flow of data is synchronized by an electronic clock. Synchronous communication takes place within the components of a computer and between computers in certain *networks*. *Asynchronous* communication is not governed by a clock signal; data is transmitted intermittently with a *start bit* and a *stop bit* signaling the beginning and end of each byte of data. Asynchronous communication can be carried out over telephone lines and is commonly used for communication between a computer and a device. See also *asynchronous*.

syntax   The spelling and grammatical rules governing a computer language. Programming language syntax is very precise, and a command that violates a grammatical rule will generate a syntax error. See also *semantics*.

SYSOP

SYSOP [SIS-op] Acronym for **system operator.** The person who manages and sometimes owns a *bulletin board system* or another type of *multi-user* system.

system A combination of components working together. A computer system is made up of all of the *hardware* and *software* that allow a computer to accept *input*, to process and store it, and to produce *output*. Within a computer, the *operating system* consists of the programs that allow the different components such as the keyboard, memory, CPU, and monitor to function together. The operating system also provides a software base from which applications can run. See table at *operating system.*

System On Macintosh computers, one of the two programs that make up the *operating system*. The other operating system program, called *Finder*, is a file and program manager.

System 7 is an updated version of the Macintosh operating system, which includes a revised version of Finder, true *virtual memory*, *multitasking*, and several other features. System 7 is a trademark of Apple Computer, Inc. See table at *operating system.*

system board See **motherboard.**

system disk See **startup disk.**

System folder In *Macintosh* computers, the *folder* that contains files for the *System*, *Finder*, device *drivers*, *fonts*, and other resources needed by the *operating system.*

systems analysis The study of a problem or task, followed by the design and implementation of computer hardware and software to solve that problem or task.

systems analyst One who performs systems analyses, designing and implementing computer systems for specific settings and requirements.

systems software   *Software* that is concerned with the actual operation of the computer as opposed to the work that is done with it. Systems software primarily includes the *operating system* and related *utility* programs, as well as *configuration files*, *compilers*, *linkers*, and other files and programs that cannot be considered *applications* software. See illustration at *software*.

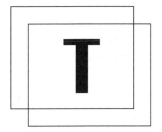

T   Abbreviation of **tera-**.

Tab key   A key that moves the cursor a preset distance, as to the next *cell* in a *spreadsheet* or to another part of a *dialog box*.

table   An arrangement of data, such as text or *fields* in a database, in rows and *columns*.

tab stop   In word processing, a position along a line of text where the cursor will stop when the *Tab key* is pressed. Tab stops are useful for indenting the first line of a paragraph, but their most important function is to make it easier to type text in columns without filling lines with spaces. Most word processors set *default* tab stops every half inch, but these can be deleted or changed. Usually they can also be set to align text *flush* left or right with the stop, centered on it, or with decimal points aligned on it.

tag   A character or *string* that is attached to a database *field* or other item of data and encodes information about that item, often used in performing a *sort*.

Tagged Image File Format   Acronym **TIFF** [tif].   A format for storing and transferring graphics images, especially *gray scale* images, as in *bit maps*. The TIFF format can be read by both Macintosh and IBM PC and compatible computers, and is commonly used in *desktop publishing*. See table at *graphics file format*.

tape   A thin strip of plastic coated with iron oxide or some other material on which data can be recorded magnetically. Magnetic tape has been used for recording sound since the 1950s and was a natural choice as a storage medium for the earliest electronic computers. But in order to retrieve data from any point on a reel of tape, it is necessary to move the entire tape until that point is reached, a process which causes continual wear and tear and takes a long time, even with high-speed drives. With the development of the much faster *random access* capabilities of the *hard disk*, tape was no longer competitive as a primary storage medium. Because of its relatively low cost and high reliability, however, it remains the preferred medium for long-term storage and *backup* for computers of all sizes. See also *QIC*, *tape drive*.

tape drive   A device that holds magnetic *tape*, mounted on reels or in cartridges, and includes a transport mechanism that moves the tape across *read/write heads* that read data from it and write new data to it. Tape drives are widely used as *backup* storage devices; they have capacities ranging up to several *gigabytes* and use tape of different sizes. *Mainframe* and *minicomputers* often use $^1/_2$-inch 9-track tape. More common types used with personal computers are 8 mm videocassette cartridge drives, 4 mm digital audio tape (*DAT*) drives, and especially the less expensive *QIC* (quarter-inch cartridge) drives, many of which can use standard audio cassette tapes. Tape backup drives were long regarded as unnecessary because the contents of a small *hard disk* could usually be restored without too much trouble in case of a failure. The increasing use of large capacity (over 100MB) hard disks and multitasking software, however, has made tape drives an increasingly valuable part of a reliable personal computer system.

target   The *destination* to which the output of a command or an operation is directed. See also *source*.

target language   The language into which a document written in another language, called the *source language*, is to be translated. The term is used to refer to a natural language as well as to the *object code* or *machine language* produced by a *compiler* or an *assembler*.

task   An operation, a job, or a process carried out by a computer or program.

task switching   A technique that allows a user to load two or more programs simultaneously and switch from one to another without having to close and open them in turn. For example, you can type a letter with a word processor, switch quickly to a *database* or *spreadsheet* to check certain information, and return to the letter without losing your place or saving and exiting the program. This technique differs from *multitasking* in that the program that is not active does not continue to run in the *background*; it is suspended until you return to it, and all of the microprocessor's attention goes to the active program. Task switching is sufficient for many activities, and is sometimes more reliable than multitasking, which is more complex. Task switching is typically performed by a *shell* program, such as the Macintosh *MultiFinder*, the DOS Shell, or XTree. Also called *context switching*.

TB   Abbreviation of **terabyte.**

tear-off menu   A pop-up menu that can be moved around the screen.

technical support   The service provided by a hardware or software manufacturer to customers who have problems with the product or questions that are not answered by the supporting *documentation*. The level and quality of technical support is an important factor to consider when deciding on the purchase of a computer system. All large, reputable companies offer telephone support to customers.

telecommunications   The transmission and reception of information, especially computer data, over telephone lines.

telecommuting   The practice of working at home by using a modem and a computer terminal connected with one's business office.

template   1. A pattern or model that is used as a starting point for an operation, with the user adding to it or modifying it as needed. Templates are often used in *word processing* programs as the basis for résumés, letterheads, business cards, and so on; in *spreadsheet* programs to do calculations for standardized procedures such as loan amortizations and investment returns; and in *databases* to eliminate the work of designing and building common structures such as address directories.   2. A sheet of paper or plastic that fits over all or part of a keyboard and contains labels describing the functions of each key within a particular *application* program or for a particular *terminal emulation*.

tera-   Abbreviated **T**   1. A prefix indicating one trillion (10^{12}), as in *terahertz*.   2. A prefix indicating 1,099,511,627,776 (2^{40}), as in *terabyte*. This is the sense in which tera- is generally used in computing, which is based on powers of two.

terabyte   Abbreviated **TB**   A unit of measurement of computer memory or data storage capacity equal to 1,099,511,627,776 (2^{40}) *bytes*. One terabyte equals 1,024 *gigabytes*.

terminal   A device, often equipped with a keyboard and a video display, through which data or information can enter or leave a computer system. The most basic configuration lacks any local data processing or storage capabilities and depends on the *mainframe* or *minicomputer* to which it is connected for these services; it is often referred to as a *dumb terminal*. Although there are many different types and models of terminals, any given central computer is compatible with only one or a few of them. It is equally possible to access these machines with a *microcomputer* by means of an *emulation* program; the computer then acts as a *smart terminal*. Most *communications software* programs provide emulation options of this sort for a number of widely used terminal types. Also called *video terminal*. See also *diskless workstation*.

terminate and stay resident   Abbreviated **TSR**   A *DOS* program that remains in *RAM* even after the program has been exited. TSRs are sometimes called *pop-up* utilities because, once loaded, they can be called up from within another application by pressing a single *hot key*. TSRs include calculators, appointment reminders, telephone dialers, notepads, screen-color programs, and spell checkers. Many of these tools are quite sophisticated and add a great deal to the convenience of operating a personal computer, but the user should be aware that they take up space in RAM that is then unavailable to the main applications that they are meant to support. The growing use of *multitasking* makes TSRs unnecessary, as any accessory program can simply be run as a standard *background* process that can be switched to the *foreground* when needed. See also *memory-resident*.

text   1. Data consisting of only standard *ASCII* characters, without formatting or any other codes.   2. In *word processing*, data in the form of words and sentences, as distinct from material such as *graphics*, tabular material, charts, and graphs.

text editor   See **editor**.

text file   A file that contains only characters in the *standard ASCII* character set and not *extended ASCII* characters, *control characters*, or formatting codes. See table at *file*.

text flow   See **text wrap.**

text mode   A mode of operation of IBM PC and compatible *video adapters* in which the display is limited to the characters and symbols of the IBM extended character set. These characters are the smallest units available to the display,

text wrap

which is divided into a number of horizontal lines and vertical *columns* of characters varying from 25 × 40 for *CGA*
adapters to 50 × 80 for *VGA*. Because the total number of
units and choices is smaller, displays in text mode are faster
than those in *graphics mode,* but text mode permits no more
graphics than straight lines and simple box drawings. Many
word processing and spreadsheet programs enable you to
switch from *character mode,* used for editing the text, to
graphics mode for viewing graphs, pictures, or text as it will
appear when printed. See also *WYSIWYG.*

text wrap   A feature supported by some *word processors* that
allows you to contour type around a graphic. Such type is
harder to read than noncontoured type, so this feature should
be used carefully. Also called *text flow, wrap-around type.* See
illustration.

thermal printer   A *nonimpact printer* that works by pushing
heated pins against treated paper. Thermal printers are used
in most calculators and *fax machines.* See table at *printer.*

thermal wax printer   A *nonimpact printer* that works by apply-
ing heated pins to a ribbon covered with usually colored wax.
The wax melts onto the paper to print an image. Although
most thermal wax printers were designed to print in color,
there are also black-and-white thermal wax printers. See table
at *printer.*

thin film transistor   Abbreviated **TFT**   See **flat-panel display.** See
also *active-matrix.*

three-dimensional spreadsheet   A program that allows two or
more *spreadsheets* to be linked together and incorporated into
another spreadsheet. All of the spreadsheets can then be
viewed at the same time. For example, monthly or yearly
reports from a number of accounts can be analyzed on separate individual spreadsheets, and then combined into a com-
posite sheet that uses *formulas* to total the data from the individual sheets. The total is automatically *recalculated* when

changes are made in any one of the single spreadsheets. Also called *spreadsheet notebook, 3-D notebook.*

throughput **1.** The rate, measured in characters or bytes per second, at which data can be processed and transferred from one place to another within a system. **2.** The ability to transfer data across all parts of a computer system. **3.** In *telecommunications,* the rate, measured in characters or bytes per second, at which data is sent and received over a given channel.

thumbnail In *desktop publishing,* a small image showing the preliminary layout of a page. It is convenient to view a number of thumbnails on the screen at once so that pages can be checked against each other for balance and consistency. See also *greeking.*

TIFF [tif] Acronym for **Tagged Image File Format.**

tiled windows *Windows* that are arranged so that they are all completely visible. Tiled windows do not overlap. See illustration at *overlaid windows.*

timed backup See **autosave.**

time-out The automatic cancellation of a process if the expected input is not received after a specified time.

time-sharing In *multi-user systems,* the process by which *CPU* time is assigned to each user in sequence, so that no user has to wait for another to finish and *log out* before beginning to work. Most *mainframes* and *minicomputers* use time-sharing, and it usually works smoothly enough that individual users are unaware of each other's simultaneous use of the system. At times of peak load on large systems, however, the CPU resources can be spread so thin as to cause a noticeable slowdown.

title bar   In a *graphical user interface*, a line at the top of a *window* that presents the name of the program or file in that window.

toggle   **1.** To switch from one to the other of two possible states. For example, most *word processors* and *editors* use the *Insert key* to toggle between *insert mode* and *overwrite mode*. **2.** To change the state of a bit from 1 to 0 or 0 to 1.

toggle switch   A *switch key*, or key combination that moves a function from one to the other of two possible states. For example, the *Num Lock key* switches the *numeric keypad* between its numeric and cursor control modes. See illustration at *DIP switch*.

token-ring network   A type of *local area network* in which permission to transmit over the network is contained in a special file called a token. The *ring topology* of the network allows the token to be circulated continuously from one station to the next. When a station wishes to transmit, it seizes the token, marks it as "busy," inserts its message together with the intended address, and sends the package back into the loop. All other stations on the network must pass the "busy" token along to its destination and are prohibited from transmitting any new data themselves. After the message is delivered, the token returns to the originating station, where it is once again marked "free" and returned to circulation. See also *bus, star.*

toner   A fine, electrically charged, powdered pigment that is fused to paper to form an image in *laser printers* and photocopying machines.

tool   **1.** A program used primarily to create, manipulate, modify, or analyze other programs, such as a *compiler*, an *editor*, or a cross-referencing program.   **2.** In a *draw* or *paint program*, a design element, such as a pattern, brush width, line width, color, or shape, that a user can select from a *toolbar*.

toolbar

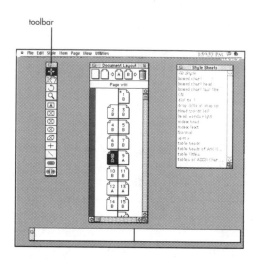

toolbar

toolbar In programs using a *graphical user interface,* a row of *icons* across the top of a *window* that serve as *buttons* to activate commands or functions. See illustration.

toolbox A set of *compiled* routines that can be used by programmers as ready-made *modules* or building blocks with which to write new software.

topology The geometric arrangement in which the *nodes* of a *local area network* are connected to each other, usually a *bus, ring,* or *star* configuration. See illustration at *network.*

touch screen A display consisting of a monitor behind a pressure-sensitive transparent panel. Touching the panel with a fingertip activates the functions represented by elements of the display. Touch screen displays are widely used for such purposes as informational displays in museums and hotels and for automated ticket purchases in airports. Also called *touch-sensitive display*.

tower configuration   A cabinet for a personal computer system that is designed to stand upright, usually on the floor, with components, such as the *power supply* and mass *storage devices*, stacked on top of each other. See also *desktop configuration*.

TPI   Abbreviation of **tracks per inch.**   A measure of the storage *density* of *magnetic media*, such as floppy disks. TPI represents the number of *tracks* that can be recorded per radial inch on the surface of the disk. Densities for common types of *DOS*-formatted disks are 48 TPI for double-density 5.25-inch disks, 96 TPI for high-density 5.25-inch disks, and 135 TPI for high-density 3.5-inch disks. As the width of disk tracks varies with density, the *read/write* heads in disk drives must be the correct size for the disk to be used.

track   One of the concentric magnetic rings that form the separate data storage areas on a *floppy* or *hard disk*. Tracks are created in the process of *formatting* a disk. *Double-density disks* formatted in *DOS* generally contain 40 tracks, and *high-density* disks contain 80. See also *cylinder, sector, TPI*.

trackball   An input device similar to an upside-down *mouse*. You move the on-screen *pointer* by rotating the ball with your fingers or palm. A trackball usually has one or more buttons that are just like mouse buttons. A trackball is stationary, however, and does not require a flat surface to operate. Consequently, trackballs are often used with laptop or notebook computers. See illustration.

tracks per inch   See **TPI.**

tractor feed   A mechanism for advancing continuous-form paper through a printer by means of two pin-studded rotating belts. The pins catch matching perforations along the edges of the paper. Tractor feed printers do not have to be fed paper as often as sheet-fed ones, but the mechanism can easily go out of alignment and require repositioning of the paper. Tractor

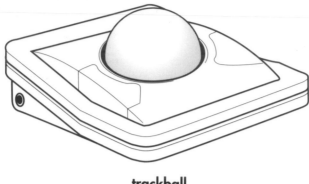

trackball

feed is commonly found in *dot-matrix printers*, many of which also provide the option of using a *friction feed* mechanism for single sheets.

transaction processing   A type of processing in which the computer responds to requests or instructions from a user one at a time as they are made, rather than in large groups as in *batch processing*. See also *interactive*.

transistor   A tiny electronic device containing a *semiconductor* and having at least three electrical contacts, used in an *integrated circuit* as a switch to create a *bit*. If electrical current passes through, the switch is on and the bit is a 1. If no current passes through, the switch is off and the bit is a 0.

translation software   Software designed to translate texts from one natural language into another. Most translation software is created in *LISP* and uses an internal dictionary to find vocabulary equivalents and *subroutines* that analyze a sentence to locate such things as the subject and verb and to identify grammatical features such as verb tenses. Translation software usually yields an approximate translation that must be reviewed and edited by a human translator.

transportable   A large *portable* computer, generally weighing over 15 pounds and able to operate from AC house current.

tree structure   A logical structure for classifying and organizing data in which every item can be traced to a single origin through a unique path. Such a structure is usually represented graphically in the manner of a family tree, with the starting point, called the *root*, at the top. The root is usually divided into subdivisions, which are connected to it by branches and may themselves be further divided. Any point where two or more branches meet is called a *node*. A node is referred to as the "daughter" or "child" of the node directly above it, which in turn is called its "parent."

Tree structures are used in computing as a way of organizing *directories* and the files they contain. The root *directory* is logically the first on a disk, with all other directories classified as *subdirectories* of it. Every directory except the root has a single *parent directory*, whose name can often be abbreviated to the sequence of two dots (..) in commands and filenames. See also *file name, folder, pathname*.

Trojan horse   A computer program that appears to be benign, such as a directory lister, an archiver, or a game, but is actually designed to break security or damage a system. A Trojan horse differs from a *virus* in that the damaging code is unable to replicate itself and spread to other programs.

TrueType   A trademark for a high-level *outline font* technology developed by Apple and available with Apple's System 7 and later releases, Microsoft Windows 3.1 and later releases, and certain laser printers. TrueType provides *scalable fonts* to both the display screen and the printer with no need for additional cartridges, printer fonts, or printer microprocessors. TrueType fonts will also print at the full resolution offered by the printer, and can print to any kind of printer. Since TrueType is an *open* industry *standard*, TrueType font packages are being developed and distributed by several different companies. See illustration at *outline font*.

truncate   To cut off the end of a number or *string* when it is too large to fit into the space allotted to it. In DOS, for example, *file names* are limited to eight characters; if more are entered,

DOS will only recognize the first eight. Truncation is most commonly applied to numbers in *floating-point notation*, which can often extend to many decimal places. If the number of digits exceeds what fits in memory, the number may be rounded off and its excess digits dropped. This method always rounds numbers downward, but the digits that are lost are normally too insignificant to matter for most calculations.

TSR Abbreviation of **terminate and stay resident.**

turnkey system A complete computer system designed for a specific application, assembled and delivered to the end user ready to run. The system includes all necessary *software, peripherals*, and *documentation*. For example, a specialized *CAD* system for commercial patternmaking or architectural drafting might include a *file server*, fast *workstations* with large *hard disks* and extra memory for *graphics* use, *plotters, digitizers*, and customized software. Turnkey systems are often designed for professional, medical, order processing, and CAD/CAM systems.

tutorial A program that instructs the user of a system or software package by simulating the capabilities of the system or software. Most large commercial *applications* provide tutorials that usually consist of a series of short, graduated lessons demonstrating how to use the features of the program. The user can repeat a lesson as often as desired before moving on to the next. Often the tutorial program and a number of sample files associated with it are loaded into a separate TUTOR or LEARN *subdirectory*, where they are kept separate from the main program files and can be deleted to save space if the tutorial is no longer needed.

type To display text by or as if by pressing keys on the keyboard, especially as the result of a command to the computer to display the contents of a *text file* on the *display screen*.

typeface The design of a set of printed letters. The typeface specifies the exact shape of each letter and character. Some common typefaces are Courier, Helvetica, Times Roman, and

Times New Roman. Typefaces that have the same shapes but differ in obliqueness (e.g., italic) and weight (bold, demi-bold, lightface, etc.) are grouped into *font families*. The two broad categories of typefaces are *serif* and *sans serif*. The growth of *desktop publishing* and the development of *outline font* technology have made a large variety of standard and decorative typefaces available for personal computers, so that the appearance of business and personal documents produced by *laser printers* can now approximate that of professionally printed ones. See also *bit-mapped font, font, lowercase, PostScript, TrueType, uppercase*. See illustration at *font family*.

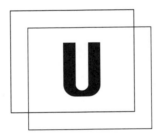

undelete   To restore text to a document, or a file to a directory, after it has been *deleted*.

underflow error   A data-processing error arising when a computed quantity is a smaller number than the device is capable of displaying.

undo   To reverse the action of a command and return to a previous state.

undocumented   Relating to a feature of a program that is not mentioned in the program's official *documentation*. In *Microsoft Windows*, for example, *double clicking* on the *title* *bar* of a *window* is a method of maximizing or minimizing the window, yet this fact is undocumented in that it does not appear in the manual. Features are occasionally undocumented through oversight; more often they are functions that were included by programmers for their own convenience but deemed unnecessary, trivial, or troublesome for customers. The largest source of undocumented features is in *operating system* software, for which large volumes have been compiled by experimenters who have discovered function calls and other information not published in the official manuals.

uninterruptible power supply   See **UPS.**

UNIX   [YOO-nicks]   A trademark for an interactive time-sharing system originally invented in 1969 at AT&T Bell Labs. When it was reimplemented in the *high-level* programming language *C* some five years later, it became the first operating system that could be moved from one computer to another easily, because *source code* written in C can be recompiled by another computer easily. Today UNIX is the most widely used multi-user general-purpose operating system in the world. There are several varieties (often called "flavors") of UNIX, among them versions developed at the University of California at Berkeley from 1979 on and AT&T's own later version, System V. More recent modifications have been made by Sun Computer and by the Open Systems Foundation (OSF). Standardization is increasing across versions.
    UNIX has long been favored in technical, scientific, and educational circles for its flexibility, power, security, and large networking capabilities. In recent years a number of more convenient *graphical user interfaces* and *shells* have been developed, such as DEC MOTIF, X Windows, and NeXTStep, which add greatly to its ease of use. See also *compile, XENIX.* See table at *operating system.*

unpack   To restore a *packed* file to its uncompressed state.

upgrade   To replace a software program with a more recently released version or a hardware device with one that provides better performance.

upload   To transfer data or programs over a digital communications link from a smaller or peripheral system to a larger or central host. See also *download*.

uppercase   Of, relating to, or being a capital letter. See also *case-sensitive*.

UPS   Abbreviation of **uninterruptible power supply.**   A *power supply* containing a battery source that will supply power to the computer in case the main supply fails. A UPS generally works for only ten minutes or so; if the main power fails it sounds an alarm and provides enough time to save important data and shut down the computer, but usually not enough to let the computer function unattended for long periods.

upward compatible   See **forward compatible.**

user-friendly   Designed to be easy for those without much experience to learn and use. User-friendly systems include such features as *menu-driven* or *graphical user interfaces*, *on-line* help, and a logical function organization that conforms to established standards.

user interface   The way in which a user enters *commands* in a given program. There are three main types of interface. In the *command-driven* interface, the user types commands from the keyboard. In a *menu-driven* interface, either the keyboard or a *mouse* is used to select an option from a *menu* displayed on the screen. In a *graphical user interface*, the user selects and activates functions by manipulating *icons* and *pop-up windows* on the screen. While the menu-driven and graphical user interfaces are generally easier to learn and use, many expert users still prefer the command line interface because of its speed and efficiency.

user memory   The portion of a computer's *memory* that is available to the user for programs. When the system starts, before any programs are loaded, a number of areas in memory are set aside for use by the *operating system*, *BIOS*, *drivers*, *video adapters*, and the like. Once these areas are allocated, the rest of memory can be used by *applications, TSRs,* and *utilities.* Memory management programs can search the reserved areas of a specific machine, locate regions that are not being used, and make them available as additional user memory.

username An identification *string,* distinct from the *password,* that is required for *logging on* to a *multi-user* system, *bulletin board system,* or *on-line service.*

utility A program that performs a specific task related to the management of computer functions, resources, or files. Utility programs range from the simple to the sophisticated, and many programmers specialize in producing and distributing them as *shareware.* There are utilities that perform file and directory management, *data compression,* disk defragmentation and repair, system diagnostics, graphics viewing, and system security, for example. Many utilities are written as *memory-resident* programs meant to serve as adjuncts to *operating systems.* Many operating systems incorporate such popular utility functions as *undeleting,* password protection, memory management, *virus* protection, and file compression. See also *pop-up utility, terminate and stay resident.*

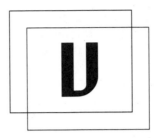

vaccine   Software designed to detect and stop the progress of a computer *virus*. Computer vaccines usually include an anti-virus function that searches files, especially *executable files*, for patterns of *code* that belong to known viruses and then removes them. The program also watches for and prevents unexpected or anomalous changes in the *file allocation table* and the area on the disk that stores *boot* information. Some vaccines can detect even unknown viruses by monitoring all executable program files and sending an alarm if an unauthorized attempt is made to change their program code.

vaporware   New products that have been announced or marketed but have not yet been produced.

variable   In programming, a *string* that represents a specified value and is treated as that value when the program is run. See also *constant*.

variable length   In *database* systems, designating a *field* whose length depends on the information it contains. See also *field length*.

variable-length record   A *record* that contains one or more *variable length fields*.

VDT   Abbreviation of **video display terminal.**   See **monitor.**

VDT radiation   The electromagnetic radiation emitted by video display terminals. Studies have shown that exposure to these emissions may have deleterious effects on users' health, but other studies have reached contradictory conclusions. Therefore debate continues over how much protection users should have from them and what levels they should be limited to. In the absence of conclusive evidence one way or the other, many monitor manufacturers have decided to comply with the strictest emissions standards currently in existence. Whatever standard your monitor meets, the advice usually given by consumer groups is to work at least two or three feet from the display screen. Furthermore, since emissions are stronger from the back and sides of a monitor, care should be taken not to place a monitor too close to a worker at another desk.

vector   An *array* of only one dimension.

vector font   See **outline font**.

vector graphics   See **object-oriented graphics.**

vertical justification   In word processing and desktop publishing, the automatic alignment of columns so that they end evenly at the bottom margin. Vertical justification is accomplished by *feathering*, the adding of space between lines of text.

very large-scale integration   Abbreviated **VLSI**   The fitting of at least 100,000, and often over a million, transistors and other electronic components onto a single *integrated circuit* or *chip*. See table at *integrated circuit*.

VGA   Abbreviation of **Video Graphics Array.**   The graphics display system introduced by IBM in 1987 that has become the industry standard for IBM PC and compatible computers. VGA works with an *analog monitor* and offers a palette of 16 to 256 continuously variable colors, far more than the *EGA*. When displaying text, VGA has a resolution of 720 *pixels* across by 400 down. When displaying graphics and using 16 colors, VGA has a resolution of 640 pixels across by 480 down. With 256 colors the resolution is 320 × 200. Some VGA circuit boards come with an extra nine-pin port that allows them to be attached to a *digital monitor*. VGA is downward compatible with all earlier IBM graphics display systems. See table at *video standard*.

VGA Plus   See **SVGA**.

video adapter   An *expansion board* designed to provide or enhance the display of graphics and text on a *monitor*. A video adapter, however, is only as good as the monitor permits; a monochrome monitor, for example, will never display colors, no matter what video adapter you use, and a *digital monitor* will never offer the same resolution as an *analog monitor*. Most video adapters offer at least two *video modes*, one for text and one for graphics. Within each mode, some monitors offer two or more different resolutions. With higher resolution, the image is clearer but fewer colors can be displayed. Many video adapters come with extra modes for *backward compatibility*, but if you need to run programs designed for particular *video standards*, you should make sure that your adapter can run under those standards. Some video adapters also come with their own memory so that they do not have to compete with applications for RAM.

video display terminal   Abbreviated **VDT   1**. See **monitor**. **2**. See **cathode-ray tube**.

Video Graphics Array   See **VGA**.

video mode   The form in which a *video adapter* displays information on the *monitor*. Video adapters generally offer at least two modes, one for text and one for graphics. In text mode, the adapter can display any letter, number, or symbol in the ASCII character set. In graphics mode, it displays *bit-mapped graphics* using *pixels*. Some video adapters offer two or more graphics and text modes that differ in resolution and the number of colors that can be displayed simultaneously.

video standard One of a set of *standards* establishing the resolution and number of colors that can be displayed simultaneously for any given system of graphics display in a particular
mode. Most video standards require *backward compatibility*
and call for separate *video modes* for graphics and text. Most
video standards for IBM PC and compatible computers are
now being set by the Video Electronics Standards Association
(VESA), although some are *proprietary*. Proprietary standards
usually suit specific applications rather than general use. Bear
in mind that video standards require tripartite cooperation:
the *video adapter, monitor*, and applications must all support
the same standard. Table 23 compares the features of various
common video standards.

Table 23. Widely Used Video Standards

Video Standard	Resolution	Mode	Simultaneous Colors	Characteristics
MDA (Monochrome Display Adapter)	720 × 350	Text	1	• Provides clear, readable text • No graphics capability
CGA (Color Graphics Adapter)	640 × 200 160 × 200 320 × 200 640 × 200	Text Graphics Graphics Graphics	16 16 4 2	• Designed for computer games • Low-quality text
EGA (Enhanced Graphics Adapter)	640 × 350 720 × 350 320 × 200 640 × 200 640 × 350	Text Text Graphics Graphics Graphics	16 4 16 16 16	• Emulates CGA and MDA and has additional high-resolution modes • Maximum palette size of 64 colors
PGA (Professional Graphics Adapter)	640 × 480	Graphics	256	• Used primarily for CAD applications
HGC (Hercules Graphics Card)	720 × 348	Graphics	1	• Similar to and compatible with MDA • High-resolution graphics capability
MCGA (Multicolor/ Graphics Array)	320 × 400 640 × 200 640 × 400 320 × 200	Text Text Graphics Graphics	4 2 2 256	• Emulates CGA and MDA and has two additional modes • Used in IBM PS/2 Models 25 and 30

Table 23. Widely Used Video Standards

Video Standard	Resolution	Mode	Simultaneous Colors	Characteristics
				• Maximum palette size of 262,144 colors
VGA (Video Graphics Array)	720 × 400	Text	16	• Uses analog signals
	360 × 400	Text	16	• Emulates EGA
	640 × 480	Graphics	16	• Used in most IBM PS/2 models
	320 × 200	Graphics	256	• Also available for conventional IBM computers
				• Maximum palette size of 262,144 colors
SVGA (Super VGA)	800 × 600	Graphics	16	• Emulates VGA and has one or more additional high-resolution modes
	1,024 × 768	Graphics	256	• Used in IBM PC-compatibles
8514/A	1,024 × 768	Graphics	256	• Provides 64 shades of gray on monochrome display screen
				• Uses interlacing
XGA (Extended Graphics Array)	640 × 480	Graphics	25,536	• Emulates VGA and has additional models
	1,024 × 768	Graphics	256	• Used in IBM PS/2 Model 90 and up
	1,056 × 400	Text	16	
TI 34010	1,024 × 768	Graphics	256	• Supports same resolution as 8514/A but is noninterlaced

video terminal See terminal.

view *n.* In *database management systems,* a display of information requested in a *query* and organized as specified by the user. For example, if you had a database to keep track of the flavors, quality, delivery options, prices, and brands of ice cream offered at your neighborhood stores and cafés, you might request a table showing the quality and prices of ice cream at each place that offered take-out. Your query would yield a particular view, which you could then save for future reference.
—*v.* **1.** To request and peruse such a view. **2.** To peruse a file without making changes in it. Some word processing pro-

grams have a different command for viewing documents than for accessing them.

virtual **1.** Capable of functioning or being used as, but not constituting, the physical object or entity represented. For example, *virtual memory* is memory that a microprocessor can use, but it doesn't correspond to actual chips in RAM. *Virtual reality* mimics reality so as to let a user respond to it and thus practice techniques that would be appropriate to the actual situation being simulated. For example, pilots train on the ground with interactive computer systems that imitate flight conditions. **2.** Of, relating to, or existing in *virtual reality*.

virtual address An *address* in *virtual memory*. The operating system must *map* the virtual address onto an address in a physical storage device, such as a hard disk drive, in order to access the necessary data and transfer it to *RAM*.

virtual disk See **RAM disk.**

virtual machine **1.** A *virtual* computer simulated by an actual computer that runs two or more operating systems, or two or more copies of the same operating system, at the same time and thus functions as if it were two computers. **2.** A software program that simulates a hardware device not physically present.

virtual memory Functional computer memory that does not correspond to actual chips in RAM but that is keyed by *virtual addresses* to memory in a storage device, such as a hard disk drive, from which data can be transferred to the RAM chips as necessary. When this transfer occurs, the data that has stayed in RAM without a summons to the microprocessor for the longest period of time is returned from RAM to the storage device to make room for the incoming data. This moving of data back and forth between RAM and the storage device is called *swapping* or *paging*. Virtual memory effectively increases RAM and so lets the user run programs that require more RAM than is physically available. Certain word processing programs, for example, will not open a document that won't fit into memory, but will open a document that fits into virtual memory. Similarly, applications that require more RAM than a computer has can run on computers with enough virtual memory to make up the difference.

virtual reality An interactive computer system that simulates reality by using such I/O devices as gloves that transmit information about the position of the user's hands and fingers, goggles that use a small display screen for each eye to provide a stereoscopic view of the virtual world, and headphones. Both the simulations and the responses to user input take place in *real time* so as to allow the user to practice techniques that would be appropriate to the actual situation being simulated. For example, pilots train on the ground with virtual reality systems that imitate flight conditions and respond to their input as an actual airplane might.

virus A series of commands that duplicate themselves and can therefore use up enough RAM to prevent any other program from running or enough disk space to interfere with ordinary data storage. The commands may be more or less damaging; they may erase all your data or do nothing but reproduce themselves. Most viruses work by attaching themselves to one program after another, including the operating system. They often replicate themselves over long periods of time before any of the commands is actually carried out, so that they may be in a system for months before they are detected. Many virus protection programs are now available to identify and remove the most common viruses. Bear in mind, however, that you put your system at risk whenever you place a disk from a dubious source in your drive or download a program that has not first been checked for viruses.

VLSI Abbreviation of **very large-scale integration.**

voice mail An interactive computer system for answering and routing telephone calls, recording, saving, and relaying messages, and sometimes paging the user. The section of the hard disk reserved for an individual's messages is called a "voice mailbox." Also called *V-mail*. See also *electronic mail*.

voice recognition See **speech recognition**.

volatile memory Memory that loses its data when the power is turned off or disconnected. *RAM*, for example, consists of volatile memory, whereas a hard disk stores *nonvolatile memory*.

volume **1.** A predetermined amount of memory on a tape or disk. The volume usually comprises all the memory on the storage device, but sometimes a single disk is divided into two or more volumes, and sometimes one volume is distributed over two or more disks. **2.** A disk or tape used to store data.

volume label The name assigned to a specific disk or tape in order to distinguish the disk or tape in question from other storage devices. Usually, the user chooses a volume label when formatting the disk or tape. Also called *volume name*.

wait state A period of time when the *CPU* waits idly for data from RAM or an I/O device such as the keyboard. A wait state occurs, for example, when the CPU processes data faster than RAM can supply it. A CPU that works with memory at maximum efficiency so as to have no wait states is called a "zero wait state" machine or microprocessor.

WAN [wan] Acronym for **wide area network**.

warm boot The process of restarting a computer without turning the power off. When you do a warm boot, your computer
erases everything from RAM, including all your data, whether
or not you have saved it. Then the computer reloads the operating system into RAM. On IBM PC and compatible computers, pressing Ctrl-Alt-Del causes a warm boot. On Macintosh
computers, you can start a warm boot by selecting RESTART
from the SPECIAL menu.

weight The degree of thickness of the strokes used to form the
characters of a font. For example, boldface characters have
thicker strokes than lightface characters.

whitespace **1.** The space on a piece of paper where no characters or graphics appear when a document, record, or file is
printed. **2.** Any of the characters that cause blank space to
appear on the screen or in print. Tabs and spaces, for example,
are whitespaces.

wide area network Acronym **WAN** [wan]. A *network* that
uses such devices as telephone lines, satellite dishes, or radio
waves to span a larger geographic area than can be covered by
a *local area network*. BITNET, InterNet, and USENET are
wide area networks.

widow In *word processing*, a last line of a paragraph that
appears as the first line of a page. See also *orphan*.

wild card A symbol that stands for one or more characters,
used in many *operating systems* as a means of selecting more
than one file or *directory* with a single specification. In *DOS*,
a question mark (?) can stand for any single character and an
asterisk (*) can stand for any number of characters. For example, "FIL?.DOC" would refer to FILE.DOC, FILL.DOC,
FILM.DOC, and so on. "*.DOC" would refer to all file names
ending in the *extension* .DOC. Most word processors also use
wild cards in *search* and *search and replace* procedures.

Winchester disk   An early hard disk developed by IBM. It had two spindles, each with a disk capacity of 30 megabytes, and was thus named after a Winchester .30-caliber rifle known as a ".30-30."

window   A rectangular portion of a *display screen* set aside for a specific purpose. Many *operating systems* and *applications* that have *graphical user interfaces* allow the user to divide the display screen into several windows and work with a different file or part of a file within each one. In *multitasking* environments, which can run several programs at once, each window can display output from a different program. To enter input into a particular file or program, the user *clicks* on the file or program's window to bring it into the *foreground*.

Each window often has its own *menu* or other controls, as for size, shape, and positioning. A window can be reduced to an *icon* representing the program running in the window in order to save space on the display screen. The icon can then be expanded back to a window. See also *overlaid window*, *pop*, *tiled windows*, *zoom*. See illustration at *graphical user interface*.

windowing   Designating an environment that allows the user to create *windows*. Macintosh computers and Microsoft Windows, for example, both offer a windowing environment.

Windows   A trademark for the *Microsoft Windows* operating environment.

word   **1.** In *word processing*, a group of characters with spaces or punctuation on both sides.   **2.** A unit of *memory*, measured in *bits*. The length of a word for a given computer is equal to the largest amount of data that can be handled by its *CPU* (central processing unit) in one operation. The most common word lengths for personal computers are 8, 16, and 32 bits. A larger, more powerful computer may use words that are up to 64 bits long.

word processing   Abbreviated **WP**   The act or practice of using a computer to create, edit, and print out documents such as letters, papers, and manuscripts. With a *word processor* the tasks of deleting, inserting, and moving sections of text can be made through a few keystrokes instead of through laborious retyping, as with a typewriter.

A simple word processing program such as an *editor* has several basic features, such as inserting and deleting text, defining page size and margins, *word wrap, cut and paste, search and replace, copy,* and *print.* More sophisticated *applications* can check spelling, find synonyms, number pages, create page headings and footnotes, generate form letters, and *merge* text or *graphics* in other files. See also *WYSIWYG.*

word processor Abbreviated **WP** A program or computer designed for *word processing.*

word wrap In *word processing,* a feature that automatically moves a word to the beginning of a new line if it goes beyond the margin of the document. The feature rearranges lines to avoid breaking a word, unless the program supports *hyphenation.* Word wrap makes pressing the *Return key* at the end of each line unnecessary, contrasting in this respect with the functions of a mechanical typewriter. When the margins or other layout parameters of the document are changed, word wrap automatically rearranges the text to fit the new specifications.

workgroup A group of individuals working together on a single project. The computers of workgroup members are linked together in a *local area network* (LAN), allowing the members to share common data files and communicate via *electronic mail.*

working directory The *directory* in which the user is currently working. A *pathname* that does not begin with the *root directory* is assumed by the operating system to begin with the working directory.

worksheet See **spreadsheet.**

workstation 1. A powerful computer used for scientific and engineering *applications, desktop publishing,* and *software* development. A typical workstation has more than 32 *megabytes* of *RAM*, 500MB or 1GB of *disk* storage capacity, a *multitasking* operating system, built-in *network* capability, a *graphical user interface*, and a large display screen with high *resolution*. Workstations are often linked together in a *local area network* (LAN), but they can also stand alone. **2.** A computer connected to a *local area network*.

WORM [wurm] Acronym for **write once read many.** An optical disk that can be written to once but read many times. Once the data has been written to the disk, it cannot be changed. Because of their large *storage* capacity (up to one *terabyte*) and unchangeability, WORMs are suited for storing data *archives*. See also *CD-ROM, erasable optical disk*.

WP 1. Abbreviation of **word processing. 2.** Abbreviation of **word processor.**

wraparound type See **text wrap.**

write To copy information from *memory* to a secondary *storage device*, usually a *disk*. See also *read*.

write once read many See **WORM.**

write-protect To modify a file or disk so that its data cannot be edited or erased. A file or disk modified in this way is *read-only*; data cannot be written to the disk or appended to the file. Many operating systems enable you to write-protect an individual file using software commands. You can write-protect a 5.25-inch floppy disk by covering the small notch cut out of its lining with either a piece of tape or one of the sticky write-protect tabs packaged with boxes of diskettes. A 3.5-inch floppy disk has a small switch in one corner of its plastic shell that may be slid open to write-protect the disk. See illustration.

WYSIWYG [WIZ-ee-wig] Acronym for **what you see is what you get.** Relating to or being a *word processing* or *desktop*

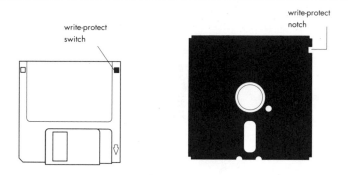

write-protect
Write-protect notch and switch on floppy disks

publishing system in which the screen displays text exactly as it will be printed. One advantage of a WYSIWYG system is that the *layout* of a document is much easier to set up.

In actual practice, the correspondence between what appears on the screen and what is printed out can be very close but not exact. For one thing, many desktop publishing systems use *outline fonts* (such as *PostScript* fonts) in printing but use *bit-mapped fonts* in displaying text on a screen. In addition, a standard *laser printer* has a *resolution* several times greater than that of the best *display screens*. Thus, what you see is usually only a good approximation of what you get.

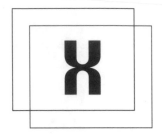

x-axis   The horizontal axis in a two-dimensional graph or coordinate system.

XENIX   [ZEE-nicks]   A trademark for an *operating system* that conforms to *UNIX*. It was developed by Microsoft for IBM PC-compatible computers. See table at *operating system*.

XGA   Abbreviation of **Extended Graphics Array.**   A *video standard* developed by IBM that is fully *compatible* with but supports higher *resolutions* and more colors than *VGA*. See table at *video standard*.

x-height   The height of the lowercase *x* in a *font*. The x-height measures the height of the body of a lowercase letter, excluding *ascenders* (strokes that rise above the top of the *x*, as in the letter *b*) and *descenders* (strokes that fall beneath the bottom of the *x*, as in the letter *g*). Since some fonts have long ascenders or descenders, the x-height often gives a better idea of the actual size of a font than the given *point* size.

Xmodem   [EKS-mo-dum]   A *protocol* for transferring files from one personal computer to another and detecting errors in their transmission. Widely available as *public domain software*, Xmodem is commonly used to *download* files from *bulletin board systems*. Xmodem operates by transmitting data in *blocks* of 128 *bytes*, each block followed by a *checksum*, a technique for detecting errors in the transmission of data. If the checksum calculated from the data received in a particular block does not match the checksum originally transmitted with the block, the same block is then retransmitted. If the checksums match, then the next block of data is transmitted. See also *Ymodem, Zmodem.* See table at *communications protocol.*

XMS   Abbreviation of **Extended Memory Specification.**   A procedure developed by Lotus, Intel, Microsoft, and AST Research for using *extended memory* and certain portions of *conventional memory* not available to *DOS.* An extended memory device such as Microsoft's HIMEM.SYS or Quarterdeck Office System's QEMM386.SYS must be installed in order for an *application* to take advantage of the additional memory.

XOR   [EKS-or or kzor]   A *Boolean operator* that returns the value TRUE if one of its *operands* is true and the other false. Table 24 shows the results of the XOR operator. Also called *exclusive OR.* See also *AND, NOR, NOT, OR.*

Table 24.   **Results of XOR Operator**

a	b	a XOR b
FALSE	FALSE	FALSE
FALSE	TRUE	TRUE
TRUE	FALSE	TRUE
TRUE	TRUE	FALSE

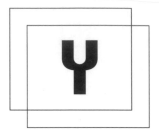

y-axis   The vertical axis in a two-dimensional graph or coordinate system.

Ymodem   [WHY-mo-dum]   An   enhanced   version   of   the *Xmodem* communications protocol that increases the transfer *block* size from 128 to 1,024 *bytes*. Ymodem also allows *batch file* transfers, whereby you can specify a list of files and send them at once. Xmodem transmits only one file at a time. See also *Zmodem*. See table at *communications protocol*.

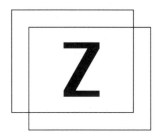

z-axis   The third axis in a three-dimensional graph or coordinate system, used to represent depth.

zero wait state   Relating to or being a *microprocessor* that has no *wait states*. The microprocessor runs at maximum speed without having to allow extra time for the memory *chips* to catch up. See also *clock speed*.

zinc-air battery   A lightweight battery that can store large amounts of energy. Zinc-air batteries have what is known as a "flat discharge voltage characteristic." They deliver a constant amount of power dependably over most of their lifetimes, rather than draining slowly.

Zmodem   [ZEE-mo-dum]   An enhanced version of the *Xmodem communications protocol* that allows faster and larger data transfer rates with fewer errors. Zmodem includes a feature called "checkpoint restart" that resumes data transfer where it left off, rather than from the beginning, if transmission is interrupted. See also *Ymodem*. See table at *communications protocol*.

zoned-bit recording   A technique for *formatting* a disk so that *tracks* on the outside have more *sectors* than tracks on the inside of the disk. Some hard disk drives use zoned-bit recording. See illustration at *sector*.

zoom   In a *graphical user interface*, to make a *window* larger by selecting the "zoom box" in one corner of the window. *Clicking* the zoom box for the first time enlarges the window to fill the entire display screen. Clicking it again restores the window to its original size.

SUBJECT INDEX

Artificial Intelligence

artificial intelligence
expert system
LISP
natural language
neural network
robotics
rule
smart
speech recognition
translation software

Communications

answer mode
AppleTalk
asynchronous
auto-redial
bandwidth
baud
baud rate
block

bps
broadcast
bulletin board system
bus
carrier
Centronics interface
characters per second
checksum
communications protocol
communications software
download
echo check
electronic mail
Ethernet
external modem
fax
fax machine
fax modem
Federal Communications
    Commission
fiber optics
full duplex
half duplex
handshaking

Desktop Publishing & Word Processing

Disks, Disk Drives, & Data Storage

Display Screens & Video Adapters

Interfaces

Keyboards, Mice, & Other Input Devices

Memory

Software